FROM THE OTHER SIDE
OF THE RIVER
A Self-Portrait of China Today

K. H. Fan edited the Anchor Press book *Mao Tse-tung and Lin Piao: Post Revolutionary Writings*. He is Professor of Political Science at College at Cortland, State University of New York.

K. T. Fan is Professor of Philosophy at Atkinson College, York University, in Downsview, Ontario.

FROM THE OTHER SIDE OF THE RIVER

A Self-Portrait of China Today

EDITED BY

K H. FAN AND K. T. FAN

ANCHOR BOOKS
ANCHOR PRESS/DOUBLEDAY
GARDEN CITY, NEW YORK
1975

D S
777.55
·F 333

Library of Congress Cataloging in Publication Data

Fan, Kuang Huan, 1932–   comp.
    From the other side of the river.

    1. China—Addresses, essays, lectures. I. Fan,
K. T., joint comp. II. Title.
DS777.55.F333 951'.05
ISBN 0-385-03743-0
Library of Congress Catalog Card Number 74-12726

Preface

The Chinese revolution is without doubt one of the greatest human experiments of our time. It is an all-encompassing revolution, affecting every aspect of life in that vast country. Many studies and eyewitness reports have appeared recently. During our visits to China we were especially impressed by the high political consciousness of the people in all walks of life. It occurred to us that a collection of writings by the Chinese themselves, providing an inside view of life in the revolutionary society, would serve, in many ways, to enlighten the West.

In understanding a society which is consciously building a new way of life, it is important to understand the self-image of the people. Collected here are articles written by Chinese from all stations covering different aspects of life in socialist China. Most of them originally appeared in various Chinese newspapers and were then translated and reprinted in one of the English publications by the Foreign Languages Publishing House in Peking. We have visited many places described in this book (we separately took two trips each from 1972 to 1974) and have talked to some of the authors. Within the limited space we attempt to include articles which are representative of the general outlook of the people. This collection is, in a sense, a self-portrait of China today.

A quarter of a century has passed since the founding of the People's Republic. In twenty-five years China has made the great leap from a semi-feudal and semi-colonial society to a socialist society. China's unparalleled speed in building a socialist economy "From each according to his ability, to each according to his work" and her achievements in many other fields are well known. And yet the Chinese are the first to admit that China still has a long way to go before she enters the goal of communism in which each receives according to his or her need. Socialism is a transitional stage between capitalism and communism. A socialist society by its very nature, is a transitional society, a society in constant change. To understand a society in transition, one must understand the past and the future of that society. During each of our various visits, we were always briefed on the conditions before Liberation or before the Cultural Revolution first, followed by a description of the present situation, and then concluded with an explanation of the goal they wish to achieve in the future. Similarly many of the articles in this collection follow this general scheme of description.

Given the transitional nature of socialist society, the Chinese Communist Party is keenly aware of the possibility of a transition back to capitalism. As Mao puts it, "Socialist society covers a fairly long historical period. In this historical period of socialism, there are still classes, class contradictions and class struggle, there is the struggle between the socialist road and the capitalist road, and there is the danger of capitalist restoration." Learning from the negative experience of the Soviet Union, Mao realized that unless and until man is transformed into the antithesis of the selfish, egotistical, and aggressive bourgeois, capitalism will be restored. Building a socialist economy is not enough, man must be changed actively, a new moral order must be created. This is the important message of the Cultural Revolution and it accounts for the high moral tone of many of the writings from China.

As a transitional society, China is guided by the future, by the goal of communism. This goal determines everything they do—"politics is in command," they say. This contrasts with the capitalist society where "economics is in command," where daily life is nonideological and de-politicized, China is a highly ideological and a most politicized society. Every aspect of life is guided by an ideology—Marxism-Leninism-Mao Tsetung Thought. Mao's thought is a summary of the experience of the Chinese revolution, an articulation of the goals of the revolution, and a strategy for achieving those goals. It provides a new socialist moral code, a dialectical world outlook, and a method of analyzing and solving problems. The pervasiveness of the influence of Mao's thought in the daily lives of the people can be clearly seen in the writings collected here. Mao's thought encourages rebellion, criticizing the status quo, and challenging authority. Continued revolution is institutionalized. The new constitution of the Communist Party states that revolutions like the Cultural Revolution will have to be carried out many times in the future.

At the moment a mass movement to criticize Lin Piao and Confucius is under way. It is the logical and necessary stage in the continuing revolution to create the new human being. The conservative philosophy of Confuciusism—the summation of the old way of thinking, old attitudes, and old habits in China, is now under frontal attack. China will no doubt undergo many more radical changes in the future, but the general direction is firmly set. We hope this book will help the readers to understand not only China today but China tomorrow.

K. H. Fan *and* K. T. Fan
September 1974

Contents

IV. LIBERATION OF EDUCATION AND PHILOSOPHY

I. THE PEOPLE

1. Family and Marriage

One of the first acts of the people's government after its establishment was to abolish the feudal marriage system. The Marriage Law (reprinted in this section) was promulgated on May 1, 1950, to establish the New-Democratic marriage system. To understand why it is called the "New-Democratic" marriage system and not the "Socialist," we need to explain briefly Mao's conception of the Chinese revolution. The Chinese revolution is conceived as a continuing revolution to be carried out in stages. There are three main stages: New-Democratic, Socialist, and Communist. The first stage was mainly anti-feudalist and anti-imperialist. It aimed at completing the democratic revolution led by Dr. Sun Yat-Sen in 1911. It was called the "New-Democratic" stage because it differed from the old one in that the working class played the leading role rather than the bourgeoisie. The political victory in 1949 marked the completion of the New-Democratic stage and the beginning of the transition to the Socialist stage.

The Marriage Law of 1950 established the New-Democratic marriage system, which is nominally the same as the marriage system in the West—i.e., monogamy based on love. But there are a number of significant differences which guarantees the equality between husband and wife. The most obvious manifestations of this equality are the practice of the wife keeping her own name and the practice of husband and wife referring to each other simply as "my lover." Since in most young families both husband and wife work outside, household chores seem to be generally shared equally by both. We noticed that in stores or parks there are usually one half men and one half women taking care of children.

According to the Marriage Law, divorce is granted when both parties desire it. There was a rush to divorce when the law was first promulgated, but now divorces are extremely rare. For example, in the whole area with 53,000 residents under the jurisdiction of the Feng-sheng Neighborhood Revolutionary Committee there was only one case of divorce in 1972. We asked the head of the Revolutionary Committee the reason for the low divorce rate. She replied, "Since a man and a woman marry only because they love each other, and usually there is a period of courtship during which they make sure they are compatible, there is usually no reason to get divorced." It's a simple matter if a couple without children want to get divorced, but when children are involved there is a strong community pressure for them to reconcile.

Most families, especially in the countryside, are extended—with grandparents or other close relatives living under the same roof. Contrary to past rumors in the West about the destruction of the family by the Communists, the family remains the basic social unit, and, as an institution, it seems to be much stronger than the family in the West. But it must be remembered that the family, like all other social institutions, changes along with the basic economic structure of a society. The family used to be a unit of production and consumption, but under socialism it is no longer a unit of production. The marriage system in China is still the "New-Democratic" system and not a "Socialist" system. We do not yet know what form the next stage will take but change is inevitable.

K.H.F.
K.T.F.

FROM THE MARRIAGE LAW OF THE PEOPLE'S REPUBLIC OF CHINA*

PROMULGATED BY THE CENTRAL
PEOPLE'S GOVERNMENT ON MAY 1, 1950

CHAPTER ONE
General Principles

Article 1.

The arbitrary and compulsory feudal marriage system, which is based on the superiority of man over woman and which ignores the children's interests, is abolished.

The New Democratic marriage system, which is based on free choice of partners, on monogamy, on equal rights for both sexes, and on protection of the lawful interests of women and children, shall be put into effect.

Article 2.

Polygamy, concubinage, child betrothal, interference with the re-marriage of widows and the exaction of money or gifts in connection with marriage shall be prohibited.

CHAPTER TWO
Contracting of Marriage

Article 3.

Marriage shall be based upon the complete willingness of the two parties. Neither party shall use compulsion and no third party shall be allowed to interfere.

* Peking: Foreign Language Press, 3rd Edition, 1973.

Article 4.

A marriage can be contracted only after the man has reached 20 years of age and the woman has reached 18 years of age.

Article 5.

No man or woman in any of the following instances shall be allowed to marry:

a) Where the man and woman are lineal relatives by blood or where the man and woman are brother and sister born of the same parents or where the man and woman are half-brother and half-sister. The question of prohibiting marriage between collateral relatives by blood within the fifth degree of relationship is to be determined by custom.

b) Where one party, because of certain physical defects, is sexually impotent.

c) Where one party is suffering from venereal disease, mental disorder, leprosy or any other disease which is regarded by medical science as rendering the person unfit for marriage.

Article 6.

In order to contract a marriage, both the man and the woman shall register in person with the people's government of the sub-district or village in which they reside. If the marriage is found to be in conformity with the provisions of this law, the local people's government shall, without delay, issue marriage certificates.

If the marriage is found to be incompatible with the provisions of this law, no registration shall be granted.

CHINA'S POPULATION POLICY*

BY CHI LUNG

Chi Lung, Deputy Representative of the Chinese Delegation to the 29th Session of the United Nations Economic Commission for Asia and the Far East (E.C.A.F.E.), made a speech on the population question at the April 16 meeting of the Committee of the Whole.

Basic Cause of Poverty and Backwardness

"The Delegation of the People's Republic of China," he said, "would like to explain here our views on the population question and to hold consultations together with the delegations of other countries."

Chi Lung went on: "We hold that, of all things in the world, people are the most precious. People are the decisive factor in the social productive forces. They are first of all producers and then consumers. As producers, they ceaselessly concentrate on production in breadth and depth and can produce more products than they consume. Under certain socio-historical conditions, some problems may arise as the population increases. This is caused by various obstacles blocking the development of the social productive forces. The entire progress of history shows that people are always able to sweep aside obstacles in the way of advance, promote the steady development of the social productive forces and create more and more wealth for society. Those views which regard people as a negative factor, that people are purely consumers and that growth in population means an obstacle to economic development do not correspond to the historical facts in the development of mankind. Those views which claim that efforts

* From *Peking Review,* No. 17, 1973.

to reduce the population's mortality rate would harm the socio-economic progress are even more absurd.

"We hold that the fundamental reason for the present poverty and backwardness in many developing countries in the Asian and Far East region as well as in other regions lies in the policies of aggression, plunder and war pushed by imperialism, colonialism and neo-colonialism, and in particular by the superpowers, which seriously destroy these countries' productive forces. The decisive conditions for changing this situation of poverty and backwardness are to get rid of aggression and oppression by imperialism, colonialism and neo-colonialism, to combat big-power hegemonism and power politics, to strive for and safeguard national independence and to develop the national economy independently. In our view, it is erroneous to say that the poverty and backwardness of the developing countries stem mainly from over-population and that a population policy is of fundamental significance and plays the main role in solving the problem of poverty and backwardness."

Malthusians Refuted

Referring to the Chinese people's own experience, Chi Lung said: "Old China's poverty and backwardness is known to all. Under the leadership of the Communist Party of China headed by Chairman Mao Tsetung, the Chinese people, after a long and valiant struggle, overthrew the reactionary rule of imperialism and its lackeys, founded the People's Republic of China and are engaged in socialist economic construction independently, self-reliantly and in a planned way. Though our population has increased relatively quickly since the founding of the People's Republic of China, the increase in production was even faster. Over the past 24 years, China's population grew from more than 500 million to over 700 million, an increase of more than 50 per cent, but during the same period, grain production more than doubled, increasing from 110 million tons to 240 million tons; cloth and other light industrial products increased by several fold, some even by more than tenfold; and still bigger increases have been registered in heavy industrial products. A look at the average annual rate of progressive increase since the founding of the People's Republic of China shows that the average annual progressive increase in population is about 2 per cent while that of grain is nearly 4 per cent, with the average annual progressive increase for the last decade being about 5 per cent. Moreover, at present China's cultivated land (which is roughly over 100 million hectares) only amounts to a little more than 10 per cent of the total area of the country. The per-hectare yield for grain is still not high and mechanization in grain production is still at a very low level. Judging from whatever angle, there are enormous potentialities for China's grain production which will grow not too slowly. China is a developing country and the living standards of her people are still rather low. However, starvation and unemployment have been eliminated. There is food, clothing and work for the people. Some Malthusians have prated that when there are too many people, the question of feeding them cannot be solved, that too many people obstruct the progress of society, and so on. Facts have thoroughly refuted such nonsense."

China's Population Policy

"Population increase in a planned way is China's established policy. We follow such a policy not because the question of 'over-population' exists in China. In China, social production is carried out in a planned way and this requires that the population increase is planned, too. It is also necessary to have a planned population increase in order to promote the thorough emancipation of women, care for mothers and women and children and bring up and educate the younger generation well, and improve the people's health and bring about national prosperity. Such a policy conforms with the interests and aspirations of the broad masses.

"To implement the policy of planned population increase requires us to develop medical and health work throughout the cities and countryside and do a good job in maternity and child care on the basis of actively developing production and raising the people's living standards and, while lowering the mortality rate of the population on the one hand, practise planned childbirth on the other to regulate the birth rate. What we mean by planned childbirth is not only birth control, but adopting different measures according to different circumstances. In densely populated areas with high birth rates, we advocate late marriage and birth control, so that the age difference between the parents and their children will be about 30 years rather than about 20 years. In national minority areas and other sparsely populated areas, we adopt appropriate measures to help increase population and promote production; guidance and help are also given to those who desire to practise birth control.

"China's work on birth control is carried out under the principle of voluntariness on the part of the masses with state guidance. The government and social organizations at all levels mobilize the masses to practise planned childbirth voluntarily through widespread propaganda and education. The state provides contraceptives free of charge and related medical services. To the few cases of sterility, active treatment is also given.

"China has gained rather noteworthy success in lowering the population's mortality rate. Initial success has also been obtained in birth-control work in the densely populated areas, but it is not developing evenly. A change has been brought about in the national minority areas where the population of some nationalities had in the past shown a sharp decline due to brutal persecution by the reactionary forces. The population in these areas has shown a fairly rapid increase and now there is a growing population and developing production. Our experience in planned childbirth is still not sufficient and we must continue in our efforts. Facts prove that our country is able to gradually achieve the control of population growth by mankind itself in a planned way."

Chi Lung added: "We hold that the drawing up of a population policy is the internal affair of the various countries. Conditions differ in the various countries, so we cannot seek a forcibly uniform policy on population. Under the premise of full respect for the sovereignty of the various countries and in accordance with the wishes of their people, it is of course beneficial to exchange experience internationally on the problems of population and family planning. We are ready to learn from the fine experience of the people of other countries."

MY FUTURE DAUGHTER-IN-LAW*

BY WANG HO-HO

Take a seat, sister, and let's have a good chat. Many's the time you've asked me about my future daughter-in-law, but you always picked a day when I was busy. Now at last I've time to tell you all about her.

To tell the truth, at first I was dead against the engagement. Not that the girl was bad-looking; no, indeed. Nor did she have a bad reputation; far from it. What bothered me then was something "odd" about her. Honest old folk like us, who've always kept on good terms with our neighbours, don't want a cranky

* From *Chinese Literature*, No. 7, 1973.
The writer is a peasant working in a commune.

daughter-in-law with no respect for other people's feelings. Don't you agree?

I was tickled pink when Hsiang-chun first told me the news. The girl's family had been poor peasants and she was branch secretary of the Youth League besides running a diesel engine for her brigade. Though I'd never set eyes on her myself, I trusted my boy's judgement.

How did they come to know each other, you ask. Well, I'll tell you from the beginning.

It all started three years ago when Hsiang-chun came home on leave. Passing through the wheat fields by Chang Family Village, he felt thirsty and decided to get a drink at the well there; but the engine pumping water out had jammed. The girl in charge—yes, you've guessed right—was my future daughter-in-law. But she was only a green hand then, just learning to operate the machine, and the breakdown had driven her frantic. She examined that engine first from one side, then from another, but just couldn't find out what was wrong. As you know, our Hsiang-chun works in a power plant. So he rolled up his sleeves and helped to check the engine. Before long he located the trouble and set it right, then switched the thing on and started it going again smoothly. That's how they became acquainted. Anyhow, they hit it off together.

But before the summer harvest this year, I was thoroughly aggravated by the girl.

It was when workers from town came down to help fight the drought. Hsiang-chun was one of them. He was too busy to go and see his girl, but just before he left I sent word to invite her over to see him off, thinking that would be a good chance for me to meet her, as all this time I'd never yet set eyes on her. I bought some lentil noodles, beancurd and beef, and steamed some buns using my best white flour. In between all these preparations I kept running to the end of the village to look out for her. But she failed to appear. When the time came for Hsiang-chun to leave, she still hadn't shown up. That's when I lost my temper. I decided, before it was too late, to call the whole thing off.

But when I told my old man, he flared up.

"Some important business must have kept her," he bellowed. "How can you blame the lass, not knowing the facts? If you want to call it off, that's your affair. I wash my hands of the business."

What way was that for the boy's father to talk? It made me madder than ever. We had no folk of our own in Chang Family Village, nobody to give me the low-down on the girl. After all, breaking off an engagement is no laughing matter. I decided to go to her village to make some inquiries myself. Hsiang-chun's father didn't care, but his mother did.

After the midday meal I hurried off. Chang Family Village lies less than two miles away from us, but it belongs to a different county. Because of this, I didn't know many of the villagers there.

As luck would have it, as soon as I reached the village I came across a woman about my age.

"May I ask you the way?" I hailed her hurriedly.

Instead of answering, she looked me over.

"Visiting relatives, eh? You must be hot and tired," she said at last.

"This is Chang Family Village, isn't it? . . ."

"That's right. Whom are you looking for? I'll show you the way."

"Do you know a girl called Hsin-hsin? I. . . ."

Before I could finish, she smiled all over her face and cut in, "I'm her mother. We've never met before. Which village are you from?"

That took the wind out of my sails. I'd come to spy out the land, instead of which I'd bumped into the girl's mother. I was so flustered that I blurted out, "Well I never! Fancy that! I'm Hsiang-chun's mother."

Overjoyed, she gripped my hand and exclaimed,

"Just the guest we've been longing for. What good wind blew you here?"

With that, she led me off. Since this would give me a chance to see the girl, I decided to follow her home.

We hadn't gone far when a voice rang out behind: "Mum!" I turned and saw a girl running towards us, smiling. I looked her over carefully as she came up. She was neither tall nor short, with a round face, two plaits and thick, attractive eyebrows. Her green jacket was clean but faded and under it she was wearing a red sweater. Her corduroy pants were dark blue and her black corduroy shoes had white plastic soles. A neat but not gaudy get-up. A fine girl, I thought.

As the girl was about to speak, her mother cast her a fond glance and cried: "Just look who's come!"

"Oh! One of our relatives, eh?" The girl darted a look at me from under arched brows. Her curved lips parted and she let out a chuckle.

I was delighted by her.

"Your sister's future mother-in-law has come to see her."

That took my breath away. Wasn't she Hsin-hsin then?

The girl turned square on me and asked, "How are you?" Then, lowering her head, she flushed.

Smiling, I took her hand. "I do declare, lass, I mistook you for Hsin-hsin."

Her mother burst out laughing and explained, "She's Jung-jung, my second daughter. She doesn't behave as well as her elder sister, though the two of them look alike. She's a spoilt child with no sense, just likes playing around."

But it was no joke, sister. What I said was true.

Then explaining that she had something important to do, she apologized for not keeping me company and told her mother, "I'll be back very soon." This said, she rushed off like the wind, calling back over her shoulder, "The tea's in the cupboard, mum."

I followed Hsin-hsin's mother into their house. She led me first to the west wing which the sisters shared. On the table and under the bed stood rows of bottles and pots, while beside the bed I noticed a first-aid kit.

"Is Jung-jung a doctor?" I asked.

Not Jung-jung, I was told. It was Hsin-hsin who had been training to be a peasant doctor ever since the "co-operative clinic" was set up there. She was so engrossed in this new job, her mother said, that she was always going off to collect prescriptions, gather herbs, prepare medicine and learn from others with more experience. She never had a moment to herself.

As she was telling me this, the door curtain was raised and in skipped Jung-jung. Hearing that we were talking about her sister, she joined in eagerly.

"Sister, eh? She's as busy as busy can be. That day when her fiancé was going back to town after helping us fight the drought, I urged her to see him off. But she said, 'Lo-cheng's dad has taken a turn for the worse, I can't leave him because of my own private business.'"

I learned that Hsin-hsin had nursed the old patient for five days and nights as if he were her own father, brewing his medicine for him and cooking his meals. I felt really ashamed of myself. My old man had been right to scold me for condemning the girl without reason.

I was so busy thinking, I quite forgot my tea. Where could she be? "Do ask Hsin-hsin to drop in on us. I'd love to see her," I told the girl's mother.

At that she urged Jung-jung, "Go and find her, child." Then she said to me, "She means to go and see you as soon as she can find time. . . . She mentioned something only last night about asking you for some clothes."

Since their engagement I hadn't given the girl a single gift. In the old days, of course, betrothal gifts were the rule; and even if girls didn't want them today the man's family still ought to offer something. It was all the fault of my old man and Hsiang-chun, who insisted that this was to be a new-style wedding. A wedding's a wedding when all's said and done. Besides, we were well-off now. When a poor couple married before Liberation, they did without fine clothes and a bridal chamber. Why, I myself got married in a "beggar's coat". But times had changed now and we poor and lower-middle peasants were our own masters. Life was getting better and better from year to year. While it would be wrong to throw money about or to give a grand feast, it was surely quite reasonable to make the bride some new clothes.

Jung-jung's return just then saved the situation. She told me that her sister had gone to North Village to take medicine to Aunt Chang, so she wouldn't be back yet awhile. Although I was sorry to have missed my daughter-in-law to be, at least I had met her younger sister who looked like her, and that was better than nothing. I saw through the window that the sky had turned dark.

"I must go or I'll get caught in the rain," I told my hostess.

In spite of her objections I insisted on leaving, explaining that our sow was due to farrow and my old man was out at a meeting. Tearing myself away at last, I hurried off.

What clothes should I get for my future daughter-in-law? This was all I could think about on the way home.

The rain was pelting down now. I'd been too preoccupied to borrow an umbrella from Hsin-hsin's mother, and she'd been so intent on keeping me that she hadn't thought of it either. The older we grow the worse our memories, as you probably know for yourself. And excitement makes me specially absent-minded.

I was wondering what to do when a cyclist rode up.

"Where are you going in weather like this, aunt?" he asked with concern, dismounting.

"I'm on my way home."

Now that the cyclist was nearer, I discovered that "he" was a girl.

"At your age, aunt, you may easily catch cold in this rain. Let me give you a lift to our place," urged the kind-hearted girl.

"Thank you, lass, but it's only a mile to my village. Don't bother."

Since I was firm, she parked her bicycle, took off her raincoat and draped it over my shoulders, so genuinely anxious to be helpful that I could hardly refuse her. Then she called out "goodbye" and rode off before I'd so much as thanked her. The young people raised in our new society by our great leader Chairman Mao are really fine! But I hadn't asked her name or where she lived. By the time this occurred to me the girl had gone. How could I return the raincoat to her later? Just think, sister, we'd never met before. I stood there at the crossroads quite at a loss.

Once home, I changed into dry things. Soon my old man came back too. Seeing the dripping clothes on the bench, he asked, "How did you get so wet? Where have you been?"

"Chang Family Village," I replied curtly.

"What? You've broken off the engagement?" He started up.

"Since you refused to go, I went," I teased him.

My old man bristled with rage, his lips quivered. Shaking his finger at me he bawled, "Woman . . . you're out of your mind!"

At that I could no longer hold back my laughter. While I told him all that had happened from start to finish, he lit his pipe and a smile spread over his face.

Suddenly I remembered the clothes that Hsin-hsin wanted.

"Give me the bank-book," I said.

"What for?" He shot me an inquiring glance.

"I'm going to buy her some clothes." I told him then what Hsin-hsin's mother had said.

He frowned at that and rapped out, "She wants clothes, so you buy her clothes. All right, now you reach me down the moon from the sky."

I ask you, what way is that to talk? I snapped back, "My son's wife will be my daughter. If you don't care for her, I do!"

My old man has a sharp tongue and he's pig-headed. "First you want to call the whole thing off," he grumbled. "Now you're talking about your concern for the girl. It seems you always know best!"

"Get away with you," I scolded, inwardly pleased. "This isn't like our marriage in the old days, when you took me out begging with you straight after the wedding and we'd only a cave to sleep in. Spring, summer, autumn and winter, I'd nothing but the one ragged jacket to wear. . . ."

By this time my old man was properly worked up too. "Very well, give that beggar's coat of yours to your daughter-in-law," he cried. "The young people today haven't been through the mill like us. They need to be taught a lesson."

Give a beggar's coat to one's daughter-in-law! Have you ever heard of such a thing, sister? "You give it her yourself," I fumed.

Guess what he said. "Very well. That's what I'll do."

I flared up again. "I'm going to buy her new clothes. No matter what you say, you can't stop me."

But I'd caught a chill after my drenching that day and I had to take to my bed. My old man was so worried, he fetched a doctor. I told him, "My illness isn't one you can cure. It comes of my old man being so aggravating."

The doctor said, "You're joking, aunt. You've caught cold. A few doses of medicine will soon set you right. But you must stay at home for a couple of days."

I did as I was told and stayed in bed for two days. I was lying there thinking about a trousseau for Hsin-hsin when I heard steps in the courtyard. Then someone called, "Mum!"

At first I thought I was dreaming. Apart from my son, who would call me "Mum"?

"Mum! Anyone in?"

I sat up and looked through the window. There in the yard stood a lad, just putting down a load of manure. He's come to the wrong place, the scatter-brain, I thought.

With firm steps he crossed the yard and came to the house. The door curtain was raised and he was in the room.

"Oh, you're in bed, mum. Why didn't you answer? Still angry with me?"

He took off his gauze mask and the white towel wrapped round his head, revealing neat bobbed hair. So it was a girl—the girl who had lent me her raincoat.

Noticing the surprise on my face, she introduced herself, "I'm Hsin-hsin, mum."

No wonder she looked so familiar, she was so like her younger sister. You can imagine how pleased and excited I was.

Holding her hand, I asked her to sit down beside me. "Are you ill, mum?" she asked with concern.

I said quickly, "It's nothing. Only a cold."

"It's all my fault. I didn't know it was you until I got home." She paused, smiling shyly, then went on, "I'm to blame. If I'd been more considerate, you wouldn't have fallen ill."

Why, sister, at those words I tingled with warmth from head to foot as if I'd drunk a bowl of hot ginger water.

While we were talking, there came a patter of feet out in the courtyard. Some children popped their heads through the open window.

"Behave yourselves! Run away!" When I called out, the children took to their heels. One of them ran back though to chant:

> *A girl visiting her*
> *Future mother-in-law*
> *Brings with her a carrying-pole*
> *And a load of manure. . . .*

Before I could box his ears, the imp scampered off.

"Why are you collecting manure, lass?" I asked Hsin-hsin.

"More fertilizer, more grain. We must catch up with the high yields of the Yangtse Valley," was her answer.

"That's the spirit," I exclaimed. "Hsiang-chun's dad would be glad to hear that."

A gruff voice sounded in the outer room, "My sentiments exactly. Spoken like a true peasant's daughter. The girl has guts." I knew, of course, that it was my old man, and the next moment in he came.

Hsin-hsin rose to greet him, saying, "You're back, dad."

He nodded, smiling from ear to ear. "High time you came. Your mum's been longing to see you. Day in day out she talks about nothing else. See, she's fretted herself ill."

It's no use trying to humour me, I thought. No matter what you say, I'll expose your true colours to your future daughter-in-law. Let's see how you wriggle out of it this time. I pulled a face at him, then turned to the girl. "Don't listen to the old fellow. I didn't fret myself ill because of you, but because somebody was so aggravating." I stressed the word "somebody". Then I went on, "Your dad's so concerned about you, when he heard that you wanted some clothes he hurried to the bank, then kept pestering me to buy some good material. I told him not to worry, I'd buy it all right, but I wanted to be sure it was something you fancied.

'Wouldn't it be better to wait and go with the lass to buy it?' I said. Then he accused me of being miserly and having no feeling for my daughter-in-law."

You might think, sister, that by then the old man would be sitting on pins and needles. But not a bit of it. He said calmly to Hsin-hsin, "Your mum's giving me credit where no credit's due. She has something ready for you in this chest." He tapped the chest beside him.

This put me on the spot. First I'd thought the old fellow was bluffing; now I remembered that my "beggar's coat" was in that chest. So he meant to have his own way after all.

In a fluster I said to Hsin-hsin, "Don't listen to him. I've not bought the material yet. Let's go to the co-op right away and get it."

But the provoking old thing stuck to his guns. "If she won't take it out, I will," he said.

Before he could do this I jumped off the bed, pushed him aside and plumped myself down on the chest.

But Hsin-hsin acted as a peace-maker. Leading me back to the bed she said, "Why buy new clothes for me? I'm not short of any. We want to carry on the poor peasants' tradition of industry and thrift in running our homes. Isn't that right, mum? Right, dad?"

I liked the way the girl spoke. It showed good sense. But in that case why had she wanted clothes?

My old man cast a triumphant glance at me. "Right!" he boomed. "Hsin-hsin is absolutely right. Caring too much for food and clothes is against Chairman Mao's instructions. That's the landlords' way, the way of rich peasants."

To spare my feelings, Hsin-hsin changed the subject. "Ever since Hsiang-chun and I got engaged, I've been wanting to see you," she said. "But I was so busy I just couldn't find the time. Even when he left for town that day, I didn't come. You must be annoyed with me."

My old man, riding the high horse now, told the girl, "Nothing of the sort! Young people have new ways of doing things, I know. Times have changed, so we old people have to change our ways too. Someone was upset by your failure to come, it's true. That someone even complained that you had no feeling for your future in-laws."

Of course, I knew very well whom he meant by this "someone". So my old man had begun to take the offensive. Never mind, now that I was sure of my daughter-in-law, I didn't care what he said.

Sensing this, Hsin-hsin turned to me with an earnest look. "I've come to ask you to give me a jacket, mum. Not a new one, but that 'beggar's coat' you wore before Liberation."

How on earth did she know about that? I was amazed.

With a smile the girl told me, "The young people in our village have never known really hard times, so we aren't on our guard against bourgeois ideas. To help raise our understanding, our Youth League Branch has decided to start a campaign for 'pouring out the bitterness of the past'. Hsiang-chun told me that you have a beggar's coat stained with your blood and sweat. It's a token of your bitter life in the old days. That's the jacket I want. Facts speak louder. . . ."

Before she had finished, my old man opened the chest and took out the ragged coat I had worn when begging. It was nothing but a mass of patches. My heart bled to see it. The dog's life I had led flashed across my mind. Tears coursed down my cheeks.

Gazing at Chairman Mao's portrait, I said to Hsin-hsin, "My bones would have rotted away long before now, if not for the leadership of Chairman Mao and the Party."

"Why not get your mum to go to your village and tell the young people all she went through?" my old man suggested.

"That would be fine," said Hsin-hsin. "We thought of that too, but I didn't like to suggest it for fear mum mightn't be willing. Will you come, mum?"

I'd better end my story here today, sister. I'll tell you about the meeting to pour out past bitterness some other day, when both of us have time.

AT THE FAMILY MEETING*

BY LI CHEN-CHUANG

My father Li Ching-feng is leader of one of the production brigades in the Talu commune in Hopei province. After the great proletarian cultural revolution began, some brigade members criticized him in *dazibao* (big-character posters). He didn't feel that what was said was correct and so he said he was not going to lead the brigade any more but would work as an ordinary commune member. When news of this reached me at my army post, I wrote to try and dissuade him from taking any such action. It had no effect on him.

Then I went home on leave. I tried to make Father see how wrong it was of him to think of giving up his responsibilities. But before I could finish my argument he blew up.

"Don't you scold me!" he exclaimed. "You would do the same if you were in my shoes!"

He refused to continue the talk.

The next day I spoke to some of the brigade members and learned that Father's main shortcoming was that he did not have a correct attitude toward the masses. He was rough in dealing with people and did not put proletarian politics above everything else. When sharply cirticized for this, instead of being willing to think it over, he felt aggrieved. In his mind, he had

* From *China Reconstructs*, February 1968.
Li Chen-chuang is a platoon leader in the Chinese People's Liberation Army.

done his duty conscientiously as a leader for eight or nine years, and even if he had no great meritorious deed to his credit, he had at least put in a lot of hard work. Now all he got was a heap of criticism. A cadre's lot was a hard one, he felt.

In our family there were various attitudes to Father's problem. Mother was on his side. My younger sister felt it was not right for him to quit, but she didn't have the courage to criticize him because she herself had once resigned as leader of a women's team, fearing meetings would interfere with her home duties. My younger brother, a Red Guard, had had several arguments with Father. But each time Father flared up at him, and he finally gave up. My wife, also a Red Guard, thought Father's attitude to criticism was wrong. But still under the influence of feudal proprieties, she could not bring herself to say this to her father-in-law.

I saw that to help Father I must first get the family to take a correct attitude. I got Mother, brother, sister and my wife together and we studied Chairman Mao's three famous articles, *Serve the People, In Memory of Norman Bethune* and *The Foolish Old Man Who Removed the Mountains,* with the aim of overcoming all thoughts of "self" by applying the teachings in them. We had several discussions. My wife came to understand that in daring or not daring to struggle against her father-in-law's wrong thinking she would show whether or not she was really loyal to Chairman Mao's revolutionary line. Remnants of feudal propriety was one of the things the proletarian cultural revolution was out to destroy, she began to realize, and it was Chairman Mao's revolutionary line that could mobilize the masses to rise and do this. My sister began to see that first she should correct her own mistake and second, that not daring to struggle against another who had made the same mistake as oneself showed that one still looked at things from the viewpoint of self-interest. My brother realized more fully that one should be firm, courageous and dauntless in making revolution. Finally all but Mother expressed eagerness to help Father.

We decided to hold a family meeting. Each of us thought over what we would say. At the meeting we first read together *Serve the People* and Chairman Mao's quotation: "Countless revolutionary martyrs have laid down their lives in the interests of the people, and our hearts are filled with pain as we the living think of them—can there be any personal interest, then, that we would not sacrifice or any error that we would not discard?"

Brother was the first to speak. "Father's behaviour in the cultural revolution hasn't been good. When he was criticized, instead of admitting his mistakes to the masses, he simply quit his post. To do this was to forget how our martyrs shed their blood and gave their lives for the revolution."

"So it's all your father's fault," Mother interrupted in an aggrieved tone. "This means all of you were right. Why don't you become cadres yourselves?"

Sister rose. "Father was wrong and yet he would not let the masses criticize him. That simply is not right." By now Father was ready to get up and leave.

To ease the atmosphere so that the meeting could go on, I said, "Father, you are a member of the Communist Party. If you make a mistake you should correct it right away. Brother is trying to help you for the sake of the revolution. Isn't it better to hear him through?" I paused, then went on. "Do you still remember, Father, what sort of life we led in the old society? If it hadn't been for Chairman Mao who helped us poor people win liberation, we wouldn't be enjoying the happiness of today and you wouldn't have been a cadre. We must never forget how the martyrs gave their lives for the revolution and we must never forget the bitter class sufferings of the past."

At the mention of class sufferings, Father began to

calm down. One could see the pain of past memories on his face. My wife urged him, "We are all too young to know much about the sufferings of the old society. Tell us about our family."

"Before the liberation our family had more than ten mouths to feed but had only two and a half *mu* of graveyard land," Father began, tears welling up in his eyes. "Your grandfather was too old to work and hobbled about begging. He finally starved to death in a deserted temple. Your grandmother was murdered in cold blood by the Japanese invaders. I worked as a hired hand for a cursed landlord for ten years. We never had enough to eat or wear. Your second sister starved to death when she had barely learned to walk. Your second brother was beaten to death by the village head because we could not pay the rent. The bitterness, the miseries we suffered—I could talk about them for days. Thanks to Chairman Mao and the Communist Party who liberated us poor people, we began to lead a better life. Indeed, as the song goes, 'Father's dear, Mother's dear, but not as dear as Chairman Mao. A thousand things are good, a million things are good, but not as good as socialism!'"

We all wept. Now that Father's class feelings were aroused, I tried to help him deepen them into political understanding. "Why do you think, Father, that we poor people suffered so much in the old society? Why is it that our life is better in the new society?"

"Because in the old society the workers and poor and lower-middle peasants did not have political power," Father said, "while in the new society we working people are the masters of the country."

"Yes," I agreed. "Without political power we have nothing. Who should be in charge of the seal of power then?"

"The workers and we poor and lower-middle peasants, of course!" Mother broke in.

"Then why don't you want Father to be a cadre?" sister and brother asked in one voice.

Mother was speechless. I then explained why the cultural revolution was so important for preventing revisionism and for consolidating our dictatorship of the proletariat. I also talked about the crimes of the handful of capitalist-roaders in the Party headed by China's Khrushchov, about how they were trying to restore capitalism in China. This aroused the whole family's hatred against these class enemies.

Father especially became deeply agitated. "I was wrong to want to run away from my responsibilities," he said. "I did not live up to the expectations of Chairman Mao, of the revolutionary martyrs, of the poor and lower-middle peasants. My attitude toward the criticism of the masses shows that I was too preoccupied with the thought of 'self' and did not follow Chairman Mao's teaching, that one should serve the people wholly and entirely. The heart of Chairman Mao's revolutionary line is one's attitude toward the masses—to have faith in them and rely on them. I am always going to stand on the side of Chairman Mao's revolutionary line and follow Chairman Mao all my life in making revolution."

Mother, too, admitted that she bore some responsibility for Father's attitude. "Don't sit and brood in the house any more," she said to him. "Go and do whatever you're supposed to do."

The whole family was happy to see that Father had realized he had been wrong. My wife suggested, "We should make it a rule in the family to give help to whoever does something not in accord with Chairman Mao's teaching. Let us all creatively study and apply Chairman Mao's works and turn the whole family into a study class of Mao Tse-tung's thought. It doesn't matter that Father can't read. Brother and I will help him."

After this round in the battle against "self", our whole family showed more concern for affairs of state and everyone took an active part in the campaign of revolutionary mass criticism. We pledged to try even harder to creatively study and apply Chairman Mao's works, carry out his instructions, follow him in making revolution and firmly keep to the socialist road.

The very next day Father asked to continue his old duties. Later he voluntarily made a self-criticism at a mass meeting. When the revolutionary masses set up a group to be in charge of both revolution and production, Father was elected to lead it.

2. Women's Liberation

The position of women in Old China can be summarized by the Confucian code of three "obeys"—obey your father before marriage, obey your husband after marriage, and obey your eldest son after your husband's death. A woman was thus under male authority all her life. The most notorious manifestation of women's oppression was the widespread practice of foot-binding. Even today one can still see the crippled feet of some old women.

Today, there is no doubt that Chinese women are the most liberated women in the world. They participate fully in all social, political, cultural, and economic life of society as equal members. They are proud, confident, and articulate. We see them working in leadership positions in all levels of government, except at the top echelon, which, for historical reasons, is still dominated by old men.

How was this radical transformation achieved? It was achieved through the socialist revolution, which is committed to the liberation of women. The first step was to give women economic independence. Thus, during the Land Reform movement immediately after Liberation in 1949, women were given equal shares of land as men. Women themselves started to cut their hair short, to wear men's clothing, and to refuse to be treated as sex objects by not using make-up. Secondly, to integrate women into the social and productive activities of the society they had to be liberated from housework and child care. Thus, a most extensive child care system was organized throughout China.

Along with these social and economic measures, men and women had to change their conceptions of each other and themselves. Women no longer accept the myth of their being the weaker sex (a myth easily shattered when you shake hands with them!) and assert themselves in all fields. They remind themselves and men by quoting their favorite quotation from Mao, "Times have changed. Today men and women are equals. Whatever men comrades can do, women comrades can too." Men and women regard each other as individuals, as comrades, and not as sex objects. A woman in China today would be insulted if you told her, "You look beautiful." Women's insistence on being treated as persons largely accounts for their desexualized appearance and for the fact that sex is strictly private and allowed only within a marriage. In all other social situations men and women meet as equals, as comrades.

China's achievement in liberating her women in such a short time is unprecedented. But this is not to say sexism has completely disappeared. As Chou En-lai reminded us, "Some old attitudes and habits of thought are not easy to change. For example, some people still value boys more than girls so that if they have only girls they keep trying for a boy. And most men are still reluctant to adopt vasectomy as a means of birth control because of their male chauvinist ideas."

K.H.F.
K.T.F.

FROM THE MARRIAGE LAW OF THE
PEOPLE'S REPUBLIC OF CHINA*
PROMULGATED BY THE CENTRAL
PEOPLE'S GOVERNMENT ON MAY 1, 1950

CHAPTER THREE
Rights and Duties of Husband and Wife

Article 7.

Husband and wife are companions living together and shall enjoy equal status in the home.

Article 8.

Husband and wife are in duty bound to love, respect, assist and look after each other, to live in harmony, to engage in production, to care for the children and to strive jointly for the welfare of the family and for the building up of a new society.

Article 9.

Both husband and wife shall have the right to free choice of occupations and free participation in work or in social activities.

Article 10.

Both husband and wife shall have equal rights in the possession and management of family property.

Article 11.

Both husband and wife shall have the right to use his or her own family name.

* Peking: Foreign Language Press, 3rd Edition, 1973.

Article 12.
    Both husband and wife shall have the right to
inherit each other's property.

WOMEN'S LIBERATION IN CHINA*

BY SUNG CHING-LING

History has proved that Women's Liberation in
China—women obtain equal status with men—began
with the democratic revolution, but will be completed
only in the socialist revolution.

What is the democratic revolution? It is a revolution
to overturn the feudal rule of a landlord class, a revolution participated by the people at large under the leadership of a political party. It first took place in China
in 1911, when a monarchy was overthrown, the emperor—the biggest landlord in the entire land—was de-
throned, and the aristocracy was dispersed. But this
revolution was not completed until 1949 when about
that time the land of all big landlords was confiscated.
Peasants and landlords were hostile to each other. The
former participated in the revolutionary movement in
1927, and only after a long period of class struggle did
they succeed to overturn the latter.

What has the overturning of the landlord class to do
with the Women's Liberation Movement? In the spring
of 1927, our great leader Chairman Mao Tsetung
clearly gave us the correct explanation: *"The political
authority of the landlords is the backbone of all the
other systems of authority. With that overturned, the
clan authority, the religious authority and the authority
of the husband all begin to totter. . . . As to the authority of the husband, this has always been weaker
among the poor peasants because, out of economic necessity, their womenfolk have to do more manual la-*

* From *Peking Review*, No. 6, 1972.

bour than the women of the richer classes and therefore have more say and greater power of decision in family matters. With the increasing bankruptcy of the rural economy in recent years, the basis for men's domination over women has already been weakened. With the rise of the peasant movement, the women in many places have now begun to organize rural women's associations; the opportunity has come for them to lift up their heads, and the authority of the husband is getting shakier every day. In a word, the whole feudal-patriarchal system and ideology is tottering with the growth of the peasants' power." Needless to say that before the democratic revolution the women in China, with the social status, were in various ways oppressed and exploited. Women of the richer classes and even the majority of the poorer classes were occupied in their families and maintained no social occupation. Women employees, especially the domestic ones, received very low wages. Indeed very few women maintained their economic independence! Meantime, very few girls were enrolled in school. The women graduates by and large returned to their homes, only a very few turned to be teachers in primary schools and girls' middle schools.

The pace of the Women's Liberation Movement closely followed the advance of the democratic revolution. Women's status in China was apparently raised by 1930, on the eve of the war against Japanese aggression. There were already at that time colleges and even middle schools where co-education was established. Women graduates, not a few of them, were employed as teachers, medical doctors and hospital nurses. Most of the graduates from Christian missionary schools and colleges, however, did not take up any occupation and remained in their families to become "social vases," then a nickname for those who were busy in social entertainments but had no profession of their own. These women, married or single, free from feudal etiquettes, turned to be social toys and bourgeois parasites. At this time, there were many women engaged in textile industries, but they were under capitalist exploitation, receiving low wages and suffering from poverty.

At the end of the war against Japanese aggression and occupation, the Chinese people under the leadership of the Chinese Communist Party accelerated the revolutionary movement. Thus numerous women threw themselves into all kinds of revolutionary work, some of them joined the military services. They gained their economic independence. Party members devoted themselves to propaganda work, in villages and factories. Many of them were women graduates from middle schools. By doing their work women won the equal status with men. They were very active in the land reform movement, they helped to do away with the land ownership of the big landlords. They were eagerly devoted to their various tasks, with self-sacrificing spirit to fulfil the orders given by the Party. It was upon the basis of this democratic revolution that the Chinese people could and did initiate the present socialist revolution.

When in October, 1949, with the defeat of the Japanese military forces, with the Chiang Kai-shek dictatorship overthrown, with the imperialistic foreign agents cleared off, the People's Republic of China was proclaimed, our democratic revolution came to its conclusion. From then on our socialist revolution began. At the very beginning of the present regime, the Minister of Justice and the Minister for Public Health were both women. Many other women entered government services in Peking as well as in the provinces. In the administration of various public utilities there was no lack of women cadres.

Within the last twenty years, more and more women enlisted themselves in the army, navy and air forces. They voluntarily entered these services after having passed a physical examination. More and more women joined agricultural field work, pasturage, mining, foundry, irrigation, communication, transportation, all kinds of factories, commerce, shop work, and various other public services. Since 1966, the first year of our Cultural Revolution, which is a part of the socialist revolution, the number of women doctors and nurses has been greatly increased. In very recent years, in a few large cities, all healthy women under forty-five have been given work in manufacture, commerce, communication, transportation, and other services for the people. Middle school graduates, boys as well as girls have been allocated to work in factories, fields and shops. Whatever men can do in these services women can equally do. By and large every woman who can work can take her place on the labour front, under the principle of equal pay for equal work. A large majority of the Chinese women have now attained their economic independence.

If we ask, however, whether Women's Liberation Movement in China has come to its end, the answer is definitely no. It is true that the landlord system has been abolished for nearly twenty years, but much of the feudal-patriarchal ideology still prevails among the peasants or rather farmers. This ideology still does yield mischievous things in the rural places and some of the small towns. Only when the feudal-patriarchal ideology is eradicated can we expect the sexual equality fully established.

In order to build a great socialist society, it is necessary to have the broad masses of women engaged in productive activity. With men, women must receive equal pay for equal work in production. Today in our country there are people's communes in rural places where women receive less pay than men for equal work in production. In certain villages patriarchal ideas still have their effect. Proportionately, more boys than girls attend school. Parents need the girls to do household work. Some even feel that girls will eventually enter another family and therefore it would not pay to send them to school. Moreover, when girls are to be married, their parents often ask for a certain amount of money or various articles from the family of the would-be husband. Thus the freedom of marriage is affected. Finally, as farmers want to add to the labour force in their families, the birth of a son is expected while that of a daughter is considered a disappointment. This repeated desire to have at least one son has an adverse effect on birth control and planned births. A woman with many children around her naturally finds it too difficult to participate in any productive labour. Another thing hampering a working woman is her involvement in household work. This prevents many women from full, wholehearted participation in public services.

From the present situation it is not difficult to understand that genuine equality between the sexes can be realized and the Women's Liberation Movement will be ended when and only when, led by a Marxist-Leninist political party, the process of the social transformation of society as a whole is completed, when the exploiting class or classes are exterminated, and when the feudal-patriarchal and other exploiting-class ideologies are completely uprooted.

WOMEN'S LIBERATION THROUGH STRUGGLE*

BY HSU KUANG

I was born in a poor family in Nankung, a small county town in southern Hopei province, and in 1936 entered the normal school there. I was very indignant at the society that allowed the bloodsucking landlords and officials to ride roughshod over the poor, while the latter, after gruelling labor, still went hungry. A teacher named Chang often talked about why class oppression

* From *Some Basic Facts About China* (Peking: Foreign Language Press, 1974).

existed and introduced me to some progressive books. The elder sister of a classmate, who I later came to know was an underground Communist Party member, told us that the Communist Party had been leading the poor to make revolution and that after a 25,000-*li* Long March the Workers' and Peasants' Red Army led by Chairman Mao had set up an anti-Japanese base in Yenan. I began to learn the truths of revolution.

It was the time of the Kuomintang white terror. Teacher Chang soon lost his job. Because I had led some of my fellow students to oppose this decision by the school principal, I was expelled and taken to the county government office where I was interrogated and beaten. I had to leave town and finally got a job as substitute teacher in a primary school in a distant village.

In 1937 the Japanese imperialists invaded Peiping and pushed southward along the railway line. Nankung was bombed, and the Kuomintang officials fled in panic. Just as I was searching for the road to revolution the Eighth Route Army led by the Communist Party marched into Nankung and set up the anti-Japanese local government there. The Party organization carried out education among us young people first. Soon I joined the revolutionary ranks. My job was to bring the women into the movement to save the nation from Japanese aggression. In 1938 the first Women's Association for National Salvation in south Hopei came into being. I was elected head of the propaganda department. In that same year I joined the Communist Party.

Smashing Feudal Shackles

The women's association sought to mobilize the women in the villages. We intellectuals had had little contact with the peasants and when we first walked through the village in our Chinese gowns or skirts the people would just stare at us and talk behind our backs.

When the village head beat gongs to call out the women to the meetings we were holding for them, only men and old women came, but no young ones. Later we found out that the landlords and rich peasants had spread slanders among the masses, saying, "They're a pack of wild women. Their words are not for young brides to hear."

In old China not only did the working women suffer the same oppression and exploitation by the landlords and officials as the men, but in addition they were fettered by the feudal concept that women were inferior to men. Marriage was arranged arbitrarily by the parents. The men ruled over the women. In southern Hopei it was very common for women to be kept from working in the fields out of the fear that they would be seen by strange men. The daughter-in-law or wife had to ask her mother-in-law or husband for every cent. Young women had no position at all in the family.

When I first started to do work among the women I felt that they would never gain any rights unless they struggled for them against their husbands, and against their families for freedom. When the women's association was faced with the job of mobilizing the women for anti-Japanese work, two opposing views arose among its members. One view supported the demands of some young women that tyrannical husbands and mothers-in-law be taken to meetings and publicly criticized. This, they felt, would strengthen the women's determination and give vent to their anger. Others pointed out that at present Japanese imperialism was the enemy of the whole Chinese people, and that this method would undermine the unity of the people against the invaders and sharpen contradictions in the family. Through discussion we finally agreed that victory in the war could be won only by uniting all those that could be united. Without national liberation, women's liberation would have no meaning. We went from house to house visiting and making friends with the women.

They came to understand us and learned to reason patiently with their stubborn mothers-in-law and husbands.

This proved a good way. The change in the family of Sister Wang Erh in Hsiaowang village, Chulu county, is an example. She was married into the Wang family as a child-bride at the age of 12. Her husband was a tenant farmer and 17 years older than she. She had been ill-treated by the family, and whenever they got a poor harvest, as payment for the rent she was sent to labor for the landlord like a beast of burden. With the back-breaking toil and unhappy family relations, she rarely said anything all day long. People called her "the dumb daughter-in-law". She was not allowed to come to our mobilization meetings because her mother-in-law was afraid she might get out of hand and neglect the household work, while her husband feared she would be attracted to other men.

When I went to visit her, her mother-in-law received me coolly and wouldn't even allow the younger woman to show herself. Some comrades contended that the only hope for Sister Wang Erh's emancipation was for her to get a divorce, return to her mother's house and join the women's association there. I refused to be discouraged and went back again and again to visit and chat with the mother-in-law. I tried to help her see that women should contribute their share to the resistance—that if the invaders took over our country we would become slaves. I described the sufferings of our fellow countrymen in the northeast, which had been forcibly occupied by the Japanese invaders, and pointed out that if we were to lose our country, families would be broken up. I also told her about my own life. When the mother-in-law learned that I too came from a poor family which had been persecuted by the Kuomintang, and that my mother had died when I was 15, she became very sympathetic. As we talked I would help her with whatever she was doing, like cooking or feeding the pig. And when she was spinning I would prepare the cotton for her. She began saying, "These women have heads on their shoulders. They are also downtrodden people and are of one heart and mind with us."

One evening the mother-in-law sent her son away for the night and had me stay over with her daughter-in-law. Sister Wang Erh poured out her sufferings to me and said she wanted to get a divorce. I tried to help her see that her mother-in-law and husband were also poor people. This formed a basis for improvement of relations. Actually the husband's own thinking was already changing under constant help from members of the Peasants' Association.[1]

In 1938 the enemy occupied the county seat of Nankung and often carried out "mopping up" campaigns in the surrounding villages. The enemy's burning, killing and looting also educated the local people. Later the husband joined the Peasants' Association and the wife and mother both joined the women's association. We students also changed in the course of doing mass work. We discarded our city dress and put on peasant clothes. We became very close to the local people and many of the elderly women "adopted" us as "daughters".

'Dumb Daughter-in-Law' to Chairwoman

After we got the women mobilized, we organized them to weave cloth and make shoes which were sold to the Eighth Route Army at cost. We also organized a self-defence unit of young women. They took turns guarding the village, tearing down town walls or destroying roads before the oncoming enemy, nursing the wounded, carrying stretchers, acting as secret messengers, hiding stocks of grain from the enemy and helping the soldiers' families. During the time of the "mop-ups"

[1] An anti-Japanese organization open to all peasants except rich peasants. Landlords, too, were not eligible.

we organized young women's guerrilla units. To confuse and frighten the enemy so they dared not remain long in the village, we took pot shots at them and threw hand grenades. Often we lit firecrackers in kerosene cans when we didn't have enough ammunition.

"Dumb daughter-in-law", Sister Wang Erh, was particularly active in supporting the front. She was a fast weaver and the cloth was very good. She could make twice as many shoes as the others. She was elected head of the village women's association. Her home and land lay just at the end of the village. One day while she was working in her garden and at the same time keeping a lookout, someone came along whom she suspected to be a spy. As she engaged him in conversation she reached for a string hanging outside her house connected to a signal in her mother-in-law's room, and pulled. This told the old lady to call the self-defence corps. They caught the man on the spot. Another time, Sister Wang Erh caught several more spies using the same method. "'Dumb daughter-in-law' has become a capable chairwoman," said the villagers.

Fighting shoulder-to-shoulder alongside the men, women made a great contribution in the struggle to repel the Japanese aggressors. This not only gave them encouragement but also educated the men and the people as a whole. In the course of the struggle the feudal thinking and customs discriminating against women were broken down. Reality also educated those of us doing women's work. We came to understand more clearly that the women's movement was an integral part of the revolutionary movement. We saw that if the women's movement had been divorced from revolution as a whole, and had fought solely for women's rights— thus becoming a struggle to wrest rights from men and making men the target of their struggle—it would have split the revolutionary ranks. Endless conflicts between the men and women, and between the young women and the old women, would have resulted. This would have been harmful to the struggle for national liberation and that for the liberation of all oppressed classes; it would have turned society against the women's struggle and put obstacles in its way.

The Same as Men

After eight years of war the Chinese people drove out the Japanese invaders. Supported by the U.S. imperialists, the Kuomintang reactionaries—who had always been apathetic about resisting the Japanese aggressors but very active in attacking the Communist-led patriotic forces—robbed the people of the fruits of their victory. Using the areas and cities taken over from the surrendering Japanese, the Kuomintang launched civil war on an unprecedented scale. This was opposed by all patriotic people. In 1948, as the People's Liberation Army moved from victory to victory, I was working in the liberated villages of southern Hopei on organizing the people to support the front and carry out the land reform, and on problems of women's welfare.

Steeled in the eight years of resistance against the Japanese invaders, women in the liberated areas were determined to carry the revolution through to the very end. Everywhere women were sending their husbands or sons off to the People's Liberation Army. One of the most moving incidents is the story of Chao Hsiu-o, chairwoman of the Chaochia village branch of the Democratic Federation of Women in Chihsien county (the name of the Women's Association for National Salvation had changed to the Democratic Federation of Women). There were only three in her family, two of whom were widows. Her father-in-law, a hired hand for a landlord, had died under the tyrant's mistreatment before the war. Her husband was killed fighting the Japanese. She had only one child, a son. The two widows were drawn together by their feelings of class and national hatred. Both Chao Hsiu-o and her mother-in-law joined the Chinese Communist Party, and she became secretary of the Party branch. Her mother-in-law would often say to me: "At home, I'm head of the family, but with matters of the revolution, it's my daughter-in-law who leads me."

Then one day Chao Hsiu-o was preparing to send her son off to the PLA. Her mother-in-law could not bear the thought. He was the only grandchild, the last one to carry on the family name. Hsiu-o sat down to talk with the grandmother and together they recalled their sufferings under the landlords' oppression. She helped the old woman see that the Kuomintang reactionaries backed up the landlords because their power in the countryside was based on the landlord class. "If we don't overthrow these reactionaries," she said, "we'll have to suffer under them again." Finally the grandmother consented to let her grandson go.

Since most of the men were fighting at the front, women became the main force in agricultural and sideline production. They also enthusiastically made supplies for the army. To meet the clothing needs of the field army they produced 800,000 bolts of hand-woven cloth ahead of time, in a month and a half. The women also nursed the wounded, filled up trenches and tore down the enemy's barricades. In all these support-the-front activities the women displayed ability they had never shown before. It made even those who had always maintained "women's place is around the stove" acknowledge that women had become an indispensable force in every period of the revolutionary struggle.

Revolution and Women's Rights

In 1947 the Communist Party Central Committee promulgated the land reform program for the liberated areas. In this struggle to thoroughly destroy the feudal system, two views arose concerning women's emancipation. As the situation developed, some women's problems such as the question of marriage, woman and child care, were in urgent need of solution. In Chaochia village a number of women said to me, "Let the Peasants' Association work on the land reform, the women's federation should concentrate on women's problems." Through discussion, we in the federation came to the agreement that while we must, of course, solve the particular problems of women—otherwise we would be divorcing ourselves from the masses and neglecting our duty—at the same time the most important of our duties was to carry out the main task of the revolution. The feudal landlord class oppressed men and women alike. Without overthrowing the landlords the working women could not really stand up either politically or economically. There would be no solution to their problems to speak of. The strength of both men and women must be concentrated on carrying out the land reform.

In the land reform the women took the lead in many ways. For example, at a struggle meeting against the landlords in Chaochia village, Chao Hsiu-o, supporting her mother-in-law at her side, was the first to stand up and accuse the landlord of his cruel exploitation. Her story of blood and tears roused the bitter memories of many and strengthened their determination to overthrow the landlord class. Every poor peasant, man or woman, was allotted a piece of land in the land reform. To emphasize the fact that women had economic equality with men we gave each woman a land certificate in her own name or wrote her name alongside her husband's on one certificate. Before, women had always been referred to by others as "so-and-so's wife" or "so-and-so's mother". Now for the first time in their lives many women heard their own names spoken in public.

At the meeting to give out the land certificates Chao Hsiu-o mounted the platform to talk about the new draft marriage law, attacking the feudal marriage system with its polygamy, concubinage, child-brides and arranged forced marriages. She called on the people to create a new kind of family based on democracy and harmony.

After the land reform the federation started work on woman and child care in a big way. In the villages, where once there was the bitter saying, "Pregnant women are seen, but no baby's laughter is ever heard", training classes for midwives were started. Before, in the villages in this area no girl ever went to school. Now we started night literacy classes and the sound of women reciting the texts could often be heard. After being allotted land the women organized themselves into mutual-aid teams for agricultural production and co-ops for manufacturing home-woven cloth. In this way they started on the road of socialist collectivization. These activities again proved that at every stage of the revolution women were an important force. Equality between men and women, freedom of marriage and other women's rights and the solution of their special problems can only be achieved step by step as the revolutionary struggle, with the women participating, achieves victory and revolutionary state power is established.

The revolutionary struggle liberated women, and steeled and trained many women activists. After the liberation those in southern Hopei became cadres of the various local governments, including heads of counties, districts or courts of justice. As for myself, I went to Tientsin and later Peking to continue to organize and mobilize women for socialist revolution and construction.

WOMEN FLIERS*

BY HSIN KUNG-YUAN

China's first squadron of women fliers was formed in 1950. They celebrated Women's Day in 1952 by flying in formation over Tien An Men Square.

* From *New Women in New China* (Peking: Foreign Language Press, 1972).

Many women fliers have matured in the 22 years since then. Conscientiously studying and applying Mao Tsetung Thought, they are developing a proletarian ideology and continuously revolutionizing their thinking. With China and the world at heart, they fly for the revolution and the building of socialism.

One of these women is Chu Hui-fen whose family slaved for generations for landlords. In 1939, when she was two years old, the Japanese invaders ravaged Chiating, her home town near Shanghai. Foreign aggression on top of class oppression left the family with no way to live. Carrying their few belongings on his shoulder pole, her father took the family and begged their way to Shanghai. He did back-breaking work for the capitalists but the family still went hungry. Then, exhausted and starved, he died, followed very soon by Chu Hui-fen's younger brother, who died of starvation. Her mother went to work as a maidservant in a capitalist family till she too died one raw, snowy day in 1944. Within three years, the vicious society had killed three of the family. The orphaned girl roamed the streets of Shanghai alone, keeping herself alive with discarded melon rinds and rotten vegetable leaves. Hatred for the exploiting classes and the aggressors of her motherland burned in her like a hot coal.

Then Chairman Mao and the Communist Party led the people to freedom. Shanghai was liberated in 1949, and Chu Hui-fen was rescued from her misery and sent to school. In 1956 she came to the air force. She stood before a portrait of Chairman Mao in her new uniform, and tears welled in her eyes. There was so much she wanted to say, but she put it all in the words, "Chairman Mao, I owe everything to you!"

Her first difficulty in training was not having enough strength. Learning to fly a twin-engined plane with only one engine running, when she had to put both feet on the rudder, she would perspire profusely and get exhausted, her feet aching for a long time after each practice. The squadron's Party branch helped her compare the present good life of the working people with the exploitation and oppression they suffered in the old society. Chu Hui-fen's simple class feeling rose to a higher political awareness of class struggle and the struggle between the two lines. She drew strength from Chairman Mao's teaching, *"In times of difficulty we must not lose sight of our achievements, must see the bright future and must pluck up our courage."* She persisted in daily physical training, running and working out on the athletic wheel with the men fliers. As she developed her strength, she redoubled her study of Chairman Mao's works and became a competent flier. On June 1, 1962, she was admitted to the Chinese Communist Party. Today she is a deputy group commander.

Chu Hui-fen and her comrades-in-arms were once assigned the urgent task of rescuing a Red Guard who had been wounded while on duty. They took off that night in face of a strong wind and after a whole day's workout.

Hui-fen said: "Chairman Mao has taught us: *'Our duty is to hold ourselves responsible to the people.'* The Red Guards have made great contributions in the Cultural Revolution. We must discharge our duty without delay."

They quickly got their plane ready and, at the order to take off, soared into the sky. The flight was of several hours' duration. Then they landed, and Chu Hui-fen helped carry the Red Guard onto the plane. The attending doctors and nurses went aboard and they took off again.

The flight back was through clouds and it was rough, but Chu Hui-fen kept firm hold on the control lever. Then she thought: "Before the liberation, I went about with a begging bowl in my hand. Now I hold the control lever of a plane for my motherland. The party trusts me. I must faithfully serve the Party and the people." With this thought she climbed higher, out of the clouds, so the wounded Red Guard would have a smoother journey.

The temperature in the plane fell at the high altitude and the crew again thought of the Red Guard. Was he warm enough? They offered to cover him with their clothes, though none of them had worn their heavy suits. Chu Hui-fen and her comrades-in-arms relaxed only after their wounded passenger was safely in hospital.

Communist Party member Yueh Hsi-tsui was already a fine flier when she had just turned 20. She constantly keeps in mind Chairman Mao's injunction to *"build a powerful people's air force to defend the motherland."* By studying hard she finished the theoretical courses in aeronautics in a short time. But just before she started flight training, she felt a numbness in her joints. The doctor diagnosed it as arthritis and advised against training for a while. Yueh Hsi-tsui was very disturbed. Would this mean that she might never fly? Urged by the leadership and the doctors, however, she finally agreed to undergo treatment.

In the hospital she studied Chairman Mao's teaching on daring to struggle and to win, and felt more confident that she could overcome her illness. She kept up her study of Chairman Mao's works and spent hours outdoors every day doing physical exercises, even in mid-winter. She practised sweeping off the hospital skating rink at rest intervals. When the treatment and exercise had improved her condition, she requested to return to flight training.

Back in her unit, having fallen far behind the others, she practised running three kilometres every day.

The leadership soon decided she could resume her flight training. How happy she was as she climbed into the cockpit! But she had trouble in landing, bringing the plane in either too high or too low. Even with her instructor's help she failed to make the grade.

Yueh Hsi-tsui turned to Chairman Mao's teaching: *"Will the Chinese cower before difficulties when they are not afraid even of death?"* She decided she must train her eyes rigorously, and would do this wherever she was.

On the bus back from the airfield she would fix her eyes on an object ahead and practise estimating distance, as she had to when landing the plane. Tired when she got back to the barracks, she would still practise with the transparent plastic map case, holding it like a cockpit windshield in front of her eyes and, taking the floor below as her runway, running up and down the stairs to train her eyes. She conquered her difficulty and took to the skies.

Communist Party member Yu Fu-lan is another staunch woman member of the squadron.

Once, when heavy rains and rising waters threatened to breach a reservoir and sandbags were urgently needed to save nearby factories and towns, the leadership decided to air-drop them. Yu Fu-lan and her comrades were given the task.

Their plane took off in the storm. The reservoir lay among hills 100 metres high and shrouded in low-hanging clouds. Getting below the clouds and into position for the drop involved the danger of a crash, but Yu Fu-lan and her comrades did not hesitate to take the plane down to 200, 100, then 80 metres. Still they saw nothing but clouds. Command then ordered them back to base to consider another plan.

On the way back, Yu Fu-lan looked at the pile of gunny bags on the plane and thought of the poor and lower-middle peasants who were waiting for them in their fight against the flood. At the base she reported to command and, backed by the whole crew, asked for permission to try again. "The people are waiting for the bags," she said. "We must deliver them!" After serious consideration, the leadership agreed. Yu Fu-lan and her comrades summed up their experience on the first flight and discussed how to cope with the problems a second time. Then they took off again.

A bold and careful navigator, Yu Fu-lan plotted the plane's course. At 80 metres there was still the blanket of dense cloud. They were already flying lower than some of the hilltops. "Drop another 20 metres," Yu Fu-lan told the pilot. They broke through the clouds and suddenly saw the reservoir in plain sight. The flood-fighters were waving their hands. Dodging the hills, the women fliers circled low over the reservoir and dropped the bundles of bags precisely on target.

HOUSEWIVES CAN MAKE ELECTRONIC EQUIPMENT*

BY KUNG YEH

The West District No. 1 Transistor Equipment Factory in Peking used to be a neighbourhood workshop where steelyards were made and scales repaired. Most of the workers had been housewives and had little formal education, but in just five years they have succeeded in turning out various electronic products which fill needs in hundreds of factories throughout the country. Some of these products have had favourable comments by friends from abroad at the Chinese Export Commodities Fair in Kwangchow.

It may be wondered how these women, who were housewives, are able now to make this modern equipment.

The Women Dare to Do

In 1965 the workshop was asked to trial-produce a diffusion furnace with automatic temperature control which had been designed by the revolutionary students

* From *New Women in New China* (Peking: Foreign Language Press, 1972).

and teachers of Tsinghua University as a project in their scientific research plan. Hearing that it was an important item for the electronics industry and had been on the list of the imperialists' embargo against China for a long time, the women workers determined to take on this task for their motherland, though none of them was an electrician, let alone a technician or engineer.

When a skeptic scoffed that it was nonsense for housewives even to think of making a diffusion furnace, the women were adamant. "Why can't we women add a brick to socialist construction?" they argued back. "Men and women are equals in the new society." And, backed by the Party branch, they decided to try. Li Hua, Wang Chin-tsai, Sung Chin-lan and some other women workers and a few newcomers who had just completed secondary school were put in charge.

The Party branch secretary, Ti Jung-hsueh, called them together to study Chairman Mao's inspiring essay, *The Foolish Old Man Who Removed the Mountains*. "The Foolish Old Man could remove mountains," he said. "What if we haven't a higher education? We're people of the new era with the spirit of the Foolish Old Man." Li Hua, a child bride in the old society, whom the Party rescued from her sadness after the liberation, was impressed. She said with conviction, "With Mao Tsetung Thought to guide us, we can overcome our difficulties and make that furnace!"

Relying on their own efforts, they started out in cramped quarters—a reed and clay cabin with asphalt felt roof, ten square metres in area.

The first step in making a diffusion furnace is to solder a device with almost a thousand components. This initial technique requires ability to read the circuit diagram. It looked to the women that they would not be able to make the first step. They went to Tsinghua University for advice. To Li Hua, who had never been to school at all, the diagram was just a maze of spider webs. With the warm and patient help of the university students, however, they soon learned to read the diagram, and they began to work. Soldering is a simple job, but when Li Hua took up the small, light soldering iron, her hand trembled, for she was used to handling 20-kilogramme weights. Following Chairman Mao's teaching: *"What really counts in the world is conscientiousness, and the Communist Party is most particular about being conscientious,"* she practised with great care. She first cut the soldering metal into very small pieces and soldered them one by one over the lead holes, finally becoming quite skilled at it.

Wang Chin-tsai, mother of three children, went to the university to learn soldering in the daytime; then in the evening she returned to the workshop where she practised what she had learned and exchanged experience with others. Thus this housewife, who had only two years' schooling, became one of the skilled technicians in this line.

Learning While Doing

Having finished their study at the university in a month, the women returned to the workshop where they were warmly welcomed by their fellow-workers. Trial-production of the diffusion furnace was to begin.

Li Hua and the other women workers had learned to make the furnace controls, but none of them knew how to make the furnace body. They studied the problem, and also sent several workers to other plants which were equipped with diffusion furnaces. They were told that it was impossible for people who knew nothing about thermodynamics to make a diffusion furnace. So they invited an expert from a research institute to teach them about that. The expert was enthusiastic about helping them, telling them many basic principles so that they learned a lot. But how to apply the principles and make a furnace?

"Let's learn while doing," they said. "Chairman Mao teaches us: *'Our chief method is to learn warfare through warfare.'*"

"That's it," they agreed. "As the saying goes, 'To see something once is better than hearing about it a hundred times, but to do a thing once is better than seeing it a hundred times.'"

They tried again and again, and finally worked out methods and made many parts of the furnace. Still they couldn't set up a constant-temperature zone without which there could be no diffusion furnace. The women worked on it day and night, but failed to solve the problem.

They reported the trouble to the Party branch comrades, who called a meeting of all the workers to put their heads together. Woman worker Kuo Ching-chih outlined for the assembled workers their progress and their difficulties, and asked for advice. There were many suggestions. When someone mentioned the long tube in the furnace and how a furnace was not like an ordinary cooking stove, Kuo suddenly got an idea. It was true, the two were different in structure, but the principles of the furnace and of the cooking stove were the same. It was easier to maintain constant temperature in the stove because the stove had no cold air in it, while in the furnace, it was hot in the middle and cooler at both ends.

Someone added, "If we change the winding of the heating elements so that there're more coils at the ends and less in the middle, that might stabilize the temperature."

This method was tried and did in fact lessen the difference in temperature inside the furnace. After over 30 experiments, they worked out a rational winding of the heating elements and produced a constant temperature zone. Thus, after more than a hundred failures and setbacks and seven months' hard work, these former housewives, who could only make steelyards, made the first high-precision automatic temperature-control diffusion furnace of advanced type.

On to Further Achievement

After crossing the threshold of the electronics industry, the women did not stop. The furnace they had made used electronic tubes. During the Great Proletarian Cultural Revolution, they proposed to the Party branch and the revolutionary committee that they try to make a transistorized diffusion furnace. The leaders supported the proposal.

They studied the diagram carefully in the light of their experience, broke through old restrictions and introduced bold innovations, overcoming one difficulty after another. The result was their first transistorized diffusion furnace, simple but of advanced level and with special features. After tests by various departments, the diagram was selected as a standard pattern in China. Tsinghua University included it in its textbooks.

The news that this small factory has produced modern diffusion furnaces, and furthermore that housewives have become electronic technicians, spread throughout the country. People have come from factories in other parts of the country to study its experience. Foreign friends have also been welcome visitors here.

WOMEN OIL EXTRACTORS OF TACHING*

BY HSIN HUA

One morning in September 1970, as glorious rays of the sun reddened the expanse of sky over Taching Oilfield, about a hundred young women oil extractors, led by the political instructor Chao Ching-chih and three veteran workers, went to the spot where "Iron Man"

* From *New Women in New China* (Peking: Foreign Language Press, 1972).

Wang Chin-hsi dug Taching's first oil well 10 years ago. They went there to learn the spirit of "Iron Man" Wang and Taching's admirable tradition of the battle for China's oil production. This was Taching's first all-women oil extracting team, formed not long ago. Its members' average age was 21. All had been brave Red Guards at the early stage of the Great Proletarian Cultural Revolution, and most had been to Peking for review by Chairman Mao at Tien An Men Square. Acting on Chairman Mao's teaching to become one with the workers and peasants, they had come to Taching from various parts of the country.

Today, guided by Mao Tsetung Thought and inspired by the spirit of Wang Chin-hsi, the women oil extractors are playing their part in the work at the Taching Oilfield. They have successfully managed dozens of oil wells and are praised as an "Iron Girls" oil extracting team.

Braving Difficulties

From the day of its formation, the young women's oil extracting team faced up to difficulties. Just before October 1 of 1970, China's National Day, the team determined to put a new oil well into production earlier than planned, regarding this as a gift at the celebration of China's 21st birthday. But the difficulties were many. Electricity was still not laid on, and at night they couldn't see their hands before their faces. The water-jacket heater for the oil pipeline needed water, and the water-tank truck had not arrived. The dewaxing equipment weighing several hundred kilogrammes was a mile away. What should they do—wait, or create the conditions? The girls talked this over and decided to be like "Iron Man" Wang Chin-hsi. "We'll beat the difficulties and see that a new oil well is producing ahead of time!" they said.

The struggle for the new oil well began. The girls

soon had the electric line up. In rain and mud they carried water, bucket by bucket, from a pond hundreds of metres away to fill the water-jacket heater, which held a ton of water. After that they moved the heavy dewaxing equipment to the well. The girls were soaked through with rain and sweat; their shoulders were swollen from carrying loads. Their legs and faces were raw and sore. But no one complained. They said proudly: "We missed the opportunity to do the pioneering work in the hard battle to open the oilfield. Neither have we experienced the test of war flames as our elder comrades did in the early days of the revolution, when they had only mouthfuls of parched flour between mouthfuls of snow to eat while fighting. Why shouldn't we stand a little hardship today, if it means more oil to support China's socialist construction and the world revolution!" After several days' intense work, the girls had their first success. At half past eleven on the night of September 30, their new oil well went into production. The sound of crude oil gushing forth and streaming into the conveyer pipe was music to the girls' ears, and they were all smiles.

Struggling against the severe cold and blizzards of their first winter, the women's team overcame more difficulties and kept the oil flowing.

Chang Tsai-feng, one on the team, was born in a poor peasant family which suffered bitterly in the old society and she had deep class feeling. Her parents died toiling for a landlord. Chairman Mao had rescued the girl from the abominable old society and trained her as an oil worker. At the oilfield, the team became like her own family. She took pride in doing hard jobs, and did her work carefully, devoting her energy to developing China's petroleum industry. One day in the winter of 1970, when the temperature suddenly dropped, she noticed a water-jacket heater not working smoothly. There was danger of the heater freezing, and the oil well to stop functioning. Braving the biting cold, she opened the outlet valve, drew out buckets of water, and returned them into the circulation system. But the well cover was crusted with ice, and there was no place to put the bucket. So she held it in her arms and was splashed all over by the steam and hot water when they spurted out. Her clothes froze stiff in the driving wind. She set her jaw and kept on working until the heater started functioning properly and the oil gushing smoothly.

Chiao Ching-lien, another of the women oil extractors, came to Taching with a strong will to be re-educated by the working class and to temper herself in difficult circumstances. She displayed the revolutionary spirit of fearing neither hardship nor death in whatever she did. Once, on an inspection tour, she noticed burning oil vapours leaking out of a separator valve. They had been set afire by a gas burner for water-jacket heating. Chiao Ching-lien ran for a fire extinguisher and rushed to the spot to protect the wells, disregarding her own safety. Her eyebrows and hair were singed, but she did not retreat half a step till she had closed the separator, preventing escape of the oil vapours and saving state property.

Scientific Management

The underground strata of the several dozen oil and water wells the team worked on were mostly under low pressure. The movements of oil, water and pressure below the earth's surface were variable and unsteady, and could mean uncertain oil production. This was a new problem on their way to continuing the work—how to manage such oil wells so as to produce more and better oil for the state. One was most difficult to manage. It had much wax, and often failed to function. The girls studied Chairman Mao's teaching: *"Practice, knowledge, again practice, and again knowledge,"* and first noted and experimented with the laws of movement of underground oil, water and pressure. Then they studied in relation to the difficult problems that arose in managing the well, while referring to veteran workers' experience in managing unruly oil wells. Thus they worked out methods and solved the problem of a well with much wax.

The women's team had not repaired oil wells or measured well pressure, both jobs being done by special teams. With improvement of their skill in managing oil wells, the girls volunteered for the jobs. To provide equipment for repairing oil wells and measuring pressure, deputy team leaders Liu Kuang-yuan and Li Chi-chih pushed carts to collect discarded used materials from the Taching grassland, from which they made a hydraulic apparatus in their spare time and used it for well repairing. Measuring well pressure is hard work and means getting up before dawn and going to bed at midnight. It involves lowering a very heavy pressure gauge to the bottom of the well, several thousand metres. It used to be done only by men workers. But the "Iron Girls" said, "If the men can measure well pressure, so can we women." With the help of veteran workers, and with practice, the girls soon learned how.

Knowing how to measure well pressure helped the girls understand better the laws of variation in the underground oil-bearing strata. They used the apparatus they had made with their own hands and measured the underground strata of every oil well to collect first-hand data, which they then studied and analysed. Now they can measure the pressure of all the team's oil and water wells by themselves. Once a heavy rain came after midnight. It was time to collect the needed data for two of the wells. Teng Yen-hsia, a Communist Youth League member, said firmly: "A delay in measuring the well means less data from which to judge the stratum. With Mao Tsetung Thought as guide and "Iron Man" Wang Chin-hsi as example, we'll certainly get the data we want." Bringing with them the pressure-

measuring tools, the girls set out in the storm and succeeded in collecting the data on the two wells. The
women oil extractors worked in all kinds of weather
and with sustained effort to learn to know the oilfield's
variation below the earth's surface. They have now
measured each of their oil wells 230 times and accumulated about 10,000 data from them, providing a large
amount of first-hand information needed for the scientific management of oil wells.

*   *   *

Nurtured by Mao Tsetung Thought and tempered in
the class struggle, struggle for production and scientific
experiment, the women oil extracting team has matured steadily in the past year and more. Many of them
have been admitted to the Chinese Communist Party
or to the Chinese Communist Youth League. Some
have become cadres of the women's team or elected
members of the Taching Oilfield Party committee.
Known among the team members as "Little Iron
Woman," Chang Tsai-feng has studied Chairman Mao's
works conscientiously since joining the team and has
been trained into an advanced woman oil worker in a
little over a year. By carrying forward the revolutionary
spirit of Taching, the young women oil extracting team
has made its contribution to the development of China's
petroleum industry. As team representative, Lu Tseng-
hua has come to Peking and had the joy of seeing our
great leader Chairman Mao, which has greatly inspired
the whole team. Now, these young women are determined to live up to Chairman Mao's hopes and make
still greater contributions to the development of China's
petroleum industry.

3. Children and Youth

from **THE MARRIAGE LAW OF THE PEOPLE'S REPUBLIC OF CHINA***
PROMULGATED BY THE CENTRAL
PEOPLE'S GOVERNMENT ON MAY 1, 1950

CHAPTER FOUR
Relations Between Parents and Children

Article 13.

Parents have the duty to rear and to educate their children; the children have the duty to look after and to assist their parents. Neither the parents nor the children shall maltreat or desert one another.

The foregoing provision also applies to step-parents and step-children. Infanticide by drowning and similar criminal acts are strictly prohibited.

Article 14.

Parents and children shall have the right to inherit one another's property.

Article 15.

Children born out of wedlock shall enjoy the same rights as children born in lawful wedlock. No person shall be allowed to harm or to discriminate against children born out of wedlock.

Where the paternity of a child born out of wedlock is legally established by the mother of the child or by other witnesses or by other

* Peking: Foreign Language Press, 3rd Edition, 1973.

material evidence, the identified father must bear the whole or part of the cost of maintenance and education of the child until it has attained the age of 18.

With the consent of the natural mother, the natural father may have custody of the child.

With regard to the maintenance of a child whose natural mother marries, the provisions of Article 22 shall apply.

Article 16.

A husband or wife shall not maltreat or discriminate against a child born of a previous marriage.

MATERNITY AND CHILD CARE*

BY YI KE

Women and children in socialist China enjoy the care and protection of the state. Maternity and child care is an important part of the health work guided by Chairman Mao's revolutionary line.

Healthy Start in Life

Children are successors to the cause of the proletarian revolution. The tremendous expansion in medical care for children guarantees them a healthy start in life.

Every year infants and young children in cities, towns and countryside receive injections of vaccines and other medicine against various common diseases. There has been a big drop in the incidence of communicable children's diseases since liberation.

Smallpox and cholera were wiped out as far back as in the early 1950s. In the district where the Peking

* From *Peking Review*, No. 23, 1972.

Children's Hospital is in charge of child health the incidence of measles has dropped to 2.3 per cent since 1959, while polio and diphtheria have been reduced to nil. These diseases have been considerably decreased elsewhere in the country. The same hospital, which treats encephalitis B by integrating traditional Chinese medicine with Western medicine, in the last 12 years has effected a cure for the disease in nine cases out of ten.

According to the well-known 73-year-old pediatrician Professor Chu Fu-tang, the Children's Hospital combines Western and traditional Chinese medicine. Modern scientific knowledge and methods are applied to analyse and sum up the rich experience of Chinese medical practice. This has helped raise the standard of pediatrics in China.

Vice-chairman of the hospital's revolutionary committee, Professor Chu notes that "like other pediatric institutions, the Peking Children's Hospital has set up a child health department to popularize hygienic knowledge to residents, schools, nurseries and kindergartens and to help organize mass health campaigns."

All over the country, a growing number of children now stay in nurseries or kindergartens, on full-time or day-time basis or organized temporarily during busy farming seasons, where they are well taken care of. In the villages of one county in Kiangsu Province, 82.6 per cent of the production brigades have established nurseries and kindergartens and 76.4 per cent of the infants and young children are in them. Youngsters there are thus brought up from childhood to love their country, the people, the collective and manual labour. In circumstances as these, children also enjoy better health.

Women in New China have equal rights with men in political, economic and cultural life. Women are entitled to do all kinds of work, except a few jobs they are not physically fit for. Working at various posts in the socialist revolution and construction, they are invariably proud of being "the other half" of the builders of socialism.

Protecting Women's Health

In the cities, women workers in factories, mines, government offices and teachers in schools, like their male counterparts, enjoy medical service paid by the state or under a labour insurance plan. The state stipulates that women employees can retire at 55, five years earlier than men employees, and draw a pension after retirement equivalent to 70 per cent of their former wages. A woman worker does not work night shifts and is given light work seven months after her pregnancy; she also receives regular pre-natal care and 56 days maternity leave (70 days in the case of labour complications) with full pay. Expenses for childbirth attendance in hospital is paid by the state. Mothers during the nursing period do not work night shifts. During working hours, mothers have one hour for feeding their babies.

In the countryside, medical expenses for women members of the people's communes are included in the funds for co-operative medical service, paid in by the commune or production brigade out of their public welfare fund. Commune members themselves need bear only a small amount of the expense. In many places, general examination and treatment of common women's diseases have effectively protected women's health.

When jobs are assigned, people's communes invariably take into consideration the physiological features of women members. During the menstruation period, women members are freed from heavy work and do not do such jobs as working in cold water or late at night.

The introduction of modern midwifery in China's vast countryside is an important measure for protecting the health of mother and infant. Before liberation, in the countryside childbirth was handled by old-fashioned midwives at home and the umbilical cord had to be severed by scissors without the use of a disinfectant. Women serfs in Tibet had to give birth in cattle and sheep pens. Maternity and infant mortality rates were appalling. Today pre-natal check-ups and modern midwifery in the rural areas have been introduced universally, as well as post-natal care, to lower the incidence of puerperal infections and tetanus of new-born babies. In rural Chaoan County, Kwang-tung Province, every production brigade now has two or three peasant midwives of their own. Quite a number of production brigades have built their own maternity wards. In some villages, not one case of tetanus among infants or a case of maternal death has occurred in more than a decade. Free medical service has been introduced in the Tibet Autonomous Region, where childbirth can be handled in hospital or at home free of charge. According to statistics prepared by the maternity ward of the People's Hospital in the region, 98 per cent of the new-born infants survive. With the improvement of the health of the Tibetan people, the population of the autonomous region has increased by more than 200,000 since 1959.

Maternity and Children's Hospitals

There are gynaecology, obstetrics and pediatrics outpatient departments and wards in all the hospitals run by counties and above throughout China. Maternity hospitals and clinics for women and children have been established in some big and medium-sized cities.

Founded in 1959, the Peking Maternity Hospital, with gynaecology and obstetrics outpatient departments, has 250 sick beds and wards for 120 new-born babies. It treats 400-500 outpatients a day and assists in 400-500 births a month. All but four of the 220 medical workers here are women, with some women doctors in charge of the work in some departments. Major operations in the gynaecology and obstetrics departments are almost all done by women surgeons.

The hospital gives medical check-ups to patients over 30 in order to discover cancer in the early stages. Medical workers visit factories and homes to treat cervix cancer in the early stage and other women's diseases.

Since the Peking Children's Hospital was established in 1953, about 30 children's hospitals have been set up in other cities. The Peking hospital has 600 beds, four times the total in all children's hospitals in pre-liberation China. Well-equipped with modern medical equipment, the hospital treats new-born babies to 14-year-olds.

Like other urban hospitals, the maternity and children's hospitals collect a minimum uniform registration fee without any distinction. The charge is ten fen, whether it is the patient's first visit or not, whether the case is an emergency or not, or whether it is diagnosed by a single doctor or by a group of doctors. Patients do not have to make advance payment; they pay one yuan a day for hospitalization. The fee for a normal childbirth is five yuan, for a chest operation on a child 30 yuan. Prices of medicines, which have continuously gone down, are now some 20 per cent what they were in the early days after liberation.

Family Planning

Party and government encouragement of family planning is a firm policy for socialist construction in China. Thus women can be freed from much child care and their household chores for more and better participation in the cause of revolution and construction. This is also good for the health of women and children and for bringing up the younger generation.

Family planning includes advocacy of late marriage and birth control. Women are encouraged to marry at over 23 and men when they are over 25. Health workers give birth control advice in the light of age, health condition, number of children and living habits of married couples, and each chooses the methods best suited to them. If a woman becomes pregnant in spite of attempts at contraception, she can apply for an abortion for which the health department must undertake the necessary operation.

Contraceptives and operations for birth control are free. People after such operations are given a certain time of rest with pay, according to the kind of operation undergone and their health condition. Similarly, commune members receive subsidies from the commune or production brigade.

People who are sterile can get medical treatment if they wish.

YOUTH SHOULD STAND IN THE FOREFRONT OF THE REVOLUTIONARY RANKS*

BY TAN WEN

The Chinese people's great leader Chairman Mao delivered his well-known speech *The Orientation of the Youth Movement* on May 4, 1939, China's Youth Day.[1] In it, he developed his ideas on the question of

* From *Peking Review*, No. 20, 1972.

[1] The May 4th Movement, a great revolutionary movement against imperialism and feudalism by the Chinese people, broke out on May 4, 1919. Thousands of Peking students gathered and demonstrated in Tien An Men Square that day to oppose the traitorous actions of the warlord government that was going to sign the Versailles "peace treaty" which the imperialists had prepared to encroach upon China's sovereignty. This movement later developed into a mass movement with the working class as its main force. It marked the beginning of China's new-democratic revolution. In the initial stage of the War of Resist-

the Chinese revolution, summed up the historical experience of China's youth movement since the 1919 May 4th Movement and formulated the correct line for the youth movement. It was the programme of the youth movement during the democratic revolution and also is its guiding principle during the socialist revolution. In China at present when work concerning the youth is going forward vigorously and youth league congresses have been convened in various provinces and municipalities, restudying this article will enable our work on the youth to advance in a still better way along Chairman Mao's revolutionary line.

Chairman Mao pointed out in the article: *"What role have China's young people played since the May 4th Movement? In a way they have played a vanguard role—a fact recognized by everybody except the die-hards. What is a vanguard role? It means taking the lead and marching in the forefront of the revolutionary ranks."* He also said that young people are *"an army on one of the fronts against imperialism and feudalism, and an important army too."* *"What then is the main force? The workers and peasants."* Chairman Mao's brilliant thesis on the youth movement's role in the people's revolutionary movement is the Marxist viewpoint required by us to understand the youth movement correctly.

Making up 90 per cent of the population, Chinese workers and peasants are the main force of revolution. Without them we can neither win the fight against imperialism and feudalism, nor can we seize victory for the cause of socialism. The youth movement is always a part of the proletarian revolutionary movement, either in the period of democratic revolution or social-

---

ance Against Japan (1937–45), May 4 was adopted as China's Youth Day by the youth organization of the Shensi-Kansu-Ningsia Border Region under the leadership of the Chinese Communist Party. It was officially proclaimed China's Youth Day after the founding of the People's Republic of China in 1949.

ist revolution. Sensitive to politics, youth have great revolutionary enthusiasm. However, to play their revolutionary role of an important army, they *"must unite with the broad masses of workers and peasants and become one with them."* Youth movement is sure to be led astray if the role of youth, divorced from the main force of workers and peasants and from the Party leadership, is incorrectly emphasized. On the other hand, negation of the youth's revolutionary role and abolition of the youth movement is also very harmful to the revolutionary cause of the proletariat.

In the struggle against imperialism and feudalism, thousands upon thousands of China's young people gradually deepened their understanding of integration with the workers and peasants. They *"went into their* [workers' and peasants'] *midst and became propagandists and organizers among them,"* standing in the forefront of the revolutionary movement. During the period of socialist revolution, not only has the role of youth not been weakened, but it has been brought into fuller play. Guided by Chairman Mao's revolutionary line, China's youth have persisted in integrating with workers and peasants and receiving re-education from them. They have thus tempered themselves and played an important part in socialist revolution and socialist construction. The emergence of young heroes like Huang Chi-kuang,[2] Lei Feng,[3] Chin Hsun-hua[4] and Chen

[2] A fighter in the Chinese People's Volunteers. During the battle of Sangkamryung in Korea on October 20, 1952, he silenced enemy machine-gun fire with his own body and thus ensured victory in the battle. He was honoured with the title of "Hero, Special Class" by the Chinese People's Volunteers.

[3] A great proletarian revolutionary fighter and an outstanding member of the Chinese Communist Party. A squad leader in an engineering corps of the Shenyang Units of the Chinese People's Liberation Army, he died a martyr at his post in August 1962. On March 5, 1963, Chairman Mao's inscription *"Learn From Comrade Lei Feng"* was made public.

[4] An example for the revolutionary youth. A Shanghai edu-

Taishan[5] fully shows the revolutionary outlook of China's younger generation nurtured by Mao Tsetung Thought. During the Great Proletarian Cultural Revolution, the Red Guards stepped forward to rebel against the revisionist line and became revolutionary pathbreakers to write another chapter in the history of China's youth movement. The struggle in the past two decades shows that China's youth who make up one-fifth of the population are shock brigades on every front. It is justified to call them a vigorous, important army in the whole revolutionary contingent.

The proletariat is the greatest class in the history of mankind and has the brightest future. It has always attached great importance to the youth and has faith in them. It has guided the revolutionary youth movement to link up with the entire revolutionary movement, making it an indispensable component part of the whole revolutionary cause of the proletariat. On the contrary, all the decadent reactionary classes, out of the needs of their own classes, always fear the struggle by revolutionary youth and try to disintegrate, utilize and sabotage their movement. In pushing ahead with their erroneous lines, the ringleaders of various opportunist lines in the Party always count on the youth and do their best to undermine the youth movement which is guided by Chairman Mao's revolutionary line. Alternating coercion with praise and cheating, Liu Shao-chi and other political swindlers tried to induce young people to be their tools in restoring capitalism. However, the future awaiting the opportunist ringleaders who sabotaged the revolutionary youth movement was not a good one. Their schemes were crushed, their absurdi-

---

cated youth who went to settle in the Shuangho Brigade in Heilungkiang Province in 1969. Not long after he was there, he gave his life to save state property during a flood.

[5] An excellent young worker at the Changchun No. 1 Motor Vehicles Plant. He died heroically while saving state property in a fire at the end of 1971.

ties criticized and turned into good teaching material by negative example.

Chairman Mao has pointed out: *"The young people are the most active and vital force in society. They are the most eager to learn and the least conservative in their thinking. This is especially so in the era of socialism."* Paying attention to bringing the revolutionary role of youth into play and strengthening work concerning them is not only required for the needs of present socialist revolution and construction, but is also a matter of fundamental importance in training millions of successors to the cause of proletarian revolution and in preventing and combating revisionism. The establishment of China's socialist system emancipates the youth politically and ideologically. The spread of Marxism-Leninism-Mao Tsetung Thought and the ever-deepening socialist revolution on the political and ideological fronts provide young people with the best conditions for mastering revolutionary theories in their resolute fight against the bourgeoisie and revisionism. The vigorous development of socialist construction makes it possible for them to develop their talents to the full and increase their ability in battling nature. All this is favourable in training and educating the young people, mobilizing their revolutionary initiative and encouraging them to be in the forefront of the revolutionary ranks in the period of socialism. We should act according to Chairman Mao's instruction and make full use of these conditions to guide the young people to perform their role as a revolutionary army on one of the fronts.

As a revolutionary army in the historical period of socialism, in order to *"fight bravely and resolutely for the great cause of socialism,"* young people must, under Party leadership, firmly bear in mind the Party's basic line in the historical period of socialism and regard the consolidation of the dictatorship of the proletariat and prevention of capitalist restoration as their most important task. The existence of class enemies at home and abroad determines the protracted and complex nature of the struggle between the proletariat and the bourgeoisie, between Marxism and revisionism and especially the struggle in the ideological field. To win victories, the proletariat as well as the youth should act according to Chairman Mao's instruction of *"criticizing and repudiating the bourgeoisie"* and *"criticizing revisionism,"* stand in the forefront of the ever-deepening socialist revolution and carry the struggle against the bourgeoisie and revisionism on the political and ideological fronts through to the end.

Nurtured by Mao Tsetung Thought, the younger generation is the least conservative in its thinking. It is eager for socialist new things and dares to challenge everything decadent. As soon as it grasps the truth, the younger generation will destroy all resistance. Since the founding of New China, the young people have contributed their share in the three great revolutionary movements—class struggle, the struggle for production and scientific experiment—and in criticizing the bourgeoisie and revisionism and capitalist tendencies in the realm of the superstructure. Previously unknown, large numbers of revolutionary young people in the Great Proletarian Cultural Revolution have acted in accordance with Chairman Mao's instructions and carried out timely and powerful criticism of the revisionist line. In the last few years, millions of educated young people have gone to settle down in the countryside, pounding away at the centuries-old concept of despising manual labour and workers and peasants through their revolutionary actions. All this shows that young people are able to shoulder together with workers and peasants the glorious task of criticizing the bourgeoisie and revisionism. These actions of theirs are good indeed! In order to continue the revolution under the dictatorship of the proletariat and to guarantee that our socialist motherland will never change its political colour, China's young people must, under the guidance of Marxism-Leninism-Mao Tsetung Thought, regard criticizing various bourgeois and revisionist ideas as their regular and important task. In the struggle, they should keep to Marxism and oppose revisionism, keep to the socialist road and oppose the capitalist road, uphold the proletarian world outlook and oppose the bourgeois world outlook. Young people should be daring in pitting themselves against all action and speech divorced from socialism. They should raise their vigilance against, be good at discerning, resolutely criticize and guard against erosion by bourgeois ideas and the evil practices of the exploiting classes. During the present movement of criticizing revisionism and rectifying the style of work, it is especially necessary for young people to be with the workers and peasants, read and study seriously and have a good grasp of Marxism. They must firmly grasp the essence of the revisionist lines of Liu Shao-chi and other political swindlers, carry out deepgoing revolutionary mass criticism to enhance their consciousness of class struggle and the struggle between the two lines, thus becoming more conscientious in implementing Chairman Mao's revolutionary line in their work.

Another historical and glorious task of youth during the period of socialism is to become a heroic shock brigade, in the true sense of the term, in the socialist construction of the motherland. Guided by Chairman Mao's revolutionary line, we have smashed the old China and built a socialist new China with initial prosperity. Yet China is still a developing country. To further develop our socialist economy, consolidate the socialist system and the dictatorship of the proletariat and to fulfil our bounden great internationalist task of helping the world's oppressed and exploited people, we must speed up the tempo of construction so as to build China in the not too distant future into a strong socialist country with a modern industry, agriculture, science, culture and national defence. Historically, this glorious yet arduous task has fallen on the shoulders of the younger generation and all our people. As Chairman Mao has taught us: *"We must help all our young people to understand that ours is still a very poor country, that we cannot change this situation radically in a short time, and that only through the united efforts of our younger generation and all our people, working with their own hands, can China be made strong and prosperous within a period of several decades."* Young people working in every field of socialist construction must respond enthusiastically to Chairman Mao's great call with deeds and resolutely integrate with workers and peasants in the struggle for production and scientific experiment as well as at every post. They should defy difficulties, work selflessly, study hard, display the revolutionary spirit of daring to think and to act, be brave in making innovations and take the road their predecessors have never travelled, so as to build China into a strong and prosperous country with their own hands.

Socialist construction and battling nature is not plain sailing. However, so long as we, under Party leadership, make up our minds to go through hardships for a good future for the motherland and people, display the revolutionary spirit of fearing neither hardship nor death, take veteran revolutionary Iron Man Wang[6] of the Taching Oilfield as our example and play the role of a shock brigade and work with a down-to-earth spirit

[6] An excellent representative of the Taching workers and the first leader of the oilfield's drilling team No. 1205. Praised for his revolutionary spirit of fearing neither hardship nor death in his work, Wang Chin-hsi was called the "iron man." Elected a Member of the Central Committee of the Chinese Communist Party during the Ninth Party Congress in 1969, he died of illness in November 1970.

like the "iron girls" team[7] in Tachai, we can overcome any difficulty, no matter how big. To achieve greater, faster, better and more economical results in building socialism, young people should not only work with a soaring revolutionary spirit, but make efforts to master knowledge in modern culture, science and technology in order to be both red and expert. The most eager to learn and full of initiative, young people are a vital force. Since ancient times, those who dare to make inventions by toppling superstitions have frequently been young people at the beginning. This is especially so in the socialist era. Young people should make efforts to study culture, science and technology for the revolution and advance continuously.

Referring to the youth movement in Yenan as the model for the youth movement throughout the country, Chairman Mao emphasized in his article: *"The youth of Yenan have achieved solidarity and unity."* Under the guidance of Chairman Mao's revolutionary line, the great unity of the revolutionary youth of the whole country and their close unity with all the other people in the land is an important guarantee for winning new victories in China's socialist revolution and construction. The Communist Youth League should be the core of uniting and educating the young people. Its task is to pay attention to the characteristics of the young people in organizing and leading them to stand in the forefront of socialist revolution and construction while fulfilling the Party's central tasks. In accordance with Chairman Mao's instruction to *keep fit, study hard and work well,* it should pay attention to young people's health, to young workers' and peasants' political study and raising their educational level, to the life of the

[7] A shock production brigade organized by some young women of the Tachai Brigade in Hsiyang County, Shansi Province. They are acclaimed as the "iron girls" team for their good work in removing hills to fill gullies and in transforming farmland.

educated youth who have gone to settle in the countryside, and further uniting and organizing the young people around the movement of criticizing revisionism and rectifying the style of work and around various tasks in socialist revolution and socialist construction. The Communist Youth League should not only unite the progressive youth, but should also be good at uniting with young people who are not so advanced for the time being to make progress and struggle together.

The brilliant thinking elaborated in *The Orientation of the Youth Movement* by Chairman Mao illuminates the road forward for China's youth. Revolutionary youth will live up to the expectations of the Party and Chairman Mao, shoulder the historic task, devote their youthful vitality to the great cause of socialism and always stand in the forefront of the revolutionary ranks.

"Young people of the whole country, bestir yourselves!"

(*A translation of an article originally published in "Hongqi" No. 5, 1973.*)

THE YOUTH—FOR THE CAUSE OF SOCIALISM*

1. FINDING FOUNTAINS OF HAPPINESS

BY WANG LIANG

After I graduated from junior middle school I began to think about what job I should do in the construction of my socialist motherland.

I have been fascinated by water for some time. Not only is it vital to human beings, there is so much farm work that cannot be done unless water is put to use. My mind was already turned towards the subject when I was enrolled at a vocational school in hydro-geology.

* From *Peking Review*, No. 19, 1972.

And when I got into it, I grew to like what I was studying.

Like others in 1958, I graduated on May 4th, Youth Day in China, two months before the semester officially ended and was assigned work.

After taking up my job in Shansi Province I learnt much about the importance of water to the national economy. Water was short in this province and it was in real need of hydro-geological workers.

It wasn't long before I found that I needed more studying to be really adept at my job. In September 1958, while continuing my work, I enrolled in a correspondence course from the Institute of Geology in Changchun, which I completed in 1964. The benefits of this course were innumerable.

In 1963 the leadership had suggested I do trade union work. This would have meant less activities in the open air. I said I preferred working outdoors in a more strenuous environment. When the leadership agreed to this, I looked forward to doing some hard work.

Water was as precious as oil in the Taihang Mountains in Shansi. Drinking water had to be brought in from two kilometres away. When there was a dry spell, people had to walk five or ten kilometres to get it. The county leadership organized truck and tractor contingents to get it.

Our team went to a village to prospect for water. Approaching it, we found a group of people coming near, beating drums and gongs. We thought somebody was getting married, but they were coming to welcome us.

We made some investigations. Old people in the village told us that an earthquake several years before had left a chasm in a courtyard. After careful observation, we decided on a well-site alongside the chasm. After finishing it, 200 buckets of water a day met the drinking water needs in this small village.

Yangcheng County was dry nine years out of ten. Educating the masses through Chairman Mao's teaching that *"irrigation . . . is the life-blood of agriculture,"* the county revolutionary committee used the example of Nankuan Commune which got high grain yields by building ponds on a mountain to retain water. This generated the people's enthusiasm to build water conservancy works.

The first thing we did in the county was to find water together with members of the Chengkuan Commune which had often been hit by drought. Not long after that, we dug five wells to pump clear water for irrigating dry farmland. Several days later we were overjoyed to find that the crops had turned from yellow to green. Later we helped train a peasant-technician for each commune. After several months' training, they were able to survey and decide independently on a well-site. The county leadership was pleased that we had left a group of hydro-geological personnel who would never leave.

As a result of our deepening a well for a brigade, the quality of the water improved and the quantity increased. Pumping for three days running couldn't dry it up. The peasants said: The Party and Chairman Mao have sent us water from Peking.

Everyone in our hydro-geological team is proud of our work which is indispensable to the national economy and the people's lives.

2. MAKING WASTE WATER USABLE

BY FENG YI-HSIN

When I came to the Peking General Petro-Chemical Plant early in 1969, I was fascinated by the magnificent sight of a rising petro-chemical complex. Delighted as I was to become a petroleum worker, I felt somewhat frustrated when I learnt I was assigned to the waste-water treatment works where I had to handle dirty, stinking water all day long.

Veteran workers knew little more than I did about purifying waste water, but they thought differently about the matter. "Waste water from the plant," they told me, "is a danger to people as well as animals and crops. China is a socialist country, we must solve this problem somehow and make good use of it as part of our contribution to the people." Their words helped me realize the significance of my work.

But how could such harmful substances as phenol, sulphur and oil be removed from effluent so that it could be used for irrigation? Workers at this newly built plant lacked practical experience in this respect. We young people and technicians and veteran workers began tackling the problem with the help of scientific research departments.

A key to solving the problem is the cultivation in activated sludge of micro-organisms which are used to dephenolize the waste water. The more activated the sludge, the better the effect in dephenolizing. But some-one said: "Micro-organisms are very feeble and easily die when the temperature is too high or too low or when there isn't enough oxygen or there's too much oil in the water." This did not discourage us. We held that since everything was governed by some law, the law of the growth of micro-organisms could surely be grasped if we made careful observations and analyses. To get enough food for the micro-organisms, many comrades worked without a let-up for days on end. In spite of setbacks, we continued our experiments and finally succeeded in cultivating tougher micro-organisms which absorbed and continually reduced the amount of phenol in the waste water.

Our confidence increased, we went on with de-oiling. We carried out more than 600 experiments and greatly reduced the oil content in the waste water. This was another step ahead in purifying waste water.

While experimenting with desulphurization one day, there was a hitch in an engine, and suffocating gas, hydrogen sulphide and sulphur-bearing waste water gushed out. Young workers on the spot rushed over to it and did their best to get the engine working properly. Continued experiments in desulphurization yielded the desired result.

Treated effluent, purified and clear, now flows to the fields around our plant. We are delighted to see ducks and goldfish swim in this clean water. Experiments by scientific research departments in conjunction with local people's communes show that using this water to irrigate the fields has led to a general increase in output of crops.

Three years at the waste-water treatment works has made me realize that we still have to redouble our efforts in purifying the waste water discharged from our plant and that there are other pollution problems we young people have to tackle. Constantly encouraging ourselves with the words "Working at our posts in treating waste water, we have the whole world in mind and the interests of the world's people at heart," we are determined to do our work still better.

3. I'LL STUDY TO BECOME A GOOD DOCTOR

BY HSU YUN-HSIN

I was a "barefoot doctor"[1] in my village before I went to college.

I had taken a short hospital training course to start

[1] "Barefoot doctors" are peasants trained to give medical and hygienic advice locally without leaving their farm work. Their main job is to popularize hygiene, improve sanitation and prevent and cure common diseases. Such doctors first appeared in the rice-growing east China region where, with their medical kits, they often went barefoot in the fields, as was the custom. Their peasant-patients fondly called them "barefoot doctors," a term now used all over China.

with, and then got clinical experience and learnt the use of various folk prescriptions as I went along.

Acupuncture was in great demand at my people's commune. So I studied it, learning from experienced acupuncture doctors, and applying the acupuncture needles on various points of my body to obtain experience. Through such repeated practice, I came to know thoroughly several dozen points on the human body and experienced the sensations of numbness, swelling, aching and pain at each point.

A patient with stomach ulcers came in one night. He was having spasms of excruciating pain. I gave him several different drugs, but all to no avail. He then asked me if I could do acupuncture. I told him that up to now I had only used it on myself. He asked me to try it on him. I inserted needles at three different points in his body which could cure ulcers. After I had made two insertions, he felt the pain diminishing, and when I had left the needles in the different positions for 20 more minutes, he declared it had completely stopped. This initial success gave me great encouragement.

High blood pressure had plagued 68-year-old Uncle Chen of my village for years. In 1969, he became partially paralysed. No amount of medicine worked. He could not go often to the commune hospital because of his condition, so the hospital sent a doctor to teach me how to give him acupuncture treatment. I went regularly to Uncle Chen's, using the new acupuncture treatment method on him as well as needling the ear. The old man got better. A month later, he recovered. I was indescribably happy to have been able to ease the suffering of poor and lower-middle peasants like him.

Though I had then mastered acupuncture and knew the use of some of the simpler drugs, both Chinese and Western, and had cured some common diseases in the countryside with them, I was unable to deal with more complicated cases. I could only give such patients preliminary aid and recommend them to go to the hospital. I often thought at the time of how nice it would be if I could study to improve my medical skill and heal more patients.

My wish came true in winter 1970. I was recommended to study at Peking Medical College, and became one of its first students from worker, peasant or soldier origin.

I will never forget the night before I left for college. My home was full of people. Many poor and lower-middle peasants had come to see me off. Old Chang remarked: "What wonderful times I have lived to see, when our children are going to college!" Another old man, Hsu, added: "There were so many epidemics in the old days. . . . How many children used to die in spring and summer! . . ." One grandmother, Li, said: "Remember 1934? Cholera must have killed dozens of people in the village that time. . . ."

So the "send-off" became a meeting in which the evils of the old society were condemned, and the good things of the new praised. It was late in the night when the gathering broke up.

Whenever my studies give me difficulty now that I'm in college, I recall that night. The accusation against the old society and the hopes the village folk placed in me always give me new strength. I've finished the basic required courses, and am now taking my clinical courses at one of the college hospitals.

Like the people back home, I, too, am looking forward to the day when I will go back a competent doctor, to heal sickness and pain among my people.

4. ELIMINATING PESTS

BY LIU CHIEN-YING

I was assigned to work at our commune's experimental farm three years ago. My job was to protect

the crops from destructive insects. Fearing I wouldn't
be up to the job, I demurred. "I'm a girl of 16," I said
to myself, "and know very little about farm work, still
less about pests. What can I do? Besides, dealing with
insects isn't pleasant work." Aware of my reluctance,
the farm director talked things over with me. "It's
the same whatever you do," he said. "You can learn
while you work. You'll never be able to master anything unless you actually do it."

Of all insects, the leaf miner is the most destructive
to peas. For many years no effective method to combat it had been found in our native village. Experiments
with several methods listed in the technical books
showed little success. An investigation group was then
organized by our farm and I joined it to find out the
leaf miners' living habits and to work out ways of
eliminating it.

Smaller than a mosquito, this insect flies off at the
least movement. I waited in vain in the pea plot several
days to observe its habits. One evening a swarm of
tiny things flew towards me. As they came near, I
saw they were the insects I was waiting for. But my
hopes were soon dashed, for they did not settle on the
peas. By luck I saw one on a leaf, but it flew off almost
instantly. Failure to get any information made me feel
the futility of my efforts.

Concerned about my work, the commune leadership
told me to study Chairman Mao's *The Foolish Old
Man Who Removed the Mountains* conscientiously.
The Foolish Old Man's perseverance and determination to remove two big mountains deeply impressed
me. Yet difficulties and fatigue seemed to have got the
better of me though I had worked only a few days.
The comparison made me feel ashamed of myself and
spurred me on.

I continued my observations in the pea plot. It was
watering time, so the ground was wet. What with the

raw spring weather, it was chilly in the morning and evening, and after watching for about a fortnight I felt weak in the legs. I was worried about not having gathered much information. But I vowed that I would find ways of combating the insect no matter what happened.

After some three weeks, I had some idea about the leaf miners' living habits on the peas: where they lay eggs, when the larvae emerge from the eggs, and when the larvae first become pupae and finally adults.

This knowledge gave me immense satisfaction. But before I could tell my mother everything I knew, she cut me short: "Leaf miners, nothing but leaf miners! What's the use of just knowing about them?" "Why," I rejoined, "knowing its habits helps me find ways to eliminate it." However, my mother's words sobered me. Would my observations of the life-history of a generation of leaf miners hold good under different circumstances? Moreover, knowledge of their habits and growth did not mean I had found effective methods of combating them. Further observation and study was necessary.

Anxious to get quick results, I used a strong insecticide, but it yielded little result. I found this was because though I knew the general law of the leaf miners' life, I had not grasped the specific law of each stage of its growth. Taking things for granted in spraying of course could not produce the desired result. Later, using different insecticides at different stages and by making comparisons and careful analyses, we gradually worked out an effective method which basically eliminated the leaf miners. Popularization of this method in other villages resulted in a bumper harvest on the commune's 4,000 *mu* planted to peas in 1970, with output double that of 1969. Another good crop was harvested in 1971.

Over the past three years, I have learnt from books, from experienced peasants as well as from my own practice and have mastered the rudiments of combating several kinds of very harmful insects. With the passage of time, I have come to like my work more and more—the work about which I had qualms at first.

4. The School Child

A GRADE OF 100*

BY HU CHIEN, A GIRL IN THE SECOND YEAR OF THE
JUNIOR MIDDLE SCHOOL

Today we got back the papers from our mathematics
test. When I saw a big red "100" up in the corner I
was overjoyed. Then, as I read through the problems,
I noticed that one of them seemed wrong. I checked
it and found that I had really done it incorrectly but
the teacher hadn't noticed it. I felt like going to the
teacher and telling him about it, but when I looked at
that bright red 100 I hesitated.

Just then someone tapped me on the shouder. I
looked around and saw it was one of my best friends.
"Hu Chien," she said, "let me see your paper." Un-
easily I passed it to her. I could feel my heart beating
very fast because I was afraid she might discover the
error. But she had wanted to see how I had done another problem and didn't notice it. "100! How wonderful!" she said as she handed it back to me.

I really didn't know what to do. "Nobody knows
anyway," I said to myself. "Let it pass." I didn't go
to the teacher that morning but ran into him at noon
after classes were over. Ordinarily I would chatter away
with him, but now I kept my mouth shut guiltily.

When I got back home I went through the newspapers looking for material for our political study and
current events class. I came across a story about a
worker who made high demands on himself. He was
a young lathe operator in a factory. One day as he was

* From *China Reconstructs*, April 1973.

going to bed he suddenly remembered that one reject part he had processed had got mixed in with the good ones and he had forgotten to tell the worker on the next shift. If that part were used in a machine it might result in a breakdown. He got out of bed at once and hurried to the shop to look for the reject.

I was very moved by this example of the working class feeling of responsibility towards the revolution. Why did this worker take the matter of this small part so seriously? Because he knew that a bad part could put a whole big machine out of commission. If you cover up even a little mistake it can bring harm to the revolution.

I thought of my mathematics test. Wasn't this also true of our study? We should be honest and modest in our studies. Wrong is wrong, and it should not be hidden. Today we are studying not for marks, but to improve our ability to analyze and solve problems. The fact that I got that problem wrong shows that my ability is not as good as it should be. This helps me learn so that I will not make the same mistake next time. If I let myself keep this 100 I haven't earned and do not have the courage to correct my mistake, some day I might cause a loss to the revolution. I determined to try to have this working class attitude of making strict demands on one's self.

The first period in the afternoon I asked the teacher to change my test paper. My mark dropped to 95, but what I learned from that math test is worth much more than 100!

PRIMARY SCHOOL*

1. GROWING UP HEALTHY IN MIND AND BODY

In a letter to China Reconstructs, *S.G., a primary school teacher in Paris, asks: How is primary educa-*

* From *China Reconstructs,* June 1973.

tion in the People's Republic of China organized? How do you educate your children? How is the curriculum arranged? How do you combine theory and practice? Do the pupils have their own organization? What do you do if they are undisciplined?

To get the answers, our reporter visited the Wenhsing Street Primary School in the western part of Peking and talked with its leaders, teachers, pupils and after-school activities counsellors.

The Wenhsing Street Primary School starts to liven up at 7 a.m., though classes don't begin until 8. The pupils on duty for the day come to clean up the classrooms, groups of colorfully dressed girls assemble in the schoolyard to play their favorite game, skipping a rope of rubber bands. A group of boys, their foreheads beaded with sweat, pursue a small football across the playing field. The morning sun illuminates eight large characters painted in white on the red brick wall of the four-story school building—Chairman Mao's admonition to the children of new China: *Study well and make progress every day.*

As soon as the bell rings the school quiets down, but soon sounds of recitation and song begin to come from some classrooms. The schoolyard and playing field are at their busiest when school lets out at 3 p.m. The air is filled with the sound of a piano, accordions, laughter and singing and the shrill blast of the athletics instructors' whistles, as the song and dance group rehearses, track and field enthusiasts practice sprinting and high-jumping, and the lower graders play games in small groups. The children often stay around till 5 p.m. when the school closes up.

Teaching Books and Children

"We want to teach subject matter, and also bring up the children right." This is what Wenhsing's teachers demand of themselves. "Since the foundations for a child's attitudes are laid in primary school," explained a teacher, "ours is a great responsibility. Therefore we give first place to ideological education." He went on to tell how, when a story of a hero is the reading matter for the Chinese class, "I have to really get into the revolutionary spirit and learn something from it myself before I can imbue my pupils with the hero's lofty ideals and be most effective at helping them master the Chinese words and expressions in the text.

"If a pupil corrects a character the teacher has written incorrectly on the blackboard, we teachers welcome this as a sign of the pupil's conscientiousness and praise him or her. We do not frown at the loss of prestige as teachers did in the old tradition. This is a stimulus to the children and it gives them at an early age an example of accepting criticism and correcting mistakes.'

It's the same in after-school activities. During a jump-rope contest the teacher tried to promote the idea of "friendship first, competition second", but found that some pupils thought that only the jumpers were "heroic", while those who swung the rope, kept score and brought drinking water were of a "lower order". He got the children to discuss the kind of thinking behind this, and the kind of attitude they should have toward division of labor. Through this little event he helped the children develop the idea of wholeheartedly serving the people.

New Teacher-Pupil Relationship

I could not help comparing all this with the primary school I attended in old China. Although that was long ago, I still retain terrifying memories of the severity of my teachers. We trembled when we had to answer a question, afraid that if we answered wrong we would be reprimanded or be made to stand as punishment. What a contrast to what I found while visiting the classrooms of the Wenhsing Street School. The teachers try in every way to arouse the children's interest in learning. When someone answers a question correctly he or she is praised by the teacher, especially if the answer shows originality. If a pupil gives a wrong answer, the teacher will say in a warm tone, "Think it over again. Isn't it like this . . . ?" In this way the pupil is led step by step toward the correct answer.

One day a girl came late. When the teacher found that the coal stove in her home had gone out and she hadn't eaten breakfast, he didn't scold her. Instead, after class he took her to the teachers' dining room to buy a roll.

On another day a boy arrived all in a sweat ten minutes late to class. Embarrassed, he admitted he had been playing. First the teacher criticized him, then she said, "Anyway you're honest about it. That's good. I'm sure you'll correct your fault and won't come late again."

These small things made a deep impression on me; they are evidences of the new teacher-pupil relationship in the school. The teacher doesn't just impart knowledge to the pupils but is concerned about them, is their understanding and helpful comrade and friend.

One boy was known throughout the school as a troublemaker. He often hit or swore at other children and sometimes his antics even disrupted class. Though only 12, he had already learned to smoke. Neither teachers nor parents could do anything with him. When his home-room teacher visited the family he found out that the boy had begun to go bad under the influence of a hooligan in the neighborhood. This made the teacher feel his responsibility all the more.

The teacher tried to get close to him and cooperated with his parents in helping him to go right. When he was sick, the teacher visited him at home. When he couldn't do his homework, he gave him individual help after school. The Little Red Soldiers in his class invited him to activities designed to educate children in revolutionary traditions, like story hours in which members of the old Red Army tell of past struggles, or a trip to the graves of revolutionary martyrs.

When the boy was undisciplined, instead of scolding him, the teacher tried patiently to get him to see the demands the children of new China should make on themselves in order to be worthy of the trust placed in them for carrying on the revolution when they grow up. The teacher encouraged every sign of progress and reported it to the parents.

One morning the boy didn't come to class. At noon the teacher went to see him and found him ill. Both parents were away and there was no one to get lunch for him, so the teacher made him a bowl of noodle soup. As he ate it the boy said, "Teacher, I was wrong. I took a bad person for a good one and thought it was heroic to hit and swear at others." Happy to see this new understanding, the teacher urged him to study well and try to become an advanced pupil.

After that the boy gradually improved. Once, on a camping trip, the weather changed suddenly and it started to hail. Ignoring his own discomfort, the boy pulled the smaller children one after another up a slippery slope to shelter in a little pavilion. His classmates were full of praise.

Bringing Books to Life

The teachers regularly get together to exchange experience and talk about ways to improve their work. They often discuss how to bring the textbooks to life, how to relate book learning to what the pupil has learned from life. That is, instead of just pouring knowledge into the pupils' heads, the teacher stimulates them to use their brains and develops their ability to think and to analyze problems.

In fourth grade, when the children are about ten, they have their first contact with natural science. The teachers carefully consider how to teach each lesson so as to increase the pupils' ability to recognize and explain natural phenomena and not just come away with a few dry principles in their heads.

One teacher began the lesson on water by pointing to a beaker of it and asking, "What color is water?" Almost all the 42 pupils in the class raised their hands, thinking this question quite simple. "Water's white," a boy hastened to say.

"Is that right?" she asked. "Then what's this?" she said holding up a test tube containing a white, milky liquid.

"Milk."

"Well, then, what color is water?"

"No color," the boy answered with an embarrassed laugh. "Water's transparent."

Holding up two test tubes containing colorless, transparent liquids, the teacher asked, "What's this?"

"Water," most pupils answered confidently. She called a girl up to smell and taste the two liquids and then asked her, "What are these?"

"One's water," she answered, "and the other's alcohol."

"Then can we say that all colorless, transparent liquids are water?" the teacher asked. Forty-two faces broke into a knowing smile, as if to say, "Now we've got it!"

On the basis of the pupils' actual experience, the teacher helped them understand the important truth that one can only differentiate on the basis of comparison. Beginning from concrete things rather than an abstract concept, she guided them to reach the same scientific conclusion as in the text—"water is a colorless, odorless, tasteless transparent liquid". Then she started on the next part of the lesson, the uses of water.

2. LIFE AT WENHSING STREET SCHOOL

Q. Who attends your school?

A. Our school, like other primary schools in Peking, takes children from the neighborhood, in our case, 20 streets with 1,300 families. If they move out of the area they transfer to another grade school. We take children at about the age of 7, though some schools take them at 6. This last term we had an enrolment of 1,040, about an equal number of girls and boys, in 23 classes.

After graduation at the end of grade school they are accepted into the local junior middle school. Before the cultural revolution they used to have to pass an examination for this, but now it is not necessary. Each year the children have two vacations of about a month, generally beginning in January and July.

Q. Do the children have to pay tuition fees?

A. Children in the city's primary schools each pay a fee of 2.50 yuan plus 0.40-0.80 yuan for books and stationery each term. This is a relatively low fee, within the reach of all. Gone are the days when a family could not send their children to school for lack of funds. The major expenses of the schools are paid out of the national budget.

Q. What do the children study?

A. Every child takes Chinese, arithmetic, music, drawing and physical training. Beginning in the third grade, every child in our school studies English. Some other schools offer French, Spanish or other languages. In the fourth grade a course in political studies is added. The reading material for it is mainly selections from Chairman Mao's writings and stories of revolutionary struggles of the past. Thus from quite early on, the children are exposed to Marxist-Leninist thought and learn to appreciate the traditions of the revolution. Another course added in fourth grade, entitled "general knowledge", deals mainly with natural science. The school day begins with setting-up exercises in the morning and has six 45-minute periods, four in the morning and two in the afternoon.

From the third grade on, pupils at our school often go with their teachers to visit factories and rural people's communes, to work in them and there to absorb the working class attitudes of the workers and peasants. This is to help them relate their book learning to life and to learn a correct view of labor. When there is a lesson on wheat, for instance, the pupils go to a commune, on papermaking, to a paper mill. Ten workers, peasants and members of the People's Liberation Army serve as permanent after-school activities counsellors.

Q. How many years does a child spend in primary school now?

A. Primary schooling used to last six years, but we have found that it is not really necessary for it to be so long. If the repetition in course material is cut out, the same amount of ground can be covered in five years. The plan is to change all primary schools in the Peking municipality over to the five-year system. The textbooks we have been using since 1970 are geared to the five-year course, and we are changing to it step by step. The children will finish the equivalent of six years' study in five years and leave primary school at 12.

Q. How about grading?

A. The guide for our work and for evaluating our pupils is Chairman Mao's directive on education: *"Our educational policy must enable everyone who receives an education to develop morally, intellectually and physically and become a worker with both socialist consciousness and culture.*" At the end of each term every pupil takes home a report card which is an all-round record of his progress, including both his scholastic achievement and character development. The latter is reported in a commentary written by the teacher and takes into consideration the child's attitude toward study and labor, adherence to discipline, the way he unites and cooperates with other children, his concern for the collective and his care of public property. In judging pupils in the upper grades, we also consider whether or not they are consciously studying for the revolution and have an interest in national affairs.

Pupils receive a grade for each course. These are based on a combination of examination results, the record of homework and attitude toward study. Pupils who fail in some subjects can get help from teachers and classmates during vacation. Before the new school term begins they can take a make-up exam. If a pupil fails again in two major subjects (political study, Chinese or arithmetic) or one major and two minor subjects, the school reviews his situation to decide whether he should repeat the same grade. If the failure is due to poor health or other unavoidable reasons, he usually remains with his class and gets help from teachers and classmates in order to catch up. If the pupil fails because he has not studied well, he will be held back a year with his parents' consent. Such cases are rare, only seven in our whole school this year.

Q. Is there an organization for children?

A. Many pupils in our school, like others throughout the country, belong to the Little Red Soldiers. Any child between the ages of seven and thirteen may apply to join. His home room Little Red Soldiers group and their teacher discuss whether the applicant has suitable moral, intellectual and physical qualifications and his admission is approved by the school. The Little Red Soldiers wear a red scarf—red, the color of revolution, symbolically, a corner of the national flag.

About 700 of our school's 1,040 pupils are Little Red Soldiers. The units are divided according to school (brigade), team (grade) and small group (home room). Leaders of each are democratically elected. The committee of brigade leaders gets direct guidance and help from the Communist Youth League group in the school. The Little Red Soldiers hold after-school activities to which applicants not yet approved are welcomed. The Little Red Soldiers must see to it that they set a good example for others in whatever they do. They should be honest, courageous, lively and promote unity among their classmates.

3. A LESSON FROM LIFE

BY MA CHUNG-LIN

For the past two years the fifth and sixth grades of the Wenhsing Street Primary School, which is in our neighborhood, have been coming to our factory, the Peking Pharmaceuticals Company's Plant No. 2. They and their teachers spend about a week with us each term, doing light tasks such as washing jars, packing medicines and making boxes. Our plant Communist Party branch doesn't regard them as a burden, it recognizes the importance of bringing up the young generation right. It assigned another Party member, also a veteran worker, and myself to teach them.

I cannot help being moved at the sight of these children, their schoolbags over their shoulders, going to school every day and then coming to our factory to learn to work so that they can serve the people better when they grow up. I am 61. In the old society my parents were too poor to send me to school. At the age of 12 I had to become a child laborer in a match factory, to be exploited and oppressed by the capitalist owners. I love these children from the bottom of my heart. All of us at the factory regard it as our duty to help them grow up well. Our job is not just to teach them how to work, but to understand why and for whom they are working.

Once master workman Tsui asked some of the sixth graders to pick bolts out of a heap of scrap iron. The pile looked as high as a mountain to them, and they became discouraged. What on earth are these rusty bolts good for, they began thinking. We came here to learn skills, not to sort out bolts. They lost interest in their work. Master Tsui saw what was on their minds. He asked them to bring some of their bolts and come into a workshop. There he scrubbed the rusty bolts in oil until they looked like new. Then he took the children around the shop and showed them how bolts are made. They also saw how a big machine could not operate if a bolt was missing. The youngsters began to feel very ashamed. "Now you see how important bolts are and how much work goes into making them. Our country is still very backward. We will have to work hard for scores of years to change it. We should work hard and be saving in everything we do."

That afternoon the youngsters worked for all they were worth until they had got out all the bolts even from the bottom of the pile. From then on whenever one of them ran across one, he saved it. When they got back to school some of them wrote an article, "A Lesson from Life", about the incident.

There are many such stories. I am happy to know that our country's younger generation is such as these, and rejoice every time I see them make progress.

4. NO ONE FALLS BEHIND

BY YANG AH-LI

Early in 1972 my pupil Chang Chu-tung became ill and had to stay home for a while. Her mother came to me, "My daughter is so worried that she'll fall behind in her studies that she often cries." I offered to come to her house to give her special tutoring, but that night after I got home, I thought it over and realized that my own time is limited. It would be better to organize others in the class to help her. I told my idea to the class and all the children volunteered. I chose three for the task.

A week later Chu-tung returned to school in high spirits. Her classmates surrounded her and asked her how she felt. They went through her exercise books and marvelled that she had done so well. I praised Chu-tung for persisting in her studies and the whole class for its spirit of mutual help.

A few days later four Little Red Soldiers came to me and suggested we organize a permanent group to help pupils who miss classes.

"How did you hit on such an idea?" I asked. A girl named Ting Tsung replied, "We worry about those who have to stay out. As Little Red Soldiers we should see to it that nobody falls behind." I was pleased to see an eight-year-old girl with such a good attitude. I encouraged them and let the four constitute themselves a tutoring group.

They were very conscientious. They took down every pupil's home address and whenever anyone was absent for a few days, they visited his or her home. In order to do their tutoring well they often asked me to go over a lesson again with them. They were so busy that for several days they didn't have much time left after school for play. This didn't suit Chang Ting-chao, the only boy in the group. One day Ting Tsung came in. "Ting-chao likes to play all the time," she said, "and is doing only a half-hearted job of helping our classmates. What shall we do?"

"Can't you make some rules so that each of you has a certain responsibility?" I suggested.

The next day they showed me the rules they had drawn up—that they wouldn't fight or quarrel when visiting other children's homes and that they would sum up their work every Saturday. They also laid out a division of labor so that some were responsible for lessons in Chinese, others for arithmetic, music and drawing. After that they worked even better and were very strict with themselves. Everyone in the class studied hard and made good progress.

In the second term another pupil named Hsuan Hung got a kidney infection and needed a long period of rest. She was very worried about missing so many classes. I visited her home with some of the children. We told her not to worry, just get a good rest and we would help her make up her schoolwork when the time came. After she got better members of the tutoring group went to her home every day for the remainder of her six-month illness. In this way she was able to do all the schoolwork just like the rest of the class. In gratitude, the girl's mother wrote the school a letter of thanks.

When the time came for the midterm exam the tutors gave her the tests. I found that Hsuan Hung had done all the arithmetic problems correctly. It gave me great joy to write a red 100 on her paper. She also did well in her Chinese test, with a 95. As I wrote the red numbers, I knew what they stood for was not just one pupil's good mark, but, more important, the spirit of unity and mutual help which we are trying to inculcate in children in our era.

AFTER SCHOOL*

What do the children do after school? How are activities for them organized?

One afternoon after school I went with Yao Yungchun, a teacher at the Kuanhsiang Primary School on Peking's west side, to visit some of her pupils' homes. In one lane we found groups of children reading picture story books, singing songs or listening to a story. In a courtyard some girls were playing the favorite game "jumping the rope of rubber bands". Further on there was a game of ping-pong on a concrete table. In other homes we saw groups of children reciting their Chinese school texts or repeating new words in English and other languages they were studying.

These are some of the educational after-school activities open to the pupils of the Kuanhsiang School. They are being started in many districts in Peking under the joint leadership of school revolutionary committees and neighborhood committees.

Since liberation all school-age children have the chance to go to school, but what happens when classes are over for the day? In some families, both parents work and they return home much later than the children. Often the youngsters used to just throw their school bags down and run out into the streets, getting into mischief, damaging trees and climbing on roofs, playing near railroad tracks and streams, getting into quarrels and fights. The school and street committee decided something should be done. They mobilized some retired workers and others in the neighborhood who had time to coordinate with teachers and parents in organizing and guiding after-school activities.

At Teacher Yao's school a meeting of teachers and after-school activities directors sums up the week's

* From *China Reconstructs*, February 1973.

work, compares notes on the children's behavior and problems and plans future activities. Their guiding principle is that the activities should be educational but not burden the children with extra homework.

In addition to reviewing lessons and cultural and sports activities, the children learn household skills like cooking, cleaning and mending, and spend some time helping people in the neighborhood.

The Story of 'Vagabond'

In the home of a construction worker we saw three girls around a desk helping a boy review his lessons. They were all Little Red Soldiers, a vanguard children's organization. How the boy became one, said Teacher Yao, was quite a story.

His name is Liu Chien-she and he is now in the sixth grade. When he was in the fourth grade he was known throughout the school for his mischief and unruliness. At class he paid no attention to the teacher; he would start humming to himself and his eyes would wander here and there, noticing every bird that flew past the window. Sometimes when the teacher was writing on the blackboard, he would start a fight with a classmate. When the teacher reprimanded him he would just make a face at her. After school he was either in the trees catching birds or swinging a stick about picking fights with people. He had the nickname "Vagabond".

How should this child be helped? The parents, teachers and neighbors were all concerned about him. Teacher Tsui from his homeroom often went to discuss the matter with his family and the after-school directors. They concluded that Chien-she was honest, strong-willed and brave. The reason he did not like to study and got into mischief was mainly that he didn't understand why he should study.

His parents started to tell him stories about the family's past. They compared present-day life with the bitter past, how in the old society they had suffered hunger and deprivation and had had to wander about begging. For generations nobody had been able to read or write; they were exploited and downtrodden by the landlords and capitalists.

The after-school director noticed that the boy especially admired the People's Liberation Army, so he asked some demobilized soldiers in the neighborhood to tell him stories of how the PLA men kept discipline and served the people. They also explained that in order to master modern military technique, one had to have general and scientific knowledge and understand things like machinery, mathematics and the weather.

Once the school took the pupils to a factory to learn some of the work there. Chien-she was to put together the parts of a flashlight, but he put them together wrong. The worker instructing him seized upon this opportunity to point out that he had not done it right because he did not know anything about electricity, and taught him some basic theory. A worker, he explained, also needed general and scientific knowledge. This was an incentive to becoming disciplined and studious.

As time went by the teacher noticed that the boy eagerly took on any job no matter how dirty or hard. She praised him for this, saying it was a first step towards growing up into a cultured worker with socialist consciousness.

Thus guided, Liu Chien-she started to change. He began to feel that it was wrong to fool around in class and pick fights, and gradually came to understand the importance of earnest study. By the fifth grade his studies showed marked improvement. In the morning he often helped tidy up the school yard and classrooms, and in his spare time after school he would haul coal for couples who were both away at work or help elderly women fetch water. Not long ago he put on the red scarf of the Little Red Soldiers.

An Enthusiastic Director

Entering the home of Ma Hsiao-wei, a fourth-grade pupil, we saw a straight, sturdy elderly man with white hair telling stories of the revolution to a group of children. They sat completely absorbed, their bright eyes fixed on the old man.

He was Shen Yu-shu, or Grandpa Shen as his neighbors affectionately call him, a retired worker now nearly seventy. In the old society he had had it hard; for almost half his life he never had enough to eat or wear. After liberation he had stood up and become master of his fate. He had been very enthusiastic in his work. After retiring he received a pension according to the labor insurance regulations and continued to enjoy various benefits like free medical care. His happy life made him want to give every bit of his remaining energy to the people.

Grandpa Shen began to work with the neighborhood committee and became a director for after-school activities. Since traffic is quite heavy along his street, every morning he calls together the pupils on his side of the street and leads them across to school. When school is out he goes to get them. Sometimes he himself visits the classes to see how the children are doing. When he notices pupils not paying attention, he seeks them out after school to chat with them and try to rouse their interest in learning.

No matter what the weather, he goes from house to house to guide the after-school activities. Some people have urged him, "A man your age should look after yourself better!" He answers, "Getting a little tired doesn't matter, what is important is helping to raise a new socialist generation."

With Grandpa Shen as their example, the other 25 directors of the Kuanhsiang Primary School's after-school activities are also very warm and enthusiastic in their work. As we arrived at the home of Yu Hui, a fifth-grade pupil, Kung Yu-lan, a director, and Miao Hsin-ju, a woman teacher, were teaching a group of upper-graders how to mend their undershirts and socks and sew on buttons. Each had a sewing kit of his own. "When I was small Mama was always busy because whenever my socks got a hole I'd just throw them in a pile for her to mend," one pupil said. "Now Mama is very pleased that I've learned to do it myself, and she has more time to study after work."

New Spirit Among Children

Through the years the close cooperation of the neighborhood and school has brought about new attitudes among the children. To study earnestly and get good results, observe discipline, love labor and show concern for the collective are the goals to strive for. In spring the children help plant trees along the streets. In summer they kill flies and mosquitoes and do other things to help maintain public health and sanitation. In autumn the upper-graders help with the cabbage harvest in communes on the city's outskirts. In winter they help clear the streets of snow, help elderly people in the neighborhood sweep their yards and do everyday shopping.

Hearing about the exploits of heroes and heroines, such as Wang Chieh, a PLA hero who had given his life to save class brothers, they want to be like them. Last summer a sixth grade after-school group and its directors went to plant trees along the moat around the former city wall. It was very hot but the children were uncomplaining and full of enthusiasm. Suddenly, Shih Sheng-ping, a Little Red Soldier squad leader, saw a small child slip and fall into the moat. He darted forward and dived into the moat. Hu Ching-sheng and Yang Chien-ping, two other Little Red Soldiers also dived in. They brought the child to safety and went to get some dry clothes for him. "You are true Little Red Soldiers!" the child's mother exclaimed gratefully when they all reached home.

Returning lost money and articles is now a common thing. At the neighborhood committee's office we saw a list of the things the pupils had found in the streets during the past year. They ranged from wallets and fountain pens to pieces of clothing. Yang Tsung-hsiu, vice-chairman of the neighborhood committee, said: "Whatever these pupils find, big or small, they do everything they can to locate the owner. If all efforts fail, they bring them here. The school, the neighborhood committee and parents praise and encourage this new spirit. We want the children to learn from very small how ugly selfishness is and to grow up with love for the people and devotion to the public interest."

A teacher then pointed out a chubby little boy playing in the yard. "His name is Chao Lien-chi. He's in the second grade," she said. "Last week while shopping with a classmate, he found a wallet at a turn in the lane. There was over ten yuan in it. He took it to the police station."

We wound up our visit as the sun was setting in the west. In parting, Teacher Yao observed, "Although these after-school activities have been going on for several years, there's still much to be done and improved to meet the needs of a developing socialist society."

II. THE PLACES

1. The People's Commune

Eighty per cent of China's population live in the countryside. The basic unit of social, economic, cultural, educational, political, and military organization in the countryside is the people's commune. The communization of the countryside in 1958 is a necessary and significant step in China's march toward communism. In the commune of the future Communist society there will be no distinction between peasant, worker, soldier, cadres; no division between industrial, agricultural, and intellectual labor. The Marxist ideal of the all-round development of the individual can only be realized in a communal type of organization.

Chinese regard the people's commune as "China's spiritual atom bomb." They believe that the new human relationship based on the new social organization will unleash unprecedented productive power. After visiting the village of Sandstone Hollow and the Red Flag Canal, we are quite convinced by the "spiritual" power of co-operative and collective labor. The stories of Sandstone Hollow, Tachai, and the Red Flag Canal described in this section, are examples of the kind of transformation China has gone through—from starvation to plenty. This transformation has been achieved through the spirit of self-reliance and perseverance.

Sandstone Hollow is a particularly vivid demonstration of the power of "China's spiritual atom bomb." It took us hours, traveling through unpaved roads and river beds, to reach this remote village in the mountains near the Great Wall. It is difficult to imagine a small herd of wild horses surviving in such a desolate place. The whole place is covered with rocks and boulders. It took twenty years for a hundred or so families of poor peasants working together to turn the rocky slopes into terraced fields.

The community is no longer on relief from the State, producing a handsome surplus which allows them to start buying tractors for the mechanization of agriculture.

What is most impressive about a commune like Sandstone Hollow is not just the neat terraced fields carved from boulders but the quality of men and women who built a prosperous community out of nothing. The experience of working collectively for the common good has transformed them into selfless new socialist human beings. Watching them working together, talking and joking, we got a glimpse of how it is to live in a *community*.

In this kind of community direct democracy is most evident. A society without bureaucracy is already a reality on the communal level. For example, Chang Kuei-Shun, the chairman of the revolutionary committee of the village, is a typical old peasant with deep wrinkles on his tanned face and calloused hands, wearing the black, pajamalike cotton dress peculiar to northern Chinese peasants. He works in the field like everyone else in the village and receives no financial reward for his political duties. Like everyone else in the commune, he receives his income according to the work he puts in. Unlike some of the cadres we met in the cities, who were elusive in their answers to our questions, Chang Kuei-Shun was frank and direct in his answers, and in fact he seemed to have a much better grasp of many ideological issues.

Another striking feature of the communal economy is its self-sufficiency. Each commune tries to be as self-sufficient as possible by producing everything it needs. This general policy is adopted for social as well as defense reasons. Mao's concept of defense through people's war requires that each commune be prepared to continue to fight even if most cities and communication lines are in enemy hands. Socially, the spirit of self-reliance is an important part of constructing socialism. We can still see the pride on Chang Kuei-Shun's face when, pointing to the elaborate banquet spread in front of us, he said, "Everything on the table is fresh from our own field!"

K.H.F.
K.T.F.

SOME BASIC FACTS ABOUT
THE PEOPLE'S COMMUNE*

1. HOW DID THE RURAL PEOPLE'S COMMUNE COME INTO BEING?

Rural people's communes in China were set up widely in the autumn of 1958. They were the inevitable result of the political and economic developments in China.

Soon after liberation China's peasants carried out land reform, led by Chairman Mao and the Communist Party. Then, in line with the principle of voluntariness and benefit for all, they went on to build a new countryside following the Party's basic line for agricultural development: the first step, collectivization; the second step, on the basis of collectivization, mechanization and electrification.

Between the land reform and 1957, China's agriculture developed from the mutual-aid team to the semi-socialist agricultural producers' cooperative and then the fully-socialist cooperative. The mutual-aid team had the rudiments of socialism. It consisted of a few to a dozen households. The means of production such as land, draft animals and farm tools were still privately owned. Members helped each other in productive labor, exchanging work for work.

The semi-socialist co-op was bigger than the mutual-aid team. Members pooled their land and other principal means of production, which were used and managed by the co-op. The owners received a certain amount of compensation according to how much they had pooled. Earnings from collective productive labor were distributed according to the socialist principle

* From *Some Basic Facts About China* (Peking: Foreign Language Press, 1974).

"from each according to his ability, to each according to his labor".

A fully-socialist co-op generally had around 200 households. Land and other principal means of production were owned collectively, and used and managed under the co-op's unified leadership. Earnings were distributed according to the socialist principle "from each according to his ability, to each according to his labor". By taking part in collective productive labor, the peasants gradually overcame the sense of private ownership based on individual farming and developed a growing desire to build the collective. Collectivization greatly promoted production. In 1957, after fully-socialist co-operatives had been formed throughout most of the country, harvests of grain, cotton and other industrial crops were all much bigger than the highest figures in history.

In 1957 the Party carried out a movement of education for socialism which deepened the peasants' socialist consciousness. In 1958, based on the excellent domestic political and economic situation, Chairman Mao formulated the General Line which called for *going all out, aiming high and achieving greater, faster, better and more economical results in building socialism*". The peasants' enthusiasm for building socialism thus inspired expressed itself in a burst of energy to speedily change the backwardness of the countryside.

From winter 1957 to summer 1958 extensive basic improvement was made to the farm land, centering around building water conservation projects. Much was done to develop industry, transport and communications, commerce, culture, education and health oriented to serving agriculture, and the organization of local militia. The fully-socialist cooperative, organized chiefly for farming, became increasingly inadequate for large-scale production. In many places the smaller cooperatives amalgamated themselves into big ones or formed federations of co-ops. Since such a co-op or federation of co-ops often embraced the households of an entire township—a total of several thousand—its managing group was combined with the township government so that the result was a unit of both political and economic organization. This was the prototype of the people's commune.

Chairman Mao promptly summed up the significance of this new creation by the masses and their experience and declared, *"People's communes are fine."* The Party Central Committee issued a resolution outlining steps and methods for the formation of communes. People's communes were organized by the tens of thousands.

2. WHAT ARE THE CHARACTERISTICS OF THE PEOPLE'S COMMUNE? HOW IS IT DIFFERENT FROM THE AGRICULTURAL PRODUCERS' CO-OPERATIVE?

(1) While the agricultural producers' cooperative engaged chiefly in farming, the people's commune both organizes the economy and does the work of the local government. It is a basic unit of China's socialist society and of proletarian political power in the countryside. The commune members' representative assembly functions as the township people's congress.

The commune not only has agriculture, but also industry and trade, and leads education and health and the militia. Its Party and administrative cadres lead and organize both political-ideological work and production. In short, the people's commune is a brand-new social organization unifying leadership of politics, economy, military affairs and culture.

(2) The people's commune is a big collective owned by all its members. With more land, more hands and more funds than a cooperative, it can better carry out large-scale basic improvement of land, experiment with scientific farming and fight natural disasters. Its far greater economic strength makes possible faster progress in water conservation, mechanization, electrifica-

tion and the use of chemical fertilizers and insecticides. It strengthens the rural collective economy, speeds up the building of socialism in the countryside and raises the peasants' standard of living more quickly.

(3) The people's commune can better carry out the policy to *"take grain as the key link and ensure an all-round development"*, that is, to develop a diversified economy of farming, forestry, stock raising, fishery and sidelines, and set up industry, repair shops and transport to serve agriculture.

(4) The agricultural producers' co-op had two levels of organization, the co-op and the production teams under it. There was ownership on the co-op level only. The people's commune has three levels of organization: the commune; a number of production brigades under it; and under each of the brigades, a number of production teams. There is collective ownership on each of these three levels, with the production team as the basic accounting unit. The land, draft animals, small farm machinery owned by a production team are managed by it, and it organizes the labor power of its members. It handles its income and distribution independently, bears its losses itself and keeps most of the profit.

Economic undertakings run by the production brigades are those which the production teams are unable to manage by themselves or which can be better managed by the brigades. These include small reservoirs and other water conservation projects benefiting the teams under the brigade, shops processing farm and sideline products, orchards, schools and health stations. Some brigades own tractors and other farm machinery.

Economic undertakings run by the communes are those which the brigades are unable to manage or which can be better managed by the communes. Serving the entire commune, these include tractor stations, hydro-electric power installations, irrigation and drainage works, farm machinery manufacture and repair shops, forest farms, stud farms, farms for experimenting with improved strains of seed, middle schools and clinics.

At present, undertakings run by the production teams account for the biggest proportion of the total assets of the commune and its teams and brigades. While those run by the communes and brigades are relatively fewer, they play a big role in consolidating and developing rural socialist collective economy.

Take the October production brigade of the Wangcheng commune in Hsishui county, Hupeh province. The brigade now owns 20 tractors of various types, 34 electric motors and 60 machines for processing farm and sideline products. This equipment provides mechanization for all the irrigation, drainage, cultivation, transport and processing of grain, cotton and fodder done by the production teams under the brigade. In 1970 this brigade harvested an average of 1,700 *jin* of grain per *mu*. It overfulfilled all state purchasing targets for grain, cotton and oil. It now has 700,000 yuan in public funds and nearly 970,000 *jin* of reserve grain. Collective income also rose markedly.

As time goes on, the dictatorship of the proletariat will become more consolidated, commune members' socialist consciousness will continue to rise, the collective economy will become still stronger. The relatively poor production teams will also gradually reach the economic level of the better-off teams, and farming will become more and more mechanized. With these prerequisites, in time the production brigade, and eventually the commune, will become the basic accounting unit. The system of collective ownership will eventually be replaced by ownership by the entire people (the state).

3. HOW IS DISTRIBUTION CARRIED OUT IN THE PEOPLE'S COMMUNE?

Distribution in the people's communes is done according to the policy set forth by Chairman Mao which pays attention to three things—the interests of the state, the collective and the individual.

The main distribution is done in the production team, at present the basic accounting unit.

After production and management costs have been deducted from the team's annual income, a small part is paid to the state as tax, a small contribution is made to the public accumulation fund of the collective, and the greater part is distributed among the members. Accumulation for the state and the collective is kept low so that in a normal year increased production will give the members increased income.

To achieve the above, the state policy in the rural areas is not to raise taxes even when production increases. In the past ten years the rate of agricultural tax for the production teams has remained the same even though every year saw a good harvest. Thus for teams in which production goes up every year, agricultural tax takes up an increasingly smaller proportion of the total income. At present it stands at 5, 6 or 7 percent. As production continues to increase, the actual rate of agricultural tax will become still smaller.

Under China's socialist planning, farm production is done in a planned way according to the needs of the economy. When there is a surplus above the state targets, the state purchases this at the same or even higher prices. Thus, in times of bumper harvest, the teams need not worry about finding a market for their surplus, or selling it at a loss. Instead, the collective adds to its income and public accumulation fund, and improves the members' standard of living. This policy of the state keeps prices stable and facilitates adding to the national reserves, which are the basis of a constant supply.

The production team's accumulation fund consists of its reserve and welfare funds. The reserve fund is used to buy small or medium-size farm machinery, or for basic construction or re-production. The welfare fund covers expenses for culture and education, items of collective welfare and aid to members who are ill, retired or unable to work. It subsidizes, for example, the rural cooperative medical system under which the members pay only about one yuan a year for full medical care. The welfare fund pays for the ever-expanding radio relay system in the rural areas. It also covers the subsidies given to members who have financial difficulties, especially families of revolutionary martyrs, dependents of enlisted men, aged people with no families, orphans and disabled or sick members.

Distribution is based on the socialist principle "from each according to his ability, to each according to his labor, more income for those who work more". At the end of the year members receive amounts based on the number of workpoints (units of payment for labor) they earn. These are awarded according to the amount, type of job, and quality of labor and members' attitude toward collective production.

Cadres at all levels of the people's communes must, according to a state regulation, take an active part in collective productive labor. This ensures that cadres do not become divorced from actual production and reality, that they maintain constant and close ties with the masses and thus avoid becoming subjective and bureaucratic in their work. This is a fundamental measure for preventing the restoration of capitalism and consolidating the dictatorship of the proletariat. Cadres at the commune level must do productive labor for no less than 60 days a year. Brigade and team cadres take part in labor for workpoints in the same way as ordinary commune members. For the time a cadre spends at public duties, he is given workpoints or a subsidy set through discussions by the members he leads.

These methods of distribution provide for funds for both the state and collective economy and for the gradual improvement of the life of commune members. The Hsichia brigade of the Tsungtsun commune in Chiangtu county, Kiangsu province provides an example. Between 1962 and 1970 the average grain yield of the brigade rose from 300 to 1,000 *jin* per *mu*. In 1970 it sold the state three times as much grain above the quota as in 1962 and its collective income was also close to three times the 1962 figure. While members' total income rose by 95 percent, the brigade's public accumulation fund reached the very substantial total of 240,000 yuan.

4. WHAT ABOUT DEMOCRATIC LIFE IN A PEOPLE'S COMMUNE?

The people's commune is run on the principle of democratic centralism. The representative assemblies of the production team, the production brigade and the commune are the organs of power at these levels. Representatives are elected after thorough discussions by the members. Every member has the right to vote and be elected. Between sessions of the representative assemblies, work is carried out by a permanent body. (In the production team it is called a leading group and in the brigade and commune, a revolutionary committee.) These permanent leading bodies are also elected by the members.

Before the start of every production year, these leading groups at each level draw up production plans based on the targets set by the state, the actual conditions in each unit and the members' needs. Unified planning gives due consideration to each of these at each level. The drafts are given to the members for full discussion, then revised according to suggestions and finalized. The figures on distribution and expenditures are made public every year. To join in discussions, approve plans and other matters, and criticize and supervise the way they are carried out is the right of all commune members. These rights are protected by law.

In addition to these democratic rights in the political and economic spheres, it is also every commune member's right to have work, rest and education and to share in social welfare.

Every member able to work has the right to take part in productive labor. Men and women get the same pay for the same work. When work is assigned, the special physical problems of women are given due consideration.

Time for work and rest are arranged according to local farming customs and vary with the seasons. Proper rest is guaranteed. Commune members give their first attention to fulfilling collective targets. In their spare time they can work at the small private plots allotted to them by the production team, raise a little poultry or a few head of stock, or do handicrafts. Members can do what they like with products from this labor.

An important democratic right for every person is the opportunity to study Marxism-Leninism-Mao Tsetung Thought and receive education for socialism. A certain amount of time each week is set aside for political study. Party organizations at the different levels are responsible not only for carrying out the Party's principles and policies but for leading and organizing cadres and the masses in political study. They give help whenever necessary so that the members will deepen their understanding of Marxism-Leninism-Mao Tsetung Thought, constantly raise their socialist consciousness and develop the proletarian outlook of serving the people wholeheartedly.

It was the spiritual power of Marxism-Leninism-Mao Tsetung Thought translated into material energy that has enabled China's millions of commune members to self-reliantly fight natural disasters and conquer difficulties and to reap bumper harvests for ten years in a row.

A VISIT TO THE TUNGTING PEOPLE'S COMMUNE*

1. ITS FORMATION AND GROWTH

To help our readers obtain some idea of China's people's communes, we publish here the first instalment of a report on this people's commune south of the Yangtze

* From *Peking Review*, No. 13–18, 1973.

*River. Five more instalments will follow in subsequent
issues. They will cover a series of topics—the commune's functions and powers, its collective ownership
of the means of production, and facts about its production brigades and teams, members' incomes and life.*

We visited the Tungting People's Commune in
Wuhsien County, Kiangsu Province, early this year.
A merger of 20 advanced agricultural producers' co-
operatives in the Tungshan area, this peninsular commune lapped by the waters of Lake Taihu was set up
in September 1958. It covers an area of 35 square kilometres and has 11,000 families with 45,000 people.
Under the commune are 30 production brigades and
237 production teams engaged in farming and other occupations—some producing mainly food grains, others
mainly growing fruit and tea and still others in which
fisheries are the main line.

Miserable Bygone Days

During our visit, we put up in a hostel at Tungshan
town, where the commune headquarters is situated. An
old compound, it was taken over by the people after
liberation. Illustrations of historical stories eulogizing
feudal rules of etiquette are engraved on the brick or
wooden gate tower, doors, window frames and eaves
of the main building. Behind it is a rock garden complete with ponds, zigzagging bridges and other natural
or artificial scenes.

This "carved mansion," the local people told us, was
built in three years' time by landlord-capitalist Chin
Hsueh-chih some 50 years ago with 3,700 taels of gold
robbed from the labouring people. Wealthy as he was,
he did not top the list of the rich in the locality. Before
liberation, the most notorious and richest landlords and
gentry there came from four families whose surnames
were Weng, Hsi, Liu and Yen. Chin ranked sixth.
These insatiable vampires owned over 75 per cent of

Tungshan's cultivated land and built many luxurious villas. Riding roughshod over the people during their lifetimes, they were not reconciled to relinquishing their hold on the land even after they were dead. Their tombs took up as much as 1,800 *mu* of good farmland!

But what about the peasants in those days of darkness? Apart from paying exorbitant rents to the landlords, they were also subjected to all kinds of exploitation by profit-seeking merchants. No matter how hard they worked all year, they could scarcely keep their heads above water. "When the tangerines turned red, we still had nothing." "After the rice harvest, we went to bed with empty stomachs." This is the way the peasants recall those days. Of the 427 peasant families in Tuchiao Village, for example, 81 had been reduced to begging, 18 were forced to sell their children and 92 became farm labourers.

People's Communes Are Fine

Liberation brought tremendous changes to the Tungshan area after land reform was carried out and mutual-aid teams and agricultural producers' co-operatives formed. We learnt from a responsible commune cadre that in the three years following the establishment of advanced agricultural producers' co-operatives, total output of fruit, tea, fish, silkworm cocoons and grain rose 47-90 per cent as compared with the time of agricultural producers' co-operatives of the elementary type.[1] These initial achievements gave the cadres and

[1] These were co-operatives of a semi-socialist nature which came into being after 1951. The co-op members pooled their land and major means of production as shares. Besides remuneration from labour, they received a certain amount of payment for the land and other means of production they had pooled.

The advanced agricultural producers' co-operatives of a socialist nature began to emerge in 1956. Co-op members worked together and were paid on the principle of "from each according to his ability, to each according to his work." All land

peasants greater enthusiasm to take the socialist road of collectivization and develop farm production faster. Handicapped, however, by the small scale of the advanced co-ops and their limited manpower and financial resources, the peasants were eager to organize bigger ones.

Prior to the birth of the people's communes, many advanced co-ops were already overcoming difficulties they could not cope with alone through mutual help. For example, the Hungkuang No. 2 Co-operative which lacked manpower reclaimed 1,500 *mu* of barren hillsides with the help of 800 members from five neighbouring co-ops. Short of funds, the Hsinmin Co-op borrowed 300 yuan from two other co-ops to buy a much-needed 30 h.p. diesel engine. These and other instances opened the eyes of the cadres and peasants. They came to realize that more people meant greater strength and bigger co-ops could do more than smaller ones.

From the winter of 1957 to the summer of 1958, farm capital construction centring around water conservancy projects reached a new high throughout the countryside. Through their own experience the peasants became more and more aware that co-ops such as theirs could no longer meet the needs of increased production on a large scale. So in many places they merged their small co-ops into bigger ones on their own initiative; some covered a whole *hsiang*[2] and were integrated with the *hsiang* government administration.

Under the impact of the Great Leap Forward in socialist construction, four co-ops in the Tungshan area amalgamated into one big one in the spring of 1958 on the basis of their close mutual-help ties. Later, another 13 co-ops joined into one.

This being the case not only in Tungshan but in

---

and major means of production were collectively owned and payment was no longer made to those who had pooled them.

[2] An administrative unit below the county level before the people's communes were formed.

other parts of the country, Chairman Mao summed up in good time the experience and creativeness of the masses when he pointed out: *"People's communes are fine."*

On August 29, 1958, the Central Committee of the Chinese Communist Party adopted the "Resolution on the Establishment of People's Communes in the Rural Areas." It pointed out: "The people's communes are the logical result of the march of events. Large, comprehensive people's communes have made their appearance, and in several places they are already widespread. They have developed very rapidly in some areas. It is highly probable that there will soon be an upsurge in setting up people's communes throughout the country and the development is irresistible."

Responding promptly to the call of the Party Central Committee and Chairman Mao, Tungshan's peasants made their pressing demand to set up a people's commune known.

When word came that the authorities had granted their request, over 3,000 families totalling some 30,000 people applied for membership in the commune in three days. Applications and pledges kept pouring into the preparatory office of the commune. Many co-op members lost no time in coming by boat and made their applications at night. Their long-cherished hope came true on September 21, 1958 when the inaugural meeting of the Tungting People's Commune was held. To their great joy and satisfaction, they spoke of this memorable occasion as resulting from the guidance of the Party's general line of going all out, aiming high and achieving greater, faster, better and more economical results in building socialism.

After the Birth of the Commune

Just as Chairman Mao has pointed out, the people's commune is characterized by being *"big and public."* "Big" means it is much bigger in size than the advanced co-ops. With more land, more people and more funds, it can use manpower and the means of production more rationally. "Public" means it has a higher degree of public ownership than the advanced co-ops.

Commune cadres took us around and showed us fields and factories. What we saw and heard spoke volumes for the many-sided changes since the commune came into being.

Terrace upon terrace of well-laid-out fields and groves of tangerine trees met the eye in the hilly areas. In fishing and rice-growing areas, commune members were casting their nets in the fish ponds or applying fertilizer to crops. They told us that their commune had had an all-round good harvest last year. Output of all their major items of production—rice, wheat and barley, rapeseed, fruit, tea, silkworm cocoons, pigs and sheep, and aquatic products—was up and, with the exception of aquatic products, all hit all-time highs.

Reclamation has put more land under use. Orchards, mulberry groves and fish ponds, each covering an area of 8,000 *mu* in 1958 when the commune was formed, have now each been expanded to 9,000 *mu,* while 12,000 *mu* of paddyfields have been added to the original 8,000 *mu.*

The commune's 980 *mu* of tangerine groves yielded one million kilogrammes of fruit in 1958. The area has doubled and yearly output is up 4.5-fold. Kwang-chialin Ridge in the Hsinmin Production Brigade, which used to be an execution ground where the Japanese imperialists slaughtered Chinese, has been turned into terraced fields with stone embankments thanks to the efforts of the commune members who put in 43,000 work-days since 1964. They are now covered with a profusion of tangerine trees.

Since the commune was set up, due adjustment has been made of the marginal land between production teams, according to fair and reasonable principles. A typical example was the Chienkuo Production Brigade, whose fish ponds were scattered alongside 16 streamlets. Some were five or six kilometres from each other, making them very difficult to look after. After consulting with the production brigades and teams concerned, the Chienkuo Brigade now has all its fish ponds located alongside one streamlet. At most two to three kilometres away from each other, they are within easy reach of management; this has boosted catches.

Practice over the past 14 years has given ample proof that the people's commune has greater strength than the advanced co-ops in combating the elements and ensuring production. The original 7,000 *mu* of fish ponds, nearly 3,000 *mu* of mulberry groves and 2,500 *mu* of cropland in the fishing areas all were on the fringes of Lake Taihu. Every water table rise was a threat to the fish ponds. Floodwaters in 1954 carried away all the fish and caused other damage. To do away with the flood menace, the commune pooled the efforts of the production brigades and teams concerned to enclose ponds and affected portions of mulberry groves and cropland with 5,800 metres of embankments containing five sluice-gates. They put in 350,000 work-days in the winter of 1964 and the spring of 1965 to do this.

A rarely seen heavy spring snowfall hit the Tungshan area in March 1970, damaging and breaking parts of some 30,000 citrus and other fruit trees. Under the commune's unified organization, manpower and material resources were concentrated to tie them up. Thanks to meticulous care, there was a bumper fruit harvest that year. Comparing this to the 1924 winter snowfall which, though much lighter, had destroyed all 200 *mu* of tangerine groves, the commune members said jubilantly: People's communes are really fine!

More people, funds and other resources have enabled the commune to expand production faster. From their own experience, the Tungting cadres and peasants are all the more aware of this. In recent years, the commune's total income has nearly doubled that of the advanced co-ops and the production brigades have been able to buy big and medium-sized farm implements and machinery. The whole commune now has 134 diesel engines for irrigation purposes, 8 grain and fodder processing factories, 139 power-driven threshers, 14 tractors and 1,200 sprayers of various types. All this accounts for the gradual mechanization and semimechanization of drainage and irrigation, threshing, food and fodder processing and plant protection. The degree of mechanized farming keeps going up and commune-run factories and other enterprises are rising in number.

Increased production is accompanied by a constant rise in commune members' living standards. Before liberation, the per-capita annual income of the peasants was the equivalent of 36 yuan today. It rose to 80 yuan at the time of the advanced co-ops. It has jumped to the current figure of 146 yuan (not including income from side-line occupations). There was only one middle school and a negligible number of primary schools in the old days. The poor and lower-middle peasants could not afford to send their children to school. Today the commune has 8 middle schools and 36 primary schools. Medical and public health work have also made much headway. The introduction of a co-operative medical system has provided free treatment to the peasants for an annual fee of 3 yuan (1.5 yuan is paid by themselves, the rest comes from the public welfare funds of production teams). A fairly complete medical and public health network has been formed by the commune hospital, production brigades' clinics and production teams' health workers.

Considering the drawbacks of a small-peasant economy in the past, Tungting's commune members take great pride in their achievements. They say: "An eagle flies much faster than a sparrow."

2. A SOCIAL STRUCTURE COMBINING GOVERNMENT ADMINISTRATION WITH COMMUNE MANAGEMENT

The Tungting People's Commune administrative set-up is in the centre of Tungshan town.

We went there to interview the commune leaders the afternoon of our arrival. However, except for the civil affairs office where one comrade was registering a young couple to be married, all the offices were closed. A demobilized armyman and a middle school graduate were waiting to be assigned work.

The one comrade around was busy answering the phone and going in and out of the office looking for people. "Our commune cadres," he told us, "generally do their work in the production brigades and teams or take part in collective labour in the daytime. They won't be back until dusk, and I'm the only one on duty here."

Interview With the Party Secretary

When we met him in his office that evening, Comrade Hsieh Wen-hsiung, chairman and Party committee secretary of the commune, was glad to see us. The bed at one end of the small room indicated that his office also served as a temporary bedroom.

We were given a general rundown of the commune. Before it was set up, Comrade Hsieh told us, the township's people's council was the grass-roots unit of socialist state power in the rural area; the advanced agricultural producers' co-operatives were the basic economic organization. This meant that the township administration carried out the administrative functions, while the latter was in charge of production; that is, government administration and economic management were under separate departments. When the commune was formed in 1958, it consisted of many advanced co-ops which, by and large, were within the confines of a township. The commune was directly led by the county and gave leadership to the production brigades and teams.

The people's commune performs the functions of state power and at the same time organizes commune-wide production, distribution, consumption and other economic activities. This is what we usually refer to as integrating government administration and commune management, and combining industry, agriculture, commerce, education and military affairs.

The 36 members on the revolutionary committee, the leading organ of the Tungting People's Commune, include representatives in industry, agriculture, commerce, education and military affairs. Led by the commune Party committee, they practise collective leadership with responsibility for various fields of work divided up among them.

To be more specific, the commune revolutionary committee has under it offices in charge of production and construction, finance, grain, trade, civil affairs, education and public health, public security and militia work. In production work, for instance, the commune helps production brigades and teams work out production plans and supervises and checks up on their implementation, helps them improve administrative and financial work and do a good job of accumulation and distribution, popularizes effective measures to increase production and advanced experience, and organizes the supply of the means of production and livelihood. All other work, too—political, economic, cultural and educational, public health, military affairs, etc.—are carried out though the commune.

Other Cadres Talk to Us

Secretary Chiang Wan-sen called a special meeting on behalf of Party committee secretary Hsieh. Responsible personnel from various offices were invited to tell us the advantages of integrating government administration with commune management.

Teacher Hsueh who is in charge of education was the first speaker. After the commune was set up, he said, our schools were put under the dual leadership of the county culture and education bureau and the commune. In this way, the commune has the initiative in deciding where schools are to be located and in building them and training teachers according to the principles laid down by the state and in the light of its own specific conditions and the commune members' needs. This has helped increase enrolment and improve teaching quality.

In its early days, the commune had only one middle school and one primary school for several brigades. Now each brigade has its own primary school and the commune runs eight middle schools. Before 1958, the number of teachers, who were all appointed by the county, was not enough for our needs. After the commune was set up, we trained young commune members to be teachers. Poor and lower-middle peasants were invited to give lectures and take a direct hand in running schools. Their representatives often came to classes to listen to lectures and help teachers correct the students' homework, and also educated students in various ways out of school.

Comrade Chou from the commercial office talked about his experience: It had been difficult before for the commercial department to co-ordinate its work with the agricultural producers' co-operatives because each went its own way. Now that the commune is in charge of both farm production and trade, close ties have been established between the commercial office and the production brigades and teams. After working out their plans, the production teams report on them to the commune. And the commerical office bases itself on these plans to supply the teams with chemical fertilizers, insecticides, farm implements and whatever means of production are needed. In the same way, it purchases in good time farm and side-line products and makes proper arrangements for their sale, thereby boosting production by doing a good job of supply and marketing.

Following the principle of "taking grain as the key link and ensuring an all-round development," he told us, the commercial office also helps production teams develop industrial crops and side-line occupations. For example, when the market demand for timber went up, it proposed that measures be taken to plant more trees. Accordingly, the commune Party committee decided to increase bamboo acreage another 400 *mu* and cedar and paulownia another 1,000 *mu* under its 1973 plan. Assignments were then given to the production brigades according to local conditions. To help fulfil the task, the commercial office bought the needed saplings in time.

As to industry, Comrade Yeh who is responsible for the industrial office said there were no factories here before the commune. It was not until 1958 that some dozen factories were built one after another by the collective strength of the commune, which was bigger than that of the co-ops. These have been a direct impetus to farm production. The fodder processing factories, for example, have played a big role in developing pig-raising. The commune sapling nursery is now able to supply all the saplings needed to afforest its hilly areas and even sell a portion to other regions. Comrade Yeh specially mentioned the fruit processing factory because it shows all the more clearly the advantages of commune-run industry. During harvest time in the past, a good deal of fruit often dropped off trees because of sudden weather changes. Piling up on the ground, they began to rot before peasants had time to ship them out, causing great losses. With the completion of this factory, such fruit is processed into semi-finished products which can be kept longer and then sent to processing factories in several cities. This not only adds to the production teams' income but also helps the commune accumulate funds.

Comrade Chen Ah-szu who heads the financial office told us: "With industry, agriculture, commerce, education and military affairs combined under the unified management of the commune, the various offices get to know each other's work and are thus able to act in unison." To illustrate, he cited an example: The commune's 1972 all-round good harvest brought members their highest income in history. The production teams' bank savings totalled more than 2 million yuan. When the time comes for distribution, they will draw 1.4 million yuan to distribute among their members. So we have to get the sum ready for them. According to past findings, it is estimated that half the sum will be deposited in the bank as personal savings soon after it is distributed, 200,000 yuan will be kept by members for daily use and the rest will immediately be spent on the markets.

"When it comes to our work," Comrade Chou, in charge of commerce, took up where Comrade Chen had left off, "we have to organize the timely supply of goods. First we send out several groups to find out what the commune members need. Investigations show that most of the Hungchi Brigade members want building materials and sewing machines, and there is a general demand in the Weitung Brigade for Shanghai-made '555' alarm clocks and wrist watches, while transistor radios are a favourite item in the Chantou Brigade. . . . Having made an inventory, we place orders with Shanghai, Soochow and other places for as much goods as possible to meet their needs."

Comrade Chiang Wan-sen who presided over the meeting rounded it out with a brief talk on military affairs. All production brigades and teams have part-time militia organizations. Militiamen and women are playing a key role in defending the dictatorship of the proletariat and defending the fruits of collective labour as well as in productive work. "All we told you just now," he concluded, "shows from different angles the great superiority of combining industry, agriculture, commerce, education and military affairs in consolidating the socialist system and promoting production."

From the talks by these and other comrades, it can be seen that under the unified leadership of the commune Party committee and revolutionary committee and with the integration of government administration and commune management, all fields of work are closely co-ordinated and go forward in step for the common goal of building a new socialist countryside. Facts over the 14 years since the birth of the Tungting People's Commune have borne out that the people's commune is a brand new social structure which has enormous vitality.

3. ITS THREE-LEVEL OWNERSHIP

During our stay in this lakeside commune, we made the rounds of a number of commune-run enterprises and went to a production brigade and one of its production teams to get some idea of the commune's system of ownership.

Collective ownership of the rural people's commune in its present stage in general falls into three levels—commune, production brigade and production team. Farmland, forests, water and its resources, farm tools and machinery, draught animals, small factories and mines and other means of production are shared between the commune, brigade and team. Collective ownership at the team level rather than that at the other two levels is at present the basic one. This is generally known as the "three-level system of ownership of the means of production in the people's commune, with ownership by the production team as the basic form."

Commune Ownership

So far as production is concerned, the commune mainly helps production teams develop agriculture, animal husbandry, forestry, side-line occupations, fisheries and other work. Usually the means of production owned by the commune are a small number of enterprises and facilities which production brigades and teams are unable to handle or which are more advantageous for the commune to run. At Tungting, these include a farm machinery repair workshop, a sapling nursery, a fish hatchery, a fruit-processing plant, several fodder-processing factories, a public service centre (making briquettes, fluffing cotton and doing other work), a workshop making reed mats, a brick and tile kiln, a construction centre, an irrigation station, a veterinary station and an environmental sanitation centre, as well as several small quarries producing granite, kaolin and sand. Most of these directly serve farm production and the peasants' daily life, with only a few providing industrial raw materials for state-owned enterprises. They are playing no small part in consolidating and developing the rural socialist collective economy.

We went by boat to the fish hatchery. Fishery is one of the commune's major lines of production and many production teams have their own fish ponds, covering a total of about a quarter of the area in use. Before the hatchery was set up, the various production teams had to send a total of 300 members to the upper and lower reaches of the Yangtze River to buy fry. This took them two or three months a year and cost the teams more than 200,000 yuan. With technical help from a state research institute, the commune built the hatchery in 1965. After several years of experiments, it now produces all the fry the production teams need and is able to sell a portion to other provinces. This not only saves on cost and manpower, it also ensures better breeds of fish with higher output.

The fruit-processing factory is a big help to the production teams which used to worry about fruit rotting if it was not shipped out in time. In 1971, for instance, three days and nights of heavy rainfall held up the loquat shipments. The factory processed them into syrup, thus saving the teams any loss. Although the teams involved did their best to ship out last year's bumper harvest of arbutus in time, they were still left with 25,000 kilogrammes on their hands. The problem was again solved by this factory which processed them.

Starting virtually from scratch in several small rooms, the factory had no funds in its early days. It at first processed fruit sent in by production teams and paid them after selling its products. Thus it gradually accumulated funds to expand workshops and buy more equipment. With an annual processing capacity of 750,000 kilogrammes of fruit, the factory has accumulated 270,000 yuan for the commune since it started.

The greater portion of the profits from commune-run enterprises goes into expanding reproduction. The fruit-processing factory was the only industry in 1958. It was later joined by the fish hatchery and farm machinery repair workshop before the Great Proletarian Cultural Revolution began. With funds accumulated by these three enterprises, the commune now runs enterprises and facilities with 500 workers doing 15 kinds of work. These enterprises and facilities are an indispensable part of the three-level ownership of the commune economy.

Ownership by Production Brigade

We went to the Chenkuang Brigade, one of 30 under the commune. It consists of eight production teams formed by and large within the confines of former villages and has a population of 1,263.

The accountant accompanied us on visits to the brigade's fodder-processing factory, farm tools factory and boat repair yard which are on a smaller scale than the commune-run enterprises. Brigade-run enterprises and undertakings, he explained, are those which are beyond the capability of production teams or are more advantageous for the brigades to run. These together with a tractor and a pump are for the teams' use.

The function of the production brigade is, under commune leadership, to take care of its teams' production and administrative work. Among other things, it helps them work out production plans; guides, examines and supervises the teams' production, distribution and financial work; helps them improve management; builds and runs brigade-wide water conservancy and other farm capital construction projects; and organizes necessary co-operation between them.

Comrade Han Chang-nan, brigade Party secretary and revolutionary committee chairman, greeted us warmly. He told us he had just been at the No. 4 team which obtained another 430 kilogrammes of rice by re-threshing stalks which had already been through the thresher. The purpose of such an on-the-spot meeting was to educate cadres of other teams who neglected the idea of re-threshing as output promised to be good without it. After seeing for themselves the advantages of re-threshing, they all pledged to do the same. This is one instance of how the brigade leadership leads farm production.

In addition, the brigade is also in charge of other work, such as civil affairs, militia, public security, culture and education and public health. Whatever it does, it puts stress on political-ideological work and helps the teams implement the Party's policies and principles. When the commune asked the Chenkuang Brigade to plant 30 *mu* of watermelons in 1972, the plans submitted by the production teams, however, all but doubled the assigned figure. They obviously saw greater profits in watermelons. But this would in turn necessitate using some cropland. Getting the wind up, the brigade called a meeting of team cadres to study the Party's policy of "taking grain as the key link and ensuring an all-round development." (This means that the people's commune, while keeping a tight grasp on grain production, should develop agriculture, forestry, animal husbandry, side-line occupations and fishery in a rational way, and handle well the relation between grain production and that of cotton, edible oil and other industrial crops.) After arriving at a correct understanding, they reasonably reduced their planned watermelon acreage.

Han Chang-nan said: "This is how we exercise leadership over the production teams. We use typical examples to induce the cadres to study the Party's policies and principles and help them do their work well, instead of issuing orders arbitrarily."

Ownership at Production Team Level

Ownership at the production team level is basic at the present stage of development. All land within their confines, collectively owned forests (except those run by the state), water and its resources and other major means of production belong to the teams. Draught animals, farm implements, small machinery and the labour force are at the teams' disposal and both the commune and production brigade cannot deploy them without compensation.

At present, commune members have their share of small plots for private use and go in for some domestic side-line occupations. Their incomes, bank savings, houses and other means of livelihood are privately owned and protected by the state.

The production team is the basic accounting unit in the commune. In other words, it organizes production and distribution and carries out independent accounting, being solely responsible for its own profits or losses. As conditions gradually ripen, the current basic ownership at the production team level will switch to that at the production brigade level and then the commune level. And collective ownership of the commune will finally pass over to socialist state ownership. Needless to say, this calls for a considerably long process of gradual development.

4. HOW A PRODUCTION TEAM CARRIES ON ITS WORK

The leader of the No. 8 Production Team of the Chenkuang brigade is 33-year-old Tsai Lung-lung whom we met during our visit.

Elected by the team members through democratic consultations, the team leadership is composed of Tsai, one deputy leader and seven team committee members who do not remain away from productive work. Six of the leadership are of poor peasant origin (referring to the economic status of their families before liberation). They carry out collective leadership and divide among themselves responsibility for political-ideological work, production, finance and accounting, work among women, the militia and other tasks.

When the leader of the team was selected to join the commune's agro-technical station in the spring of 1972, the team members decided to elect a new one. They chose 27-year-old demobilized armyman Chen Wen-fu. Hard-working as this young man was, however, he committed some unavoidable mistakes due to the lack of experience in farm work.

For example, because of inaccurate planning, seedlings ran out when early rice was being transplanted and the team had to buy some from other teams. As a result, the transplanting time was delayed. Practice over a period of time revealed that though Chen Wen-fu was a good cadre, he was not suitable to be a team leader. So after democratic consultations, he was put on the team committee and Tsai Lung-lung, concurrently a member of the brigade's revolutionary committee with more experience in farm work, was elected team leader.

One special feature of a well-watered area like the locale of the No. 8 team south of the Yangtze River, Tsai told us, is it has a large population in a small area. With 46 families consisting of 161 people, the team has only 119 *mu* of irrigated land, half of which is lakeside land reclaimed after the commune was set up. This averages less than one *mu* for each member. There are 20 *mu* each of mulberry groves and fish ponds. Over the past decade or more, the team has used its reserve fund to buy a walking-tractor, an electric motor and a green-fodder crusher, two rice and wheat threshers, a cement boat and several hundred small farm implements, and has built among other things a cement threshing floor, a storehouse, a pigsty, a chicken yard. All these belong to and are used by the team. Under no circumstances can land be leased or bought and sold.

Production Plan

A big chart in Tsai-Lung-lung's living room showed the lay-out of the crops sown in 1972. The team's land was divided into 82 pieces, with each specifically marked out for use in different seasons. (Generally speaking, the production teams have no office and team cadres do their routine work in the fields or at home.)

"This chart fully expresses the struggle between the two lines," Tsai said. "Every year the production team has to decide what crops should or should not be sown and allocate their acreage accordingly. This involves the question of whether we should take grain or money as the key link. All this is reflected first of all in this chart."

He then described how the chart was made. The county first assigns tasks to the commune in terms of its land, population and productive capacity. The commune then works out a proposed plan for sowing and sends it to the production brigades which in turn make their proposals to the production teams. According to the state plan and the needs of its members, each team works out its own production plan which is subject to endorsement at a general meeting of team members.

Sharp struggle in the realm of ideology often took

place in the course of drawing up the plan. In recent years two crops of rice and one crop of wheat a year have been planted instead of one each as in the past. When this was introduced, most of the peasants favoured it. But a few with conservative ideas showed reluctance. To enable everyone to gain a correct understanding, the team committee organized the peasants to study and discuss the importance of boosting grain output and reserves and of being prepared against war and natural calamities. In the end, all voluntarily switched to better farming methods. The team's grain production has, therefore, kept going up in the last ten years. The 1972 per-*mu* yield (two crops of rice and one crop of wheat combined) reached 1,150 kilogrammes and total output doubled the 1962 figure. Over 30,000 kilogrammes of surplus grain were sold to the state last year as against 2,000 kilogrammes in 1962.

However, paying attention only to increasing grain output at the expense of developing a diversified economy is not the way to do things, Comrade Tsai told us. In 1969 and 1970, for instance, his team had high yields of food crops but engaged in less side-line occupations. As a result, there was no significant increase in the peasants' income and they voiced their criticisms and suggestions when the 1971 plan was being worked out. It was decided that while making continuous efforts to increase grain production, the team should raise more silkworms and more pigs and go in for other side-line occupations such as raising chickens and geese, growing mushrooms and cultivating pearls from mud clams. All this resulted in more peasant income that year. Last year saw a 50 per cent increase in income from side-line products over 1971.

As regards the 1973 production plan which has been approved by cadres and peasants, the team leader said they were going to increase output by improving strains. In the past when two crops of rice were sown a year, they mainly used low-yielding and early-ripening strains because of lack of manpower. (This manpower shortage is partly offset by using early-ripening strains to lengthen the interval between harvesting time of one crop and sowing time of the next crop.) With increased labour efficiency resulting from the use of walking-tractors and threshers, they are now able to replace early-ripening strains with late-ripening and high-yielding ones. According to the plan, the No. 8 team will grow mushrooms on 1,400 square metres of land instead of the 700 devoted to them in 1972 and raise 1,000 chickens instead of 300. . . . It thus will supply the market with more non-staple food and increase team members' income.

Year-End Distribution

The team's accountant is 22-year-old Yeh Chien-chiang who took part in farm production in 1969 after graduating from junior middle school. The team members have faith in him because he works with a high sense of responsibility. Once when a peasant was sent out to buy a boat, he spent some 30 yuan entertaining the sellers in restaurants and later asked Yeh to be reimbursed. Some cadres thought that though the peasant was wrong he had done something for the collective and a few words of criticism were quite enough for him. But Yeh insisted that every penny belonged to the collective and must not be squandered. He refused to pay the sum. The team committee held two meetings about this and finally all its members agreed with Yeh. When this became known to the rank and file, they praised him for being their "good housekeeper."

Yeh Chien-chiang talked at length about the team's distribution work. He began by showing us a number of forms and accounts he kept. Some recorded the amount of money and grain each family had received before the year-end distribution, others showed the team's balance between income and expenditure or listed each team member's work attendance. All this was made public annually so that corrections might be made if there were mistakes in figures or other errors. This is one aspect of democracy in economic affairs.

The No. 8 team's 1972 total income, he told us, was 41,593.18 yuan (including income from surplus grain, oil-bearing crops and other farm produce and from side-line products such as pigs, chickens, fish and silkworm cocoons), while total expenditure (including seed, fertilizer, insecticide and fodder purchases, fees for mechanized ploughing, overhead expenses and agricultural tax) was 17,969.69 yuan. Net income was 23,623.49 yuan or 56.8 per cent of the total income, 15 per cent higher than the year before.

Speaking of the agricultural tax, he said that its proportion to the team's annual total income was getting lower and lower thanks to the People's Government's policy of stabilizing and not increasing the tax when production rises. In 1971, for instance, the agricultural tax was 2.6 per cent of the team's total income. It dropped to 2.1 per cent in 1972 because both grain and side-line production went up.

Distribution is carried out according to the socialist principle of "from each according to his ability, to each according to his work and more pay for more work." Those who take part in collective labour are paid according to work-points earned, which are based on an assessment of the work done. The value of each work-point is fixed by the team from time to time in the light of production.

The No. 8 team called a special general meeting of its members to discuss the 1972 distribution plan one evening early this year. This is one more aspect of democracy in economic affairs.

As team leader, Tsai Lung-lung reported on the year's income, expenditure and balance and reaffirmed the state's policy regarding distribution—a policy which is to take into consideration the interests of the state, the collective and the individual and enable the peasants to receive more income year after year on the basis of increased production in normal years.

Greatly elated by what he said at the meeting, everyone present agreed to sell as much surplus grain as possible to the state in support of the areas in the north hit by natural calamities, after setting aside enough food grain, seeds and animal feed as well as a certain amount of grain reserves.

Discussions on the percentage of public accumulation were particularly animated because they involved the question of correctly handling the relations between collective and individual interests. Apart from a small portion for public accumulation, the remaining net income was distributed among the team members according to the principle of "to each according to his work and more pay for more work."

Public accumulation consists of the public reserve fund and public welfare fund. The former goes for expanded reproduction. The latter is spent on social insurance and collective welfare facilities, such as creches, canteens during the busy farming seasons, part of the medical fees under the co-operative medical system and subsidies for the old and disabled who are unable to do physical work and have no relative to support them.

During the discussions, some members said: "Our team has a bigger income than in 1971 so we should increase our efforts to get a higher degree of mechanization and electrification. We favour a higher percentage for accumulation." Others said: "Our living standards were not high in the previous years and we think we better keep our public accumulation at the same level as last year. All the rest of our increased income should be distributed among us."

After some heated discussions, they unanimously concluded that with more income, accumulation should increase to a proper extent and at the same time better living standards should be guaranteed. As a result, it was decided that last year's accumulation was to take up 14 per cent of the net income as against 11 per cent in 1971. The remainder was to be distributed among the team members who received 13 per cent more income than the year before.

The finalized plan kept Comrade Yeh busy for several days. He had to work out each individual's cash payment according to work-points. With 3,327.45 yuan deducted from net income as public accumulation, the remaining 20,296 yuan was to be distributed among the members. His calculations gave an average of 126 yuan per capita. This is not a high income, but the peasants generally spend little except for food grain and clothing. They get vegetables and eggs from their private plots and side-line occupations and live in their own houses. So they have spare money to buy some furniture and daily necessities.

Another general meeting which the peasants attended took place several days later. There they got their pay in cash (charges for food grain, payment in advance and other expenses being deducted). Each family's money was wrapped in red paper to mark this happy occasion after a year's hard work.

5. COMMUNE MEMBERS' LIVES, PAST AND PRESENT

In visiting peasant families we singled out the afforestation brigade's No. 2 production team which is mainly a fruit-producer. Compared to others in the commune, this team's living standards are rated middling.

We went by bus. It was not long before we saw hills thickly covered with loquat, arbutus, kumquat and tea trees, a sight which meant we were not far from our destination. We got off the bus and walked into the village. Making our way past new houses on both sides of clean well-laid-out roads, we came to team leader Yeh's home.

He gave us a general account of the team's production work. Its 33 families with 181 people have 156 *mu* of orchards. Before liberation, 52 *mu* had been forcibly seized by landlords and capitalists to build their tombs. Back in the hands of the labouring people after the birth of New China, the land was planted with loquat, kumquat and other fruit trees. In line with the Party's principle of taking grain as the key link and ensuring an all-round development, 34 *mu* of paddyfields have been reclaimed from wasteland by the lake since the Great Proletarian Cultural Revolution began. Instead of depending entirely on the state for their food grain as they did in the past, the fruit-growers produced a fairly large amount of rice in 1972, or one-fifth of their yearly supply of food grain. Tea, kumquat, loquat, arbutus and other fruit output also increased by 30-50 per cent compared with that of the previous year.

Speaking of commune members' work, Comrade Yeh said: "Everyone who can do physical work is taking part in collective productive labour, and farming is not just for improving their own living standards but first of all for speeding up socialist construction. They always act upon the slogan: 'Contribute more to socialism.' You can't find a single person living in idleness nowadays. Except for children and people who are too old to do physical labour, every man and woman is taking an active part in farm work."

"In winter like now," he added, "we work from 7 to 11 in the morning and from 12 to 4 in the afternoon. Apart from necessary meetings, all off-hours are at our own disposal. According to regulations, every able-bodied member has four days off every month (two days during busy farming seasons). Women members are given lighter jobs out of consideration for their physical conditions and the larger share of household chores they shoulder; in the morning they can knock off an hour earlier than the men to prepare lunch."

Turning to the topic of the peasants' lives, team leader Yeh said: "Our team members' income has been rising steadily due to increased production. Average per-capita income last year was about 160 yuan.

"Half of the 33 families used to live in thatched huts or tumble-down houses which are now completely gone. Twelve have moved into new homes and six others have rebuilt their old ones. Pan Ching-yu, an old poor peasant and the team's representative to the brigade's poor peasant association, never had his own house when he was a hired farmhand before liberation. In the years immediately after land was distributed to him, he still had economic difficulty and lived in a rented house. It was after the formation of the agricultural producers' co-operative and then the people's commune that he saved enough money to build a new tile and brick house with three rooms in 1962."

Continuing, the team leader said: "The production team gives all possible help to those who build new houses, such as helping them get the builders and the necessary material. Generally speaking, however, the peasants rely on themselves to build their houses from their own savings."

Comrade Yeh took us to two families so we could see how the peasants live. Old peasant Ku Cheng-hsiang was the first. There were eight—wife, two sons, one daughter, one daughter-in-law, two grand-daughters and himself—in the family. The house was well furnished. Each of the bedrooms had a carved mahogany bed (each cost two to three hundred yuan), a wardrobe with a big mirror, a chest of drawers, a bedside table and other items. There was a new bicycle in his unmarried younger son's room. Ku told us that last year, apart from the income of his elder son's family, the workpoints earned by his wife, younger son, daughter and himself amounted to 1,200 yuan. They had some 500 yuan left over after buying whatever they needed. This plus income from side-line occupations made life quite easy.

With more people working, team leader Yeh explained, Ku's family received a comparatively higher income as a result of implementation of the principle "To each according to his work and more pay for more work." The family's living standards are rated at the top of the middle category in the No. 2 team, he said.

Next we went to see 50-year-old Yeh Kun-fang who had been a poor peasant before liberation. His family which had had the hardest time among those in the locality then is now leading an average life. He and his five-year-old grandson were happy to see us.

His three-room house—with the living room in the middle and two bedrooms on both sides—and a kitchen were built in 1964. It cost about 2,000 yuan which the family had saved over several years.

He spoke of his miserable life in the old society. "My father owned a dozen *mu* of arbutus garden," he said, "but he had to sell it to a capitalist who turned it into his family cemetery. I myself became the caretaker and eked out a living by selling fruit and firewood which I was allowed to gather in small quantities. Several years later, the capitalist hired someone else and that was the end of my job. I made a living by doing odd jobs and selling firewood.

"When the reactionaries ruled, we fruit-growers were subjected to all kinds of exploitation. When the fruit was brought to town, brokers got their commissions from us while the capitalists freely forced prices down and bought the fruit cheap. Also, the bogus local government put heavy taxes on what we sold. What angered us most were the tyrannical officials. Once a head of a *pao* (each *pao* was made up of 100 households whose neighbours were required to watch each other's activities and report them to the reactionary authorities) who had just lost in gambling spotted me when

I was selling firewood on the street. He took the fire-wood away to pay his debts."

"Where is he now?" we asked.

"Him? During the land reform, many peasants exposed his crimes. Now he's doing physical labour in our team under the peasants' surveillance. We poor people now have our old scores settled."

Life for Yeh Kun-fang's family got better and better after the agricultural producers' co-op was set up in the village, and it has continued to improve since the birth of the people's commune. After his son got married and became economically independent, the rest of the family—himself, his wife and daughter—still earned enough to support themselves. Though they were not very well-off, they no longer worried about their food, clothing and other expenses.

Last year, the three of them did 760 work-days which were equivalent to 760 yuan. This together with another 75 yuan for 150 *dan* (one *dan* is about 50 kg.) of manure they sold to the team as an assigned task made a total of 835 yuan. Their net income was 490 yuan at the year-end distribution after expenses for food grain, firewood, cooking oil and other items were deducted. This income, of course, did not include what they got from their private plot and side-line produce, such as pigs and chickens. They had recently sold two pigs for 110 yuan. All this money was for their own use as they grew enough vegetables on their private plot for their own consumption and paid no rent for the house they owned.

The vegetables grown on their 0.21-*mu* private plot are cabbages, broad beans, rape and others, all of which belong to them and are not subject to any tax in kind or cash to the state or collective. The peasants usually work on their private plots before or after collective production work which comes first.

We asked Yeh Kun-fang how he had spent his spare cash in the last few years. Pointing to a chest of drawers, he told us that it was made in Shanghai. He showed us his wardrobe with a big mirror, dressing table, transistor radio and clock. "All these," he said, "cost me over 400 yuan. My daughter has grown up and I've been preparing a wedding gift for her."

Talking about his daughter, Yeh told us Yeh Hui-chen is a 23-year-old Communist Youth League member. She is in the brigade's cultural troupe and is also the brigade's committee member in charge of work among women as well as deputy platoon leader in the militia. Her fiance is a 24-year-old member of the same production team. According to the Marriage Law, both have reached the required marriage age. But in response to the government's call to marry late, they're going to wait two years.

Team leader Yeh told us something about cultural and recreational activities among the peasants. The 40-member cultural troupe is formed by the brigade with four to five young people from each team taking part. Aside from giving performances of dances and songs and theatrical items, they write and perform their own skits dealing with the peasants' daily lives. Most villagers were illiterate before liberation. But now all school-age children in the No. 2 team are in the brigade's two primary schools and a dozen or so young people have gone to the brigade's middle school. Among the younger generation there no longer are any illiterates. Other young people like Yeh Hui-chen who had some primary schooling are attending night classes to raise their political and educational level.

Team leader Yeh was cut short by the bell signalling it was time to knock off. About a dozen young women carrying loads of firewood on shoulder-poles were coming down a nearby hill. Pointing to the one in printed cottons, Yeh told us that she was Yeh Hui-chen. A few minutes later, a pretty girl with two long plaits and a pair of large black eyes came in. She was followed by her brother, a robust young fellow carrying a spade just back from planting trees. The last to come in was Yeh's daughter-in-law, a healthy and serious woman. She had gone to the creche to bring back her daughter.

This is how an ordinary peasant family in the Tungting People's Commune lives. Though it is not very well-off at present, life for the peasants will get better and better with the growing prosperity of the socialist motherland.

6. WOMEN MEMBERS

There are many lines of production and numerous kinds of work in the Tungting Commune. With every able-bodied woman engaged in collective productive labour thanks to women's initiative being successfully brought into play, there is no manpower shortage in the commune. Many commune members told us: "There is the saying that women do half the work, this is certainly true of our womenfolk here."

Chin Chih-fang, a vice-chairman of the commune's revolutionary committee in charge of work among women, talked to us about the commune's women members. A cadre who had been chairman of the women's organization during the land reform in the early post-liberation days, she had the conditions of the peasant families, especially those of women members, at her finger-tips. She impressed us as being a good talker, intelligent and capable.

Change of Political and Economic Status

Speaking of today's women and men being politically and economically equal, she said with real feeling: "This was hard-won after many, many struggles!" She recounted the past sufferings of women in the Tungting area.

"Women are always busy, either beside the kitchen stove or at the far-off riverside" was a saying in the old days. It aptly described how the labouring women were tied down from morning to night with household chores, such as cooking, fetching water and washing.

Like their sisters in other parts of the country, the women of Tungting suffered multiple oppression—they were inferior to men, had very little say in the family and were dependent on their husbands economically. Besides heavy housework, they sometimes rowed boats, fished and collected firewood and even worked as maids in the homes of landlords and capitalists in order to earn some money for their families. Landlord-capitalist Chin Hsueh-chih (see first instalment of this report on p. 14, No. 13), for instance, had more than 20 maids. Some women were so poor that they had to leave six-month-old babies at home and become wet nurses for capitalists' children.

Liberation brought Tungting's women political emancipation. The vestiges of feudal ideas, however, still existed and exerted their influence. Women had to carry on their battle against old conventions and ideas to achieve complete equality with men.

"For instance," Chin Chih-fang recalled, "when I first took part in land reform work, some people chattered: 'How can a woman do it? Everything will be all right so long as we men do a little more work.'"

It's a different story now. Nearly 500 women, she said, hold leading posts at the commune, brigade and team levels and in the militia organizations, the Communist Party and Communist Youth League branches. There are always women among the cadres at commune, brigade or team meetings to discuss various fields of work. Women are also playing a bigger and bigger part in production. Each of the commune's 237 production teams has a woman leader or deputy leader, and women account for 46 per cent of the commune's total labour force.

Many lines of production, she continued, such as picking and curing tea, picking fruit and raising silkworms, are mostly done by women. In some production teams, more and more young women have taken over the work of growing rice and wheat and doing other farm work formerly done by men only. In this way, more able-bodied men have been transferred to heavier jobs like scooping mud from the rivers and ponds to make compost and quarrying rocks to build terraced fields. Compared with the men, young women can do a better and faster job of weeding, harvesting rice and other similar farm work.

Chairman Mao has called upon Chinese women to *"unite and take part in production and political activity to improve the economic and political status of women."* This is exactly what Tungting's women are doing.

Chin Chih-fang is a good example. While taking an active part in struggling against the landlords and distributing land during the land reform, she helped other women free themselves from the yoke of the reactionary feudal bureaucrat forces. From the time the mutual-aid teams and co-ops were formed to the birth of the people's commune, she joined with other women to struggle without a let-up against Rightist conservative thinking of every description and the spontaneous capitalist tendency in the rural areas. They were always in the front ranks in taking the socialist road.

Their constant efforts to study and temper themselves in class struggle resulted in a marked rise in political consciousness and ability in work. During the Great Cultural Revolution, in particular, they courageously defended Chairman Mao's revolutionary line and thus raised their consciousness of class struggle and the struggle between the two lines to a new high. Ten middle-aged women of the Yangwan No. 4 team, who had never used a pen before, have become prolific writers of articles criticizing Liu Shao-chi and other political swindlers. All of them pledged to do a good job in raising silkworms for the revolution.

Good at Farm Production

We heard quite a number of moving stories from Comrade Chin Chih-fang about women who have distinguished themselves by their outstanding achievements in collective productive labour.

Wang Tung-hui, an elderly woman in the Kuangjung Production Team and an old hand at raising pigs, puts her heart and soul into the job the team has assigned her. Whenever a sow gave birth at night, she would sit up looking after it. When the newly born piglings did not eat, she fed them gruel with a spoon. She always took pains to look after the sick pigs. She also carefully observed the characteristics of each pig and fed them accordingly. Thanks to her efforts, the number of pigs collectively owned by the team has increased 2.5-fold in three years.

Weng Chin-feng, a woman cadre in charge of work among women in the Hsinmin Brigade, took the lead in laying a pipeline to bring water up to the terraced fields. Since the work involved some skill and the removal of rocks, some men would not believe that women could complete the task. They said: "If women can lay the pipeline, then all work can be done without men." With firm determination, Weng and other women went ahead, learnt the necessary skill in the course of work and finally completed the planned pipeline.

Especially noteworthy were the many shock teams formed by young women who were called "capable girls of iron" by the villagers. In the fields by the Taihu Lake, we saw the "Iron Girls' Squad" of the Chienkuo Brigade's No. 2 team which is known throughout the commune for its many outstanding contributions. Led by Chin Lung-ti, all 14 squad members—strong and healthy young women with rosy cheeks and long braids—were applying fertilizer to the rape in the fields. Work on this team's 200 *mu* of paddyfield used to be done by men who were kept so busy that they sometimes had to seek help from other teams. Now part of the paddy-field is under the squad—all the girls are in their early 20s and they do all the work from transplanting to harvesting.

While fulfilling their production tasks, they also work on 1.9 *mu* of experimental plot in their spare time. In 1972, a single rice crop sown on the plot yielded 470 kilogrammes per *mu*. Their experiments have pushed scientific research activities ahead all over the commune. During the work-break, the "iron girls" got together and told us something about themselves.

The squad was set up by nine young women and later another five joined it. Working hard and unafraid of difficulties, they outpaced young men in emulation campaigns and were named the "Iron Girls' Squad" in 1970 at a general meeting of the production team.

The members were not only good in production work but were also solidly united. "At first," Lung-ti said, "we were not always in agreement since there were occasional differences among us. Later, the brigade's Party branch got us to study at the political night school. After studying Chairman Mao's works, we understood better that we were farming for the revolution and not for our individual interests. After that none of us fussed over trifles. We helped each other and made concerted efforts to build a new socialist countryside. Hence the unity among us."

Apart from working and studying together, all squad members are militiawomen. They have done their military training conscientiously and had excellent marks in their first target practice.

The "Iron Girls' Squad" always has the interests of the collective at heart. Once when sweet potatoes had been harvested, some team members after work dug up those left behind and took them home. When the girls learnt of this, they went digging too, but instead of taking the sweet potatoes home they handed them over to the team. Meanwhile, they criticized those who had taken the potatoes home and helped them realize that though what they had taken was not of much value, it involved the question of correctly handling relations between public and private interests. In the end, the team members accepted their correct criticism and of their own accord turned the sweet potatoes over to the collective.

Safeguarding Women's Interests

Both men and women members take part in productive labour and political activities on an equal footing. How then do the women arrange their household affairs and children? For an answer to this question, Comrade Chin Chih-fang took us to the Weitung Production Brigade which has 850 women members, more than half its population.

Taking into consideration women's physiological conditions, the production teams always see to it that they are given lighter jobs. Also, they are allowed to knock off one hour earlier than men. To help lessen the women's burden the brigade runs all-year-round canteens with additional ones set up during the busy farming seasons. When there is rush work during harvesting or sowing time, canteens are set up in the fields far from the villages. As to payment for work, even when women did the same work as men, they received about 20 per cent less in the past. Now all men and women get equal pay for equal work.

The Weitung Brigade has a creche in each of its eight production teams. And the brigade runs four kindergartens with 99 children under the care of a staff of 25.

We visited several creches. The No. 3 team's creche was in a clean, spacious room with small wooden beds and cradles made by the team members. Two middle-aged women looked after eight two- or three-year-olds. When we arrived at the No. 4 team's creche, two young women were teaching the tots to sing songs. Seeing us, the 12 lovely children, from three to seven, lined up and performed for us. The first song they sang was *The East Is Red*.

We interviewed Chu Feng-chu, an old woman who started taking care of children in 1955 and has always worked with a sense of responsibility. Some of the children she looked after are now in senior middle school, others are working elsewhere, while still others have enlisted in the People's Liberation Army. To this day, she still is unwilling to quit working because she feels that the more she works, the greater is her enthusiasm.

When we asked Chu Feng-chu why she continued working so hard despite her advanced age, she replied: "I myself had several children in the old society, but they all died of sickness and starvation. I regard all the children who come to the creche as my own children and grandchildren. I take good care of them and bring them up so that parents can set their minds at rest while doing production work and can contribute more to socialism. Though I'm old, I still can do my bit in building socialism. This is what brings me the most happiness!"

A COMMUNE ALONG THE RED FLAG CANAL*

Looking out over the Taihang Mountains, one can see the Red Flag Canal and its branches winding amid the peaks like silver ribbons, linking up reservoirs whose blue ripples glitter in the sun. At the foot of slopes near and far pumping stations are at work and high tension wires stretch out to every village. Lower down on the mountains trucks and tractors run along the asphalt roads.

The center of the Jentsun commune, which lies along the Red Flag Canal, is a green, shady village of cleanly-whitewashed houses. Beside them runs a small canal neatly lined with stones. The murmuring water was so

* From *China Reconstructs,* August 1974.

clear that I could see the bottom. Beside the canal a few people were washing clothes or fetching water.

When I asked a woman how the supply of water was, she smiled and replied, "Fine. Since the canal was built we can get water right outside our door."

Water Precious as Oil

Today none of the Jentsun commune's 115 villages need to worry about water. Before liberation, however, people had to carry it over the mountains on shoulder poles or on their backs. The peasants of Sangerh village had to go four kilometers to a small spring in a gully and stand in line behind a lot of others to get water.

People still tell the story of Sang Lin-mao, an old poor peasant, who set out early in the morning on the day before Spring Festival to get water for festival cooking. When it grew dark he had not come home yet. Worried, his daughter-in-law went out to look for him and met him halfway home. There had been so many people and he had had to wait so long. She insisted on taking the water from him, but just as they neared the house she stumbled and spilled the two pails of the precious stuff the old man had spent all that time and effort getting. She was so overcome with remorse that she hanged herself. The whole family left the region and never returned.

Although some villages had cisterns for storing snow and rain water, these were the property of landlords or rich peasants. They wouldn't even let others have water to drink but kept the heavy stone covers locked down. Two buckets of water could be got at a cost of between 50 and 100 coppers.

A folk song describing the people's life went:

Our mountaintops are bald,
Drinking water precious as oil,

The rich want grain for rent and payment of debt
The poor are sad night and day.

In 1942, 300 people starved to death during a serious drought and over 3,000 fled the area to escape the same fate.

After liberation the poor peasants, led by the Communist Party, carried out land reform and ended feudal exploitation. The cisterns became the common property of the peasants. After agricultural producers' cooperatives were set up people were organized to dig more cisterns, seek out mountain springs and build storage ponds. The problem, however, was insufficient sources of water and these measures could not fundamentally solve it.

The Fight for the Canal

Chairman Mao has observed, *"Poverty gives rise to the desire for change, the desire for action and the desire for revolution."* How the people of Jentsun wished they could be free from the threat of drought! They were able to make their wish come true only after the people's communes were formed in 1958.

In February 1960 the Communist Party committee of Linhsien county, responding to the people's wishes, decided to mobilize the 15 communes under it to bring in water from the Changho River north of the county. They were acting in the spirit of the General Line not long before formulated by Chairman Mao to *"go all out, aim high, and achieve greater, faster, better and more economical results in building socialism"*.

If they were to get water from the Changho they had to dam its upper reaches in neighboring Shansi province and lead the water over in a canal through the Taihang Mountains. When the county Party committee issued the call to begin the project the members of the Jentsun commune responded enthusiastically.

They raced to sign up for the labor that would "bring water to Linhsien county".

It was a time when the imperialists, revisionists and other reactionaries abroad were attacking China in chorus. Internally the national economy faced temporary difficulties brought on by natural calamities. The class struggle and the struggle between the revolutionary and counter-revolutionary lines was very sharp. Enemies of the working people began to say, "We didn't have a canal before but we went on living."

"And how did you live?" the poor and lower-middle peasants[1] shot back. "You lived by exploiting and oppressing us poor people!"

Some commune members lacked confidence because they saw only the difficulties in building such a project and were unable to see the strength of the people. The poor and lower-middle peasants replied with the ancient fable of the Foolish Old Man who moved the mountains that Chairman Mao has told. The old man wanted to remove two peaks outside his door and dug away at them every day.

"Why can't we be like the Foolish Old Man and cut through the Taihang Mountains?" the people said. "We have Chairman Mao and the Communist Party to lead us. We have the people's commune. Surely we can dig until we achieve our aim." The sabotage of the class enemy was beaten back and the commune members gained new confidence. "Build a canal. We want to build a canal," was heard all through the village.

Two thousand people from the Jentsun commune joined the army of tens of thousands of builders from elsewhere in the county at the worksites. The county Party committee leading the project assigned the Jentsun commune to work on the canal headgate, a big dam on the Changho and a canal leading from it. As the

[1] This is a political term denoting class status and not present economic status. In class struggle the poor and lower-middle peasants are the most reliable allies of the proletariat.

dam reached the point where it was to be closed, the river was so turbulent that it simply washed away 150-kilogram gunny sacks of sand and mud thrown into the water to block the flow. Two young Communists, Tung Tao-chou and Chang Li-fang, ignoring the danger, jumped into the water. Soon shoulder to shoulder in three rows, arms linked, 200 peasant builders formed a human wall which weakened the impact of the current and made it possible to pile up thousands of sacks quickly and firmly to block the Changho.

Rocks were blasted away and tunnels dug as the construction progressed step by step. One danger was loose rocks detaching themselves from the sheer cliffs after blasting and falling down on the work crews. Jen Yang-cheng, a peasant builder, learned to dangle in midair over a precipice and dislodge loose boulders and soon was leading a team of 30 doing this work.

After a hard eight-month battle the canal finally reached the county line 20 kilometers away. The people were overjoyed, but a few others were not so happy. This was the time that Liu Shao-chi and his gang, chiming in with the anti-China chorus abroad and intending to pull China back to capitalism, were making fierce attacks on the Three Red Banners for building socialism—the General Line, the Big Leap Forward and the People's Communes. Liu's agents in Honan, following his lead, ordered work on the project to stop.

Their act met with strong opposition from the peasant workers. "Chairman Mao has taught us that we should *'transform China in the spirit of the Foolish Old Man who removed the mountains',*" said Jen Yang-cheng.

"We intend to do as he says and never pull back on this project," declared Chang Li-fang, another worker. "*'Water conservation is the lifeline of agriculture.'* We will be resolute about carrying out Chairman Mao's teaching. The only way our mountain region will prosper is with water from the Changho. We'll always say No to whoever says Stop!" The revolutionary spirit of the peasants kept the project going.

The 70-kilometer main trunk canal was completed in April 1965. Auxiliary construction was finished in June 1969, just as victory in the proletarian cultural revolution was being hailed. The project was given the name Red Flag Canal by the county people's congress.

Coming of the Water

The day the water flowed through the canal thousands of cheering peasants crowded its banks. "Chairman Mao and the Communist Party have brought us the water of happiness!" they said. Eighty-one-year-old Li Hsing-wen asked his grandson to help him to the canal. With deep emotion he scooped up a handful of water. "Never in my life did I dream that the water of the Changho would run through our village!" he said.

Brigades the canal passes through began construction to conduct the water to individual villages. Nankou village in the Jentsun commune is some distance from the canal and on land higher than it. The people found they could bring the water over by building a pumping station. Now the village's 40 families no longer have to walk far to get drinking water and all their fields are irrigated. Before, 32 families who lived in another village four kilometers away used to walk over to work on the fields at Nankou. Soon the commune brigade had enough money to build three rows of new tile-roofed houses with a total of 185 rooms and these people could move to Nankou. "The water of the canal built us a new village!" the commune members say joyfully.

Today no village in the county needs to worry about lack of water. The nightmare of "water precious as oil" has become nothing but a memory in the minds of the old people.

How the Place Changed

In Sangerh village I was entertained at the home of Sang Sung-chi. The dinner consisted of noodles, deep-fat fried eggs and vermicelli made from sweet potato flour. Old Sang talked enthusiastically about the changes the canal had brought for his brigade and family. "Now we not only have drinking water but water for irrigation. Before liberation with drought nine years out of ten, we were lucky to get 500 kilograms of wheat per hectare. The yields were better after liberation but fastest progress has been since the canal was built. Last year we averaged 2,430 kg. per hectare, 750 kg. more than before the canal. This means more wheat flour for our food."

It was an even bigger surprise when I was served rice in the home of Chang Shou-teh in Panyang village. In the old days rice was grown only in south China and the valley of the Yangtze River where rain is plentiful. I never expected to find it being raised in this area.

Old Chang said that irrigation with water from the canal had made it possible to grow some rice. In 1971 the brigade planted their first crop on 2.7 hectares of land. By 1973 they had increased this to 27 hectares. They plan 53 hectares for this year. "The Red Flag Canal has brought us white flour and rice for our meals!" Old Chang chuckled.

"In the old days neither trees nor vegetables would grow in this place," he continued. "It was hard to get drinking water for humans, let alone for raising animals. Now, with the canal, we have lots of water and cattle and sheep besides."

Before the canal, of the Jentsun commune's 2,700 hectares, only 20 hectares along the Changho River could be irrigated. The average yield per hectare was less than 1,000 kg. Today 1,400 hectares are irrigated and the over-all yield per hectare reached 5,167 kg. in 1973.

Since the main canal was completed, half of the 2,700 hectares suitable for afforestation have been planted to timber and fruit trees, an average of 450 trees for every one of the 40,000 people in the commune. Last year the commune produced a total of 3,000 tons of fruit—persimmons, apples, pears and dates and also walnuts. The hillsides below the canal are dotted with orchards and green groves, giving an entirely different look to the once-denuded hills. Animal husbandry is growing rapidly. In their reservoirs and ponds some commune teams have begun raising fish, a thing unthinkable in the past.

With plenty of water, collective production at the Jentsun commune has developed rapidly and the standard of living of its members has made marked improvement. Practically every household has surplus grain and savings. Grain sold to the state rose from 395 tons in 1964 to 880 in 1973. The commune has a grain reserve of 2,100 tons and a public accumulation fund of 10,800,000 yuan.

Electricity

At dusk as I sat talking to Old Chang the room was suddenly flooded with light as the power went on. Our conversation turned to the question of lighting. "Before liberation we could not afford a lamp," Chang said. "After liberation we got a castor oil lamp and after the agricultural cooperative was formed we changed to a kerosene lamp. And now the commune has installed electric lights for us."

A little later we heard the evening news from the Central People's Radio Network and a weather forecast over the commune's rediffusion system. "Every house in our village has a speaker," Old Chang remarked, "so we know what's going on in our country and the world all the time."

The next morning I toured the village with Yuan Hsien-suo, secretary of the Panyang brigade Party branch. First we visited the brigade health center, a spick-and-span room with about a hundred drawers of Chinese herbal medicines, a cabinet of modern drugs and an assortment of medical and surgical instruments. A young woman "barefoot doctor" greeted us with a smile. Then we went to a "seven-year school" (5 elementary and 2 junior middle school grades) housed in seven new brick classrooms with whitewashed walls.

As we walked about, Yuan described the tremendous development in health and education in the brigade and the rest of the commune. Every brigade has a cooperative medical care plan and its own health center. There are 116 medical personnel in the commune, including 62 "barefoot doctors". The presence of water has improved sanitation and reduced infectious diseases, so the people's health has improved greatly. Now there are 50 schools in the commune. Everyone of primary school age is attending, and the commune has a regular middle school and 23 schools like the one I saw with junior-middle grades or classes.

We climbed the slope just behind Panyang village to the brigade's power station. The tile-roofed brick building houses two generators of 40 and 125-kilowatt capacity. I asked whether these generated enough electricity for their own use. "More than enough," replied a young worker. "At the suggestion of commune members we have linked our lines to the power grid serving the area and thereby add our surplus current to the state's supply to help develop our socialist industry."

The five small hydropower stations built by the Jentsun brigades have a total generating capacity of 331 kw. More such stations are being planned.

The brigade's small grain-processing plant and its four threshing machines run on electric power, Yuan told me. "The manpower released by use of electricity and by irrigation enables us to go in for intensive farming and improve our soil through deep plowing," he said. All of which makes for a steady rise in production.

We strolled along the canal past shady villages and large stretches of green-carpeted wheat fields. Yuan Hsien-suo, I learned, as a young man was steeled in the campaign to build the canal and is now a capable leader in his brigade. The tremendous changes already brought about by the Red Flag Canal enable him to say with pride and confidence, "We're still developing but we're determined to work harder so that we can achieve mechanization and electrification as soon as possible."

Nature Being Transformed

Since the canal was completed the people have scored one new achievement after another in changing their mountain region.

After 1965 when work began on the third trunk canal a dozen brigades also started on a 57-kilometer branch of it which would take its water eastward to 230 hectares of their fields. The main trunk canal had just been completed; blasters, stonemasons, blacksmiths and thousands of other peasant builders returning triumphantly from it set right to work on the new site.

Tung Tao-chou, one of the young men who blocked the river with his body when the dam was being completed, became an able leader of a brigade and a bold worker on the new project. He learned of the difficulties of working in a small 40-meter tunnel because the smoke wouldn't disperse after a blast and it was hard to get the stone out and immediately went himself to work at the job. When water to mix the mortar had to be carried up a steep slope, it was he who did it. His taking the lead encouraged the others to work all the harder.

There were many such who worked on the project

and many examples of moving deeds and good ide-ology.

One example is the story of the Tienchiao Canal. Usually the Red Flag Canal provides ample water for the county's 40,000 hectares under irrigation, but dur-ing periods of heaviest use there is still not enough. Most members and cadres in the four brigades near the beginning of the canal felt they should make use of their favorable location near the Changho River to build a canal directly from it and leave the water of the Red Flag Canal for brigades and communes further on. A few people, however, didn't understand. "We're near the head of the canal, all we need to do to irrigate our land is open the headgate. 'The flowers on the sunny side are always the first to bloom'."

Yang Yu-huai, Yuan Hsien-suo and other Commu-nist Party members who had worked on the Red Flag Canal project studied Chairman Mao's *In Memory of Norman Bethune* with the other brigade members. Dur-ing the discussion Yang said, "Thinking only of oneself and not of others is selfish, just the opposite of Dr. Bethune's utter devotion to others."

"The land along both the upper and lower parts of the canal is part of our socialist motherland," Yuan pointed out. "We can't think of just one brigade or commune. Standing in the Taihang Mountains we should think of the whole country and the whole world." In the course of the study those members who had opposed the new canal came to see they had been wrong.

Working several winters and springs, the brigades completed the 17-km. new canal, named the Tienchiao, in the summer of 1973. Though the water it saved in Red Flag Canal was only enough to irrigate 200 hectares, the people of the county praised these four brigades for their spirit of considering the whole.

On the worksites, where nature is still being trans-formed, and in the broad fields, this good thinking and working style can be seen not only in commune members and cadres who worked on the Red Flag Canal, most of whom are now over thirty, but also in a large number of fresh-faced younger men and women who are steadily maturing.

Chang Chi-hui is one of these younger members of the commune's Jentsun brigade. When he graduated from senior middle school early in 1971 he was filled with a lofty vision of building a new socialist countryside. Not long afterward he sought his village Party branch secretary Chang Li-fang. "The Red Flag Canal irrigates only 213 of our brigade's 280 hectares. If we were to build two small reservoirs to store rainwater and the canal water we don't normally use, couldn't we irrigate the remaining 67 hectares?" The Party secretary supported the idea and praised the young man for having the same spirit as the earlier builders of the canal. Chang Chi-hui and the Party secretary climbed the hills with veteran peasants to make a survey. When work on the reservoirs began, his vision of building a new socialist countryside spurred him to load 200 kg. of earth on his cart and run 250 meters with it, dump the cart and run back—80 times a day. He set an example that many other young men followed.

The Party branch asked Chang Chi-hui to lead an agricultural experiment group of young people who had returned to the village after finishing school. Chang agreed that this was just what was needed. "After basically solving the problem of irrigation, we must farm more scientifically if we're going to completely change our mountain district," he said.

With the help of a veteran peasant he and his companions tried hybridizing corn and finding new methods of raising sweet potato seedlings. Repeated failures made him realize that though he was a graduate of senior middle school, when it came to practical application he knew far from enough. He went into agricultural science and learned from the old peasants. Finally in the past year the group has been having some good results. "With a younger generation like you with education, drive and vision, we won't need to worry about whether or not our mountain village will be changed," brigade members say.

Advancing in Struggle

I saw a scene of "thoroughly transforming nature" along the Dew River, where thousands of peasants were at work building a new riverbank and filling in the riverbed to make fields. The place was dotted with red flags and streams of people and carts moved to and fro.

The Dew is a seasonal river. Though it is dry most of the year, the fierce mountain floods when they come have washed out a bed a kilometer wide along the 11-km. course. The desire to transform the barren riverbed was voiced by commune members and cadres who had worked on the Red Flag Canal and by the younger people as well. In this they were seeking to follow the lead of the Tachai brigade in Shansi province, a national pacesetter in agriculture. They began work last winter.

Posted on boards beside the worksite I noticed short articles and cartoons by the builders criticizing Lin Piao and his venerable master Confucius, the former who tried to restore capitalism, and the latter who over 2,400 years ago wanted to restore slavery. The worksite was also a battlefield for criticizing them. The whole commune was condemning them in speech and writing.

"In the old society the landlords exploited me so that I could not go on living here," said Kan Tsao-chuan, an old resident of Panyang village, furiously. "Trying to get away from starvation I had to go begging in Shansi. There was no way out: I had to sell my son and tell my wife to find some other way to live. The old society broke up our family just like that.

"Today, with the people's commune, I've returned to my old village and rebuilt my home. My son's been found—he's a worker in Shansi—and my wife's back home with me. That villain Lin Piao tried to restore capitalism and turn history backward. He wanted to bring the old society back and make us suffer again. But we won't let it happen!"

The mass movement to criticize Lin Piao and Confucius was brought right down and linked with the class struggle in the Jentsun brigade. The people exposed, criticized and struggled against two reactionary rich peasants who had once made an attempt to seize back property confiscated during the land reform and make a counter-revolutionary comeback. The poor and lower-middle peasants were furious. "The landlords and rich peasants oppressed us so we couldn't breathe. They would not even give us a drink of water from their wells. Lin Piao wanted to restore capitalism, wanted the landlords and rich peasants, these class enemies with bitter hatred for socialism, to rise up again and ride on our backs!"

Criticism of Lin Piao heightened the people's socialist enthusiasm and pushed the whole commune's farm production forward. In a few months during the criticism of Lin Piao and Confucius they completed one section of a firm new riverbank and filled in 80 hectares of new fields in the bed of the Dew River. Following the policy of "benefit the same year" they plowed and planted the fields as they finished them. When I was there they had already planted 27 hectares of potatoes and were going to put rice on the other 53. Progress on the project was rapid.

The brigade plans to transform the riverbed a section at a time so that the whole project will be completed next winter, a commune cadre told me. The 200 hectares of new fields created will be planted to rice irrigated by the Red Flag Canal.

"BAREFOOT DOCTORS"—GIVING MEDICAL TREATMENT WHILE TAKING PART IN FARM WORK*

"Barefoot doctor" has become a familiar term to more and more readers abroad. Just what are these doctors? How are they trained? And what role do they play in China's medical and public health work? The following stories offer some answers.

To Meet the Pressing Demand

The name "barefoot doctor" first appeared in the Chiangchen People's Commune on Shanghai's outskirts.

In 1965 when Chairman Mao issued the call *"In medical and health work, put the stress on the rural areas,"* a number of mobile medical teams formed by urban medical workers came to Chiangchen. Though it was near the metropolis, this commune had only one health clinic with about a dozen medical personnel serving a population of 28,000. When the medical teams arrived, the local peasants were glad to see them. While curing and preventing commune members' diseases, the doctors from Shanghai helped the clinic give a group of young peasants some medical training.

Later when the teams left, these peasants took their place and since then have gradually become full-fledged doctors. Taking medical kits with them, they worked barefooted alongside the peasants in the paddyfields, and they treated peasants in the fields, on the threshing grounds or in their homes. They were at once commune members and doctors, doing farm work and treating patients. Like other commune members, they receive their pay on the basis of workpoints, and their income was more or less the same as that of able-bodied peasants doing the same amount of work. The peasants warmly

* From *Peking Review*, No. 21, 1973.

welcomed them and affectionately called them "bare-foot doctors."

Renmin Ribao devoted much coverage on September 14, 1968 to this new-born thing. This set off nationwide efforts to train "barefoot doctors" from among the peasants.

Eight out of every ten people in China are in the countryside. But the vast rural areas had been short of medical workers and medicines for centuries under re-actionary rule before liberation. Over a fairly long pe-riod of time after liberation, medical personnel, medical and public health funds, medicines and medical equip-ment were mainly concentrated in the cities and medi-cal conditions in the rural areas had not improved rapidly due to the effects of Liu Shao-chi's counter-revolutionary revisionist line. Changing this situation was an urgent task confronting medical and public health work. Thus after Chairman Mao issued his call to stress medical and health work in the rural areas, prompt action was taken throughout the country. The People's Government allocated special funds for the rural areas. Factories turned out more medical equip-ment and medicines suited to rural conditions. Urban medical personnel and large numbers of graduates from medical schools went to work in the countryside. It was under these circumstances that the "barefoot doctors" emerged.

Building a New Socialist Countryside

Wang Kuei-chen was one of the Chiangchen Com-mune's first "barefoot doctors." After graduating school in Shanghai, she worked in a towel factory for three years. Anxious to build a new socialist countryside, she returned to her village to do farm work in 1961.

A group of city medical workers arrived at the height of the early rice harvest in mid-July to inoculate the peasants against summer diseases and help them im-prove environmental sanitation. Wang Kuei-chen took an active part in this work which helped keep the peasants fit during the busy farming season. She learnt that building up the rural areas meant much more than just working with hoe or sickle.

In 1965, Wang Kuei-chen who was 21 that year was chosen to attend a training course for "barefoot doctors" run by the commune's clinic. The first lesson was given by an old poor peasant who recounted his past sufferings and spoke of today's happy life. Two instances he talked about left a deep impression on her, daughter of an impoverished rural carpenter.

The first was about a poor peasant's son who had acute ulceration of the gum and cheeks before liberation. Blood and pus continually oozed from the ulcers and the child's case got worse and worse. The father went to town to get a doctor who demanded an amount of money far beyond what he could pay. He went back and borrowed the money from his fellow villagers. But by the time the doctor came that night, the child had died.

Another poor peasant's child contracted encephalitis B several years ago. There was no hospital near the village and the boy's condition rapidly worsened. He was rushed to town and hospitalized for a month. Though the family spent more than 300 yuan, the child became disabled because of delayed treatment.

These examples made a deep impression on Wang Kuei-chen and heightened her determination to do what she could for the peasants' well-being.

During her four months of training, Wang Kuei-chen and 27 other young men and women were taught to cure scores of common diseases and prescribe some 100 medicines and they learnt the fundamentals of acupuncture treatment at 30 major points on the human body. This ABC of medical science was of great use to these young people who have deep feelings for the peasants.

Back from the training course, Wang Kuei-chen continued doing farm work such as transplanting rice-shoots, weeding and harvesting together with the villagers. Wherever she worked, in the fields, at construction sites of water conservancy projects or other places, she always had her medical kit at hand. She and two other "barefoot doctors" took charge of handling all the diseases and injuries they could among the more than 1,500 brigade members. After giving prescriptions, she made it a rule to call on the patients and ask them about the effects of the medicine so as to sum up experience and improve her work. As to cases she could not handle, she always went with the patients to the city hospital.

All this was not just for the purpose of learning, but, more important, her aim was to look after the patients still better. In summer, villagers sometimes were bitten by snakes. When she was told that a worker in a factory several kilometres away could treat snake-bites with herbal medicine, she immediately went to see him. Combining what she learnt from the worker with Western medicine, she has treated more than a dozen snake-bite cases in the last two years.

Affectionately called their "close friend" by the villagers, Wang Kuei-chen was elected deputy secretary of the commune Party committee and a member on the county Party committee. Despite the change in her position, she is still a "barefoot doctor."

She has also made rapid progress in medical technique. She and other "barefoot doctors" took turns working in the commune's health clinic or getting further training in advanced courses. Last year, she spent two months studying anatomy, physiology and biochemistry in a medical college and later went to the county hospital's internal medicine department for advanced study in combination with clinical treatment.

To Serve the Peasants

Liu Han's long-standing hope was to become a peasant-doctor who serves the villagers. His desire to do so goes back to the tragic death of his mother.

Liu Han lives in Kirin Province, northeast China. When he was only nine, his mother came down with puerperal fever. His father travelled a long distance trying to get a doctor, but the doctor refused because the Liu family could not pay his fee. Tearfully, he walked another dozen kilometres to call in a quack. After feeling the patient's pulse, the charlatan scribbled a prescription for which he insisted on being paid 20 litres of rice and treated with good food and wine. The father had to borrow from neighbours to satisfy this demand. No sooner had the quack departed very drunk than Liu's mother died of eclampsia due to high fever. Liu Han said: "If there had been a doctor willing to serve poverty-stricken peasants, my mother (then in her early thirties) wouldn't have died."

When Liu grew up, he decided to become a doctor who worked for the peasants. He began learning traditional Chinese medicine from a folk doctor after finishing primary school. During the first half of the 1960s when the revisionist line was doing great damage on the medical and public health front, he was not allowed to practise medicine by a handful of capitalist roaders on the pretext that he had not had any regular training. The Great Proletarian Cultural Revolution fired him with soaring revolutionary enthusiasm and he became a "barefoot doctor." Instead of waiting for patients to come to him, he always made the rounds of peasant families and went to the fields to treat patients. He used a small cart to carry a large box holding over 100 kinds of medicinal herbs so that patients could get their medicine immediately after their cases had been diagnosed.

To know the properties of various medicinal herbs and find the optimum dosage, Liu Han time and again tasted the herbs to check their reaction on the body.

"Barefoot doctor" Jentso who belongs to the Tibetan nationality lives on the Chinghai Plateau some 4,500 metres above sea level, an area with very low temperatures and only one or two snow-free months. In addition to strong winds all year round, there is snow, hail or sandstorms in different seasons. What with the herdsmen living far apart, a "barefoot doctor" has to overcome many difficulties to see the patients. From the day she began practising medicine, Jentso has made light of journeys across mountains, valleys and grasslands to treat 36,000 patients.

She always keeps in mind the example of the Canadian internationalist Dr. Norman Bethune. In 1968 soon after she had given birth, word came that influenza with gastro-intestinal disorder had broken out in an area some 40 kilometres away and was spreading. Aware that it was the busy lambing season, she immediately left her baby with her neighbours and set out on foot for the affected area in the teeth of a howling wind. As soon as she got there after walking a whole day, she called on one family after another and gave the necessary treatment. Five days later, the situation was under control.

A homeless orphan, Jentso started tending the herd-owners' flocks at the age of seven. Because of malnutrition, her hair turned brown. The herd-owners and so-called "living Buddhas" regarded this as an ominous sign and cursed her as a devil. She was not even allowed to stand near the livestock sheds. After liberation, she was sent to many medical training courses run by the commune, county and autonomous *chou*. She is now able to cure local common diseases, give acupuncture treatment and deliver babies. "Though there are difficulties in my work," she said, "they are nothing compared with what we herdsmen and women suffered in bygone days." She always shows warm concern for the patients on her calls. Apart from helping them boil water and cook meals, she encourages them to build up their confidence in conquering illness.

A Communist Party member, Jentso seldom mentions the difficulties she encounters or gets conceited about her achievements. She takes an active part in collective productive labour, milking, spinning wool and doing other work, and is paid according to her workpoints just as other commune members. Time and again she has declined subsidies offered her by the production brigade.

At the county's Party congress in May 1971, Jentso was elected a member of the county Party committee.

Study in the Course of Practice

Generally speaking, "barefoot doctors" are given three to six months of short-term training before starting to work. Training classes with fewer but well-selected courses are run by the commune's clinic, county hospital, mobile medical teams from the cities or medical schools, according to the principle of linking theory with practice. The aim is to give the trainees the ability to do practical work as quickly as possible and to lay the foundation for advanced study.

For "barefoot doctors," in addition to taking part in short-term advanced study (one to several months) by turns and with full pay, most of their study is always tied in with problems that crop up in their everyday work. Many of them have made rapid progress through hard work and diligent study.

Chulaimu Niyatse who is of Uighur nationality returned to her native village in Sinkiang's Kuche County after graduating from junior middle school. Before becoming a "barefoot doctor," she had studied for only 35 days in the class run by the commune's clinic and she could only handle injections and minor injuries.

After 1966, she began studying medicine in the clinic every Wednesday while learning from the doctors and the medical team members whenever there was the opportunity to do so. She and the "barefoot doctors" from other brigades were required to report on the villagers' health conditions and the clinic's experienced doctors gave them lectures on how to prevent, diagnose and cure diseases. There once were five cases of diphtheria in her brigade and she administered medicine to the sick children and at the same time isolated them from the others whom she inoculated against the disease, thus checking it. Another time she used the same method to prevent meningitis from spreading. She now not only can use Western medicine to cure the local common diseases, but can prescribe traditional Chinese medicine and give acupuncture treatment. She also has learnt to deliver babies.

Together with four other "barefoot doctors," she took charge of a medical centre for a production brigade of 1,600 people. Last year, they gave medical treatment on over 7,000 occasions, including complicated cases such as tuberculosis of the bones and paralysis. There was one woman whose placenta was retained after giving birth and whose uterus bled profusely. Chulaimu brewed some medicinal herbs for her and got her out of danger.

"Barefoot doctor" Chang Hsiang-hua in the countryside around Yenan in northwest China had only learnt some elementary knowledge and technique of Western medicine in a training class. In the course of practice, he found that there were many effective prescriptions of traditional Chinese medicine used by the local people who lived in a hilly village where many medicinal herbs grew. If these traditional methods were put to good use, he thought, it would produce very good results in curing certain diseases and save the patients much expense. So he and his colleagues set about learning from veteran practitioners of traditional Chinese medicine and experienced herb-pickers in the locality. As a result, they were able to recognize 240 herbs and learnt to give herbal prescriptions and cure diseases by acupuncture. They themselves picked the needed herbs and later planted them. Last year, they went a step further. Based on efficacious herbal prescriptions, they processed herbs into easy-to-use pills, powders and liquid medicines to stop bleeding and coughing, induce lactation and cure burns.

In 1970, Chang Hsiang-hua had the opportunity to learn from a traditional Chinese doctor of a medical team that had come from Peking for six months. He worked together with this old doctor every day, diagnosing and curing patients. He also spent one to two hours listening to his talks on the theories of traditional Chinese medicine. Studying this way helped Chang quickly increase his ability.

For a period of time, he and other "barefoot doctors" in the brigade co-operated closely with medical teams from Peking, making an overall investigation of an endemic disease. They learnt to give every brigade member a cardiographic check-up and carried out auscultatory and oral investigations from house to house. They gave decoctions of herbal medicine twice a day to 28 patients who had varying symptoms. Carefully observing the effects, they continued studying ways to improve the prescription's ingredients. After 150 days, all the patients were better. In this way, the young "barefoot doctors" learnt how to diagnose, cure, treat and prevent this disease.

Study through practice, as shown by the above-mentioned examples, is the basic way "barefoot doctors" are trained. This quick and effective method makes up for the drawbacks due to medical schools being unable to train large numbers of doctors in a short time. In a developing country like China, the first step to change backwardness in medical work in the rural areas is, so to speak, "sending charcoal in snowy weather," not "adding flowers to the embroidery." "Barefoot doctors" are a new-born force which has bright prospects.

Every rural people's commune today has its "barefoot doctors" who are either children of the once impoverished peasants and herdsmen or city-bred middle school students who have settled in the countryside. These peasant-doctors are playing an important role in the rural areas where doctors and medicine are in great demand.

2. The Cities

Our first impressions of Chinese cities are their cleanliness, greenness, safety, and all those bicycles. We wouldn't go so far as to claim that there are no flies and mosquitoes in China (as some visitors have claimed), but there are very few of them. The old Chinese bad habit of spitting on the street has almost disappeared, but again, we wouldn't say it has disappeared completely. All the streets and roads are lined with trees, even along the very narrow old streets of Shanghai. We were told that the average summer temperature in Peking is 3°C cooler, thanks to the innumerable number of trees planted in the last twenty years. For those of us who do not dare to walk in a city park or on a sidewalk without first checking for canine droppings, it was quite a relief to know that dogs are not allowed in cities. It was also a relief to cross busy streets without worrying about being hit by a car.

These outward changes are impressive, but they are only expressions of a more important inner change—the change in the soul of the people. The transformation of human beings brought about in only twenty-five years by the revolution can be illustrated by our experience in Shanghai—a city which contributed to the English lexicon a verb meaning "to obtain something by unscrupulous means." One of our friends traveling with us lost his wallet with Chinese money equivalent to about forty-five U.S. dollars (which is more than an average worker's monthly income). Our guide told him calmly and confidently, "We would find it anywhere in China, except maybe Canton" (where bourgeois influence is still strong as a result of the large number of overseas Chinese visitors from Hong Kong). Two days later his wallet was returned to him with every penny in it. Streets in Chinese cities are probably the safest in the world today.

The transformation of city life has been accomplished by full participation of the people. We visited a basic street organization in Peking, the Fengsheng Neighborhood Revolutionary Committee, which runs a neighborhood with 53,000 people, to find out life on the street level. We don't remember all the statistics and figures Hsu Chung-chi, head of the Neighborhood Revolutionary Committee, ticked off for us, but we do remember the real sense of community in the neighborhood. Hsu Chung-chi, an author of the selection on "Our Neighborhood," looks like a typical middle-aged housewife with short hair and cloth shoes. She spoke with confidence and had all statistics at her fingertips. As she took us to visit some homes, kindergartens, a street factory, and the street hospital, we sensed the obvious rapport between her and the people.

Every aspect of life in the city is organized. The Neighborhood Committee not only organizes matters such as child care, birth control, etc., it also organizes ideological study groups for housewives and retired workers. The current campaign to criticize Lin Piao and Confucius, for example, is not just an affair for the academics and the press but involves everyone on the street and in the commune. In these study groups ideological and philosophical issues are not discussed in abstract but are always related to their immediate work and daily life. These neighborhood meetings are an important means by which the political consciousness of the people is raised.

K.H.F.
K.T.F.

OUR NEIGHBORHOOD*

THE NEIGHBORHOOD REVOLUTIONARY COMMITTEE

What is the neighborhood revolutionary committee?

It is the basic-level organ of people's political power, the lowest level of government administration in the city. Peking is divided into nine districts, five city and four rural. Fengsheng is one of nine neighborhoods in the West City District, its administration is called the Fengsheng Neighborhood Revolutionary Committee.

How big is the area under your committee and how many people live in it?

Our neighborhood covers 1.5 square kilometers. It contains two main streets and 132 lanes. There are 14,136 households with 52,978 people. Of these, 22,-808 are workers in industry, commerce and service trades or government cadres, teachers, doctors or theater people. We have 16,262 primary, middle school and college students, 6,146 pre-school children and 7,762 of what we call "neighborhood people"—retired people, old people and housewives who stay at home because they have many children to look after.

When was your neighborhood revolutionary committee set up? How is it organized?

It was formed in March 1968 during the cultural revolution. Its 27 members were elected after many meetings and consultations by the "neighborhood people" and those who work in neighborhood-run factories and units. Ten are government workers who were assigned

* From *Some Basic Facts About China* (Peking: Foreign Language Press, 1974).

to the locality and later elected to the committee. The rest are workers in neighborhood-run factories, teachers in the local schools, workers in the clinics and "neighborhood people". They participate in government as representatives of the local people. Those who have jobs in neighborhood-run factories or other units continue in them, so they are in a good position to know the opinions and demands of the people and pass them on to the committee. In this way they help the people exercise their revolutionary supervision over this basic-level organ of government.

Among the committee members are some who have been doing community work for years as well as young people who became activists during the cultural revolution. Thus it has elderly, middle-aged and young people. More than half of the members (16) are women.

What is a residents' committee?

Our neighborhood is divided into 25 residential areas. Each takes in from one to eight lanes with 400-800 households, about 2,000 people. Every such area has a residents' committee which works under the neighborhood revolutionary committee. The residents' committee is a self-governing people's organization, not a unit of government, which does the actual day-to-day work of serving the people in the locality, as assigned by the neighborhood revolutionary committee. This residents' committee serves all the people who live in its area, but those most active in it are those who work in neighborhood-run enterprises and the "neighborhood people". For the latter, the residents' committee serves as the center for collective life in the same way that the place of work does for people employed in non-neighborhood enterprises. The "neighborhood people" elect from among themselves the 15 to 25-member residents' committee which serves without pay. Most of the members were once workers or cadres and are now retired, or members of their families who have been active in service to the people.

Every residents' committee has three to six subdivisions of about 120 households each which serve as a basis for groups of 50 to 60 "neighborhood people" for study and other matters.

What do the neighborhood revolutionary committees do?

These are the main tasks of the neighborhood revolutionary committees: They organize workers, teachers, students and cadres in neighborhood-run units as well as the "neighborhood people" to study works by Marx, Engels, Lenin, Stalin and Chairman Mao, to discuss national and international affairs and to carry out the policies of the Communist Party and the people's government. They set up such small factories and other production units as fit into the state plan. They operate nurseries and kindergartens to supplement those run by the city and large places of work, as well as dining rooms and household-service shops. They administer the cultural, educational and health affairs of the neighborhood and safeguard the people's lives and property.

Under our Fengsheng revolutionary committee are seven factories, a household-service shop with eight branches, four nursery-kindergartens and a neighborhood hospital. All of these were set up by the local people in 1958 and are collectively owned by the revolutionary committee. We also administer 10 primary schools set up by the government in our area before 1958.

How does the neighborhood revolutionary committee do its work?

We try to carry out the principle of simple administration with as few people as possible. A chairman and three vice-chairmen divide the work and lead collectively. Important questions are decided in general meetings of the committee. Leaders and staff members must not sit in offices. They join the local study group, go into the streets and lanes and talk with the residents to find out about local conditions.

One of the tasks of the members of the neighborhood revolutionary committee is to pass the opinions and demands of the masses on to the committee and to convey to the people the decisions of the committee and directions from higher organs. Those who work full time for the committee spend one day a week working in some neighborhood factory or other unit to keep in close touch with the people.

The residents' committees are an important link between the neighborhood revolutionary committee and the people. The residents' committees take on the job of making known to every household the policies of the Party and government and tasks assigned by higher organizations. They hold discussions among the people on how to carry these out locally. Their aim is to see that every man, woman and child understands the reasons for the policies and tasks in relation to both the country and the individual. This understanding leads to everyone thinking up ideas and methods, and to conscious individual and collective effort for reaching the objective.

Most of the affairs of the neighborhood which we handle concern the interests of the people themselves. Since they participate in and control the management of their own neighborhood, the revolutionary committee has almost total support in whatever tasks need to be carried out.

SERVING THE PEOPLE

BY WEI FENG-YUN

I am an ordinary housewife with five children. My husband drives a three-wheeled motorcab. In 1949 the

Chinese Communist Party and Chairman Mao liberated the working people and of course my family. My husband began to have a steady wage and the family did not have to worry about food and clothing anymore. From then on, after I finished my housework I began to go out to do community service.

When our neighborhood set up its revolutionary committee in 1968, the people elected me to represent them on it. Thus I began to take part in the management of our neighborhood. I thought: I am what I am today because of the political understanding the Party has given me. Because the people trust me so much, I will work all the harder to serve them wholeheartedly.

Each of us in the revolutionary committee is responsible for certain areas. I am in charge of contacting three residents' committees in Mengtuan, Wuting and Shuncheng lanes with altogether 1,433 households—5,417 people. Right after every meeting of the revolutionary committee I go to the leaders of these three residents' committees, tell them the decisions and discuss with them how to accomplish the tasks assigned.

The people elect the neighborhood revolutionary committee, trust it and have a great interest in its work. They constantly give us suggestions for improving our work. I take criticisms and demands raised by the people to the neighborhood revolutionary committee which studies them and tries to solve the problems as quickly as possible.

Let me give some examples. Residents in old-style houses in Shuncheng Lane had to go down the lane to fetch water for cooking, washing clothes and baths, and there were no nearby drains to empty dirty water. The problem was quite serious in the summer when they used more water. We told the public utilities bureau about it and they installed more taps and dug more drains in the lane.

The grocery store in the lane was too small and there was no public telephone. They had to walk some distance to another store for even such small items as needles, thread and buttons. We wrote to the municipal trade bureau and asked that the local store be expanded to include other items and that a public telephone be installed. Very soon we saw men setting up telephone poles, and a telephone appeared. Now the local grocery store handles more items, more varieties of vegetables and other nonstaple foods, and they are fresher.

The cultural revolution brought new ideological awareness to the "neighborhood people". They show a high degree of initiative in doing their part in building socialism. At the request of the local people, production groups and health stations were organized in all 25 residents' areas in the Fengsheng neighborhood. All the women in the neighborhood who can work are employed.

My children are no longer small and there is not so much housework now. I want to do more for the people, but it is hard for someone without much education to do this work well. Last spring the neighborhood revolutionary committee set up a night school where housewives who are leaders of the residents' committees can study politics and improve their general education.

I joined the classes at once and never missed if I could help it. We never dared to dream of such a thing in the old society. My memory is not what it should be—I am 50 already—so it's pretty hard to learn and my hand doesn't want to obey me when I try to write. But I'm stubborn—because I want to do more for our neighborhood.

STUDY BRINGS A BROADER VIEW

BY LIU JU-CHIN

On the mornings when our study groups get together, the members start coming after breakfast carrying their little stools. There are white-haired retired people, mothers carrying babies and grandmothers pushing tots in carriages. They sit in a circle, laughing and chatting, until the group leader declares the class in session.

The "neighborhood people" are divided into four groups according to where they live along our lane. Each group chooses its own leader and guide, usually people who have retired. We meet for study 2 hours 3 times a week, usually from 8 to 10 in the morning. Since families are especially busy over the holidays such as the Spring Festival or National Day, the study stops for a week or so.

Our studies are along the lines of the general program followed throughout the country by groups like ours. We read and discuss articles from the newspapers or *Red Flag* magazine, or works by Marx, Engels, Lenin, Stalin and Chairman Mao. The guide explains difficult points. Sometimes the period is used for transmitting Party and government policies and directives or to organize activities in our lane.

In the current movement to criticize revisionism and rectify the style of work, every group held at least two or three meetings to criticize and repudiate swindlers like Liu Shao-chi. Scathing denunciations were illustrated with facts from the members' own experience.

In the past, when we housewives in the lane ran into one another at the market or on the street, we usually talked only about everyday matters such as food, fuel and kids. But now we often discuss questions that come out of our studies or national and international problems. Whenever we can't come to a session because of sickness or other business, we always feel we've missed something.

We try to relate our studies to our lives and put what we learn into practice. Grandmothers now say, "It's not enough just to see to it that our children eat properly and dress neatly. They've got to be taught to love their studies, love labor, have concern for the collective and fight against bad people and bad actions. Otherwise there's going to be revisionism and we working people will suffer again."

Such study broadens the vision of the members. More and more people are showing concern for others and the collective. One day after study, Chi Yen-yun of group 4 thought, "Chairman Mao urges unity but the two families in our yard aren't getting along just because of a quarrel between their children. They have no conflict of basic interests, why can't their differences be solved?" When she brought the question up with the other members of her study group, they urged her to help unite the two families. With much patient effort she finally brought the families together to talk it over. Each said that they bore part of the responsibility and the misunderstanding was cleared up.

Sun Fu-lun, living at No. 27 in a courtyard of six families, doesn't go out to work because she has a number of children to take care of. All the husbands and wives in the other five families go out to work, and when their children come home from school there is usually no one home. So Sun Fu-lun has boiled water on hand for the children to drink and helps them to do things like prepare meals and buy groceries. Her grateful neighbors do all they can after work to help her with her household chores, and knit sweaters for her children in spare moments. Coming from different places and working at different jobs, the six families did not know each other before, but now they feel very close to each other. Since Sun Fu-lun is always at home, the other families leave their keys with her and she has become the yard's "housekeeper".

HOW OUR CLINIC WORKS

BY YEN CHIU-HUA

Our clinic was set up by our Brick Tower Lane Residents' Committee in 1969, along with similar ones in other areas in Fengsheng. This was in accordance with the principles of putting prevention first and integrating public health work with mass movements. We got a lot of help from the area's residents and the big People's Hospital nearby. Three months of preliminary training at the People's Hospital gave us housewives an initial knowledge of acupuncture, injections, and the prevention and treatment of common illnesses.

We are located in a sunny room in the same courtyard as the office of the Brick Tower Lane Residents' Committee. We have two beds which serve as examination and treatment tables. Our big glass cabinet is filled with medicines and medical equipment. The two of us in charge are doctor, nurse and pharmacist at the same time.

One day a couple with a year-old baby were passing through our lane when the child suddenly went into convulsions. His eyes rolled up and he stopped breathing. We rushed out, examined the child and gave him acupuncture treatment. When he finally began to cry, we knew he would be all right again.

Since our clinic started, people no longer have to go out of the area to get treatment for such common illnesses as headaches, colds and coughs. Residents who get their free medical care through their place of work and are resting at home due to illness can get prescriptions filled, injections, dressings changed, blood pressure tested, etc. at our clinic for five *fen*.

In the citywide health care network, we belong to the section covered by the People's Hospital, and its doctors often visit the area to give treatment or to offer us guidance and help solve our technical problems.

If someone is seriously ill and we cannot diagnose it or handle it ourselves, we immediately arrange for him to be sent to a hospital. To help invalids, old people, babies and others who are being treated at the People's Hospital or the Children's Hospital but cannot get there easily, we make home calls or deliver medicine. In advance of the seasons when common and epidemic diseases occur we spread knowledge of preventive measures among the residents and in street factories, nurseries and primary schools. We help the People's Hospital with their preventive work by giving vaccinations and inoculations and also do education on birth control.

Through several years of practice our ability in prevention and treatment has improved. The people constantly encourage us and this spurs us on to do all we can to serve them better.

OUR LANE HAS CHANGED

BY TUNG HSIU-CHING

I'm seventy years old this year and have been living in Nanyutai Lane for 33 years. What great changes I've seen!

Before liberation, our lane had three "manys"—many poor people, many slum houses and many children. People made their living by selling their labor—pedalling pedicabs, doing odd jobs, running small stalls. None of them had a fixed job. Many families did not know where their next meal would come from. The houses they lived in were in a terrible state, with the wind whistling through the cracks in the winter and the rain leaking through the roof in the summer. But in those days who cared about us?

With liberation in 1949, we working people stood up and became masters of the new society. As soon as the People's Liberation Army men entered the city, they provided us with food, money and clothes. They got us together and explained the revolution to us. The people's government began solving the problem of unemployment and we all got steady jobs. Some went into factories and others joined producers' co-ops. With stable monthly wages, our life improved steadily.

Take my old neighbor Sun Meng-hsueh, for example.

He was a pedicab man, trying to feed his mother, a wife and four children. The seven of them huddled in a room about to fall down. Every day the family had to wait for him to come back with money before they could buy the day's food. If he had no luck, they would go hungry. To try and help, the three daughters picked over the cinders in rubbish heaps for unburned pieces of coal.

But now Sun is the dispatcher at a three-wheeled motorcab station and earns 60 yuan a month. They live in two nice rooms facing the south. His four older children are married and the two younger are in junior middle school. His wife, who suffered from asthma for many years, is now receiving good treatment at the People's Hospital. The whole family leads a happy life.

Our people's government thinks of everything for us. More than 100 families in our lane have moved into new apartments or houses. The homes of the others have been well repaired. The street's housing management office always asks for the opinions of the neighborhood representatives before they distribute or renovate housing. If anything goes wrong with the electricity, water or drains, we just tell the office and it sends repairmen right away.

Before liberation the rent collectors hounded us like baying dogs. They yelled and shouted whenever they stepped through the door. You had to pay the rent first, even if your stomach was empty. But today the rent we pay doesn't even cover the cost of maintenance and repairs! What a striking contrast with the old society!

Children of the poor in our lane used to run about naked or half naked. But now they are all well-clothed and healthy. When it is time for inoculations, the People's Hospital and the neighborhood clinic arrange everything. When children reach school age, the teachers go from house to house to enroll them. Before liberation the husband of Chang Chun-ching, vice-head of the lane residents' committee, a worker, was so poor he couldn't afford to send his children to school. But in the new society three of his children have graduated from college and the fourth from a secondary technical school.

My husband died when I was 31 and we had no children. But I enjoy a happy life though I'm getting on in years. The people's government always shows concern for me, members of the neighborhood revolutionary committee come to see me often and my neighbors take good care of me. The world has changed and so has our lane.

STREET FACTORIES

"We want to build socialism!" These were the words of Cheng Hsiu-lan, 15 years ago a housewife who could neither read nor write. Today she is vice-chairwoman of the revolutionary committee of the Fengsheng Spring Factory. Her words reflect the wishes of the neighborhood's housewives.

Under the Fengsheng Neighborhood Revolutionary Committee are six other factories for insulating materials, rubber products, adult and children's clothing, powder metallurgy and cardboard boxes. They all have some common features: a mixture of unimpressive buildings old and new; both modern machinery and equipment they made themselves; and over 80 (in some, 90) percent of the workers and staff made up of women, most of whom live less than a 15-minute walk away.

Each year these women produce millions of yuan worth of products for the domestic and foreign markets, complementing large plants. They have become an indispensable part of the national economy.

It is hard to believe that in 1958 these plants were just groups of women who had organized to make simple products such as loudspeaker cones, sheet mica, children's toys and cardboard boxes. "Capital invest-ment" came from three or four-yuan donations by the members, and only the simplest tools.

Starting from Scratch

In 1958 housewives in the neighborhood were in-spired by the Communist Party's general line for build-ing socialism. "The whole country is taking a big leap forward," one of them said in a discussion about it, "can't we do anything but bend over our stoves all day? We want to do our part to build socialism too!"

When they heard there was an urgent demand for springs, Cheng Hsiu-lan and 20 other women organized a production group and started making small ones for mouse traps and eyeglass cases. They made their first batch by turning them on hand winders and heating them in a kitchen stove.

They have not forgotten their second year. The Great Hall of the People was being built in Peking for China's tenth National Day. They were given the job of making 250,000 sofa springs for its furniture. Now 68 women, they sent representatives to learn the technique from large plants and studied hard. In spite of their primitive conditions, they delivered high-quality springs 14 days ahead of schedule.

When the hall was finished, the women were invited to tour it. Entering the splendid main hall and sitting on the sofas, these mothers were as happy as children. "Our work went into these!"

"For the first time," Cheng Hsiu-lan said, "we really realized that money can't buy the happiness that comes from taking part in helping our country."

"Build socialism!" is the slogan that keeps them ad-vancing. After 15 years of hard struggle, they have automated or semi-automated most of the production process. They have built new shops and their number has grown to 270. Using wire from 0.2 mm. to 8 mm.

in diameter, they produce over 1,100 specifications of springs for dozens of models of automobiles.

Now 39, Cheng Hsiu-lan is a member of the Communist Party. She learned how to read and write in a night class shortly after the factory was started. Though she had never touched a machine in her life, she is now an experienced manager responsible for the factory's production. She reads blueprints and makes innovations.

When the Fengsheng Neighborhood Revolutionary Committee was set up during the cultural revolution, Cheng Hsiu-lan was elected to its standing committee.

Advance or Retreat?

The other factories in the Fengsheng neighborhood developed in much the same way. Like Cheng Hsiu-lan, other housewives found their horizons broadening after they came out of their homes to join in building socialism.

Everyone praises Liu Ying-pin, who is in charge of the insulating materials factory. She is the daughter of a poor peasant. Before liberation she got tuberculosis of the bone and because she could not afford treatment her left leg had to be amputated below the knee. Today she wears an artificial limb. In 1958 she and other housewives set up a small shop to make insulating material. Then, around 1960, China ran into temporary economic difficulties. A handful of revisionists headed by Liu Shao-chi thought that street factories with their "slim resources and inferior technique" were not of much use to the national economy. They said that "factories with orders should work and those without should close".

Liu Ying-pin did not agree. "Chairman Mao liberated us housewives and gave us a role in building up the country," she went around telling everyone. "We can't retreat to our homes and live off others."

Their small factory was not operating at capacity, so she and the others went to a construction site to wash clothing for the workers, even taking their sewing machines along for the mending. "We'll do anything," they said, "as long as it supports socialist construction. But we refuse to disband."

Resisting the revisionists' demand that they quit, they kept their factory going with their own hard work. Slowly they enlarged their factory until today it produces over 36 types of low-cost, high-quality insulating material in a variety of specifications. In 1965, before the cultural revolution, they turned out 556,000 yuan worth of material. Last year it was 4,300,000 yuan.

Last year Liu Ying-pin attended a national meeting in Shanghai at which orders were placed. The products of this small factory are sold throughout the country and have their place in the state's production plan.

These factories are collectively owned. The neighborhood revolutionary committee gives them unified leadership in political and ideological work and the realization of their production plans and provides a unified accounting system. Their profits are used to cover the cost of benefits for the workers and are invested in new buildings and equipment for the expansion of local production.

The development of production has improved the workers' situation. An adjustment of the wages of neighborhood factory workers last year brought them basically in line with those in state enterprises. Women who started to work at the same time as Cheng Hsiu-lan earn about 40 yuan a month.

They receive free medical treatment. A woman can send her child to a neighborhood nursery from the time her 56-day maternity leave ends until her child begins primary school. Her factory pays half the cost of care. Neighborhood household-service shops do washing, mending and other repairs. This helps liberate the women from time-consuming chores.

Everyone Can Do Her Bit

About 30 percent of the local women work in the neighborhood's factories. Fengsheng neighborhood has an embroidery workshop and has also organized older women who have difficulty in going out to work to do embroidery in their homes.

In its spacious rooms in Tacheng Lane one can see its beautifully embroidered bedspreads, tablecloths and aprons made for export. Group leader Chang Kuei-chen learned to do embroidery as a child in the countryside. The group, she told us, gets jobs from an embroidery plant and distributes the work to some 300 women in their homes.

Visiting the women regularly to see how the work is going, Chang Kuei-chen frequently comes upon the energetic bespectacled grandmothers busy over their embroidery while their grandchildren do their homework. She mentioned Tuan Hsiang-yun, in her sixties, her children all working and her family's income a very adequate 400 yuan a month. Afraid she would overtire herself, her children advised her to drop the embroidery work. "My eyes are still good," she retorted. "I can still do my bit for our country."

Fengsheng's neighborhood factories complement state-run plants and there are various residents' committee production groups which process things for these factories. Some production is concentrated, some dispersed. Through these channels all the housewives in the neighborhood who can work have a chance to make their contribution to building socialism. Through political study in the factories, learning techniques as they work, increasing their general knowledge in night school classes, the women of the Fengsheng neighborhood have developed into an energetic corps for building socialism.

SHANGHAI ADVANCES ON THE
SOCIALIST ROAD*

From the terrace of the Shanghai Mansions Hotel one has a bird's-eye view of the port city of Shanghai. Vessels of all kinds sail up and down the Whangpoo River. A continuous stream of cars, bicycles and pedestrians moves along the wide waterfront street, the Bund. Round the clock the city of more than a million industrial workers and nine million other citizens dwelling on six thousand square kilometers of land along the Whangpoo contributes its share to socialist revolution and construction. In 23 years initial success has been achieved in transforming and building the city into an integrated socialist industrial base and a vital port for strengthening the friendly ties between China and the people of other countries.

The Past

Old Shanghai was a paradise for imperialist adventurers. The story behind the city's changing skyline as skyscraper after skyscraper arose on the Bund is the story of savage exploitation and plunder of the Chinese people. The customs building was a stronghold of the power of the imperialists. They controlled China's maritime customs, their own foreign representative occupied its main post of inspector general. Only after the liberation did the Chinese people recover sovereignty in this field. Forty years ago, beside the gate of the park on the Bund, which today is open to all, was a sign reading: "No entrance to dogs and Chinese".

Under the wing of the colonialist forces, imperialist adventurers came to Shanghai empty-handed and soon became millionaires through ruthless maneuverings. A prime example was Silas Hardoon who arrived in

* From *China Reconstructs,* July 1972.

Shanghai in 1874 without a penny in his pocket. Working hand in glove with reactionary Chinese warlords and bureaucrats, he reaped a tidy profit from traffic in opium. With it and imperialist influence he bought up half the real estate on Nanking Road, the city's business artery and shopping center. He became king of Shanghai real estate. Another such adventurer was the British businessman Victor Sassoon who owned more than 1,900 buildings, including seven of the 28 buildings with ten or more stories.

To preserve and strengthen their political and economic privileges, the foreign aggressors carved "concessions" out of the city's territory. Within these they stationed troops, maintained their own police forces, levied taxes of all kinds, and exercised "consular jurisdiction". In addition to direct colonial rule in these states-within-a-state, the city's public utilities such as the water system, electric lighting, telephone service, street cars and gas were imperialist monopolies. They ran missions, hospitals, schools and newspapers in order to spread an enslaving colonial education.

But the Shanghai people never once bowed to the imperialists. After the Chinese Communist Party was founded at its first national congress in Shanghai on July 1, 1921, it was the vanguard organization for the city's working class, who waged its struggle against imperialism, feudalism and bureaucrat-capitalism under direct Party leadership. On May 30, during a series of anti-imperialist strikes, British police fired on demonstrators on Nanking Road, killing and wounding many. Two days later 200,000 workers began a three-month strike that hit hard at the imperialists. From October 1926 to March 1927 the workers of Shanghai staged three armed uprisings aimed at overthrowing imperialist and warlord rule.

From the day the Japanese imperialists occupied Shanghai on August 13, 1937, the city's working class and revolutionary people began a long struggle against the invader's rule. It provided strong support for the resistance war in the rest of the country. After the U.S.-Chiang Kai-shek gang took over Shanghai following the victory of the anti-Japanese war in 1945, its workers and other citizens, coordinating with the national armed struggle to seize power, many times launched city-wide mass movements to fight U.S.-Chiang outrages.

The Revolution Continues

The Chinese People's Liberation Army entered Shanghai in May 1949. Led by Chairman Mao and the Communist Party, the working class and other people of Shanghai began clearing out remnants of imperialist power in politics, economy and culture and transforming the semi-feudal, semi-colonial metropolis into a city of the proletariat.

The torrent of revolution quickly swept out the filth and dirt of old Shanghai, the source for crime of all kinds. The city was the den of gangsters big and small. Gambling joints, opium houses and brothels were established institutions. In the years immediately before liberation there were 90,000 vagrants and 30,000 prostitutes, and an average of 13,000 recorded crimes every year.

Beginning to exercise its power as master of the city, the Shanghai working class in the latter part of 1949 mobilized the masses to tackle problems left over from the old society. Gambling, opium-smoking, prostitution and gangster organizations were outlawed. A small number of people who had engaged in counter-revolutionary crimes were punished according to law, as were gangster chiefs who had incurred the wrath of the people for their direct dealings with counter-revolutionaries and criminals. Ordinary vagrants and prostitutes were either brought together for reform or the masses were mobilized to supervise their reform. This consisted of political and ideological education, literacy classes and training in useful skills to prepare them for productive work. Then jobs were found for them so that under socialism they became working people earning their own living.

Shanghai has always been an important arena of struggle between the proletariat and the bourgeoisie. After liberation the government confiscated the enterprises owned by the bureaucrat capitalists and turned these into state enterprises. The policy towards the industrial and commercial concerns owned by the national capitalists was to make use of them, but to restrict and transform them. The bourgeoisie, however, immediately took advantage of the economic strength they still possessed and unleashed an attack on the proletariat. Through speculation and profiteering they raked in a huge booty. Some wormed their way into the revolutionary ranks in order to engineer schemes to disrupt the socialist economy, or achieved this end through bribing and corrupting a few weak-willed cadres with money and women.

Led by the Party the Shanghai working class launched mass movements to counter the attacks. There was a "three-anti" campaign against corruption, waste and bureaucracy, followed by a "five-anti" campaign which was against capitalist bribery of government workers, tax evasion, theft of state property, cheating on government contracts and stealing of economic information from government sources.

In the winter of 1955 and spring of 1956, as part of a nationwide movement, peasants in the countryside surrounding Shanghai organized themselves into agricultural cooperatives. The proletariat had full control over the countryside. The bourgeoisie, thus isolated, were forced to accept changes in ownership of their enterprises. In 1956 all of the city's industrial and commercial concerns in 203 lines were transformed so as to be owned jointly by the state and private capital.

The question of what system of ownership for China's economy was basically solved, but the struggle between the working class and the bourgeoisie continued to deepen. In 1957 bourgeois Rightists in Shanghai, in concert with Rightists in the rest of the country, launched an attack on the Communist Party and socialism. Led by the Party and Chairman Mao, the Shanghai working class and revolutionary people repulsed it and moved ahead to new victories in the socialist revolution on the political and ideological fronts.

In 1958, guided by the Party's general line to "go all out, aim high and achieve greater, faster, better and more economical results in building socialism", Shanghai's industry and agriculture made a big leap forward. People's communes were formed throughout the surrounding countryside. But Liu Shao-chi and his agents in Shanghai, representing the bourgeois forces, never ceased their attempts to restore capitalism. They interfered with every advance of the revolution either from the Right or the "Left" and worked against the proletarian dictatorship and taking the socialist road.

The proletarian cultural revolution begun in 1966 opened a new chapter in the history of Shanghai. Carrying on its tradition as the main force in the revolution, the city's working class, uniting with the revolutionary masses and cadres, criticized and repudiated the bourgeois reactionary line pushed by Liu Shao-chi and his agents. In January 1967 they seized the power of the then municipal Party committee and municipal people's council which had been held by the capitalist-roaders, and set up the Shanghai Municipal Revolutionary Committee. Many workers and poor and lower-middle peasants[1] became leaders in the new organs of political power—revolutionary committees—of various levels.

In August 1968, in answer to Chairman Mao's call that *"the working class must exercise leadership in everything"*, the Shanghai workers formed Mao Tse-tung Thought propaganda teams to lead the struggle-criticism-transformation movement in the cultural, art, education, journalism and health fields. The working-class leadership thus brought to these fields created conditions for using Marxism-Leninism-Mao Tsetung Thought as a guide for transforming them.

Revolution Spurs Production

Production, too, has made rapid progress.

The electrical engineering industry is an example. In the 35 years from 1914 to 1949 no electrical motor bigger than 50 kilowatts was ever manufactured. The Kuomintang ruling clique talked for ten years about making a 1,000-kw. turbo-generator, but nothing materialized. Five years after the working class took over, China's first 6,000-kw. turbo-generator was built. In the 1960s the industry was capable of producing a 125,000-kw. generator with inner water-cooled rotor and stator. More progress has been made in the last two years.

Shanghai's industrial development has not been without its ups and downs. In the shipbuilding industry Liu Shao-chi pushed the revisionist line that "it is better to buy foreign ships than make our own, still better to charter foreign ships than buy them". The influence of this line held back progress so that in the 17 years from 1949 to 1966 only one 10,000-ton ocean-going vessel was built.

During the cultural revolution the shipbuilders repudiated this line and took a big stride forward. The

[1] The term poor and lower-middle peasants refers to original class status, not present economic position.

Shanghai Shipyard planned a 10,000-ton freighter but its building berth could accommodate nothing larger than 3,000-ton vessels. Some people were for constructing a big berth, which would cost the state five million yuan and take a year to complete. The workers, however, felt they could find a way to build the big ship in the small berth. "Chairman Mao says we should follow our own road in developing industry," they said. They lengthened the berth with old and scrap material. In the last two years Shanghai has put out eleven ocean-going freighters in the 10,000-ton class.

Today Shanghai has more than 9,000 factories, big and small, producing steel, machinery, electronic equipment, meters and instruments, ships, chemicals, textiles and light industrial goods. The total value of the city's industrial output for 1971 was 14.5 times that of 1949 and an increase of 78 percent over 1965, the year before the cultural revolution. Today the value of Shanghai's industrial output in one month is higher than that of a whole year for old Shanghai after a hundred years of industry. The average monthly output of a single rolling mill today equals a whole year's rolled steel production of pre-liberation days. The city is now making many kinds of high-grade alloy and stainless steel, as well as shaped steel, steel wire, cold-rolled steel and cold-bent shaped steel of many specifications. Besides tapping the potential of existing industries the city has gone into many new lines, aiming at high-grade and high-precision products and sophisticated technology.

Agriculture in the city's surrounding countryside reaped its tenth successive outstanding harvest in 1971. Greater Shanghai supplies all its own edible oil and vegetables.

Shanghai's thriving port is the result of the efforts of its working class in strengthening mutual support and internationalist friendship among the people of the world. Trade with more than 130 countries and regions passes through it and it has contact with more than 200 ports around the globe. The 1971 average monthly volume of goods handled by the port was one and a half times that of the annual figure in early liberation days.

Life Is Better

An army of unemployed numbering in several hundred thousands was a permanent part of old Shanghai. At the time of liberation the imperialists had prophesied that the Chinese people could never solve the problem of unemployment. In answer Chairman Mao said, *"In places like Shanghai, the problem of unemployment, or of feeding the population, arose solely because of cruel, heartless oppression and exploitation by imperialism, feudalism, bureaucrat-capitalism and the reactionary Kuomintang government. . . . revolution plus production can solve the problem of feeding the population."*

As soon as the city was liberated the Party and government organized the unemployed for productive labor so that they could support themselves, and provide relief to reduce economic hardship. Some were given training in skills to fit them for work. The unemployed found jobs and gradually more and more others joined the labor force. In the past ten or so years 500,000 housewives have gone out to work. Under socialism the threat of unemployment is a thing of the past. All who are able to work are working. It is considered an honor to labor and to serve the people.

Wages have gone up and labor insurance and other benefits to working people have been increasing. Shanghai industry's expenditures for medical care, pensions, labor insurance and other benefits are equivalent to about 20 percent of the city's total wages. Altogether 2,600,000 workers and office personnel are covered by labor insurance and free medical care, and 1,600,000 of their family members get medical care at half the cost.

Prices have been stable in the past 23 years in Shanghai as in the rest of the country. In recent years the government has more than once reduced prices on farm machinery, medicine and certain industrial goods. Purchase prices for farm and sideline products have risen while the selling price has remained basically the same. This has brought an improvement to the life of the people in both town and country. Residents who knew the old Shanghai cannot help contrasting the stability of today with inflation and skyrocketing prices of the Kuomintang days. In 1937 under Kuomintang rule 100 *fapi* bought two oxen; in 1947, only one little coal ball; in 1949 it was not enough to buy a single grain of rice.

Housing for the working people has improved greatly. In the past 23 years Shanghai added 10 million square meters of new housing, providing new homes for over a million people. Much of this is in 45 new workers' communities, each with 50,000 square meters or more of floor space. There are more than 30 on a slightly smaller scale.

The New Tsaoyang Villages begun in 1951 were the first workers' residential areas built after liberation. They consist of two to five-story buildings with a total floor space of 840,000 square meters. The apartments have running water, electric lighting, toilets and kitchens with gas stoves. Rent is about six percent of a worker's wages. The community is served by seven middle schools, 14 primary schools, 13 nurseries and kindergartens, two hospitals and eight health stations, also a theater, parks, banks, post offices and a variety of stores. Before liberation many of the residents of the area lived in huts made of straw mats, dilapidated boats or shelters made of several straw mats haphazardly patched together and humped up barely high enough for people to crawl under.

For Wang Hsiao-ti, who now lives at Apartment 81 of the No. 1 Village, a hole in the ground was "home" before liberation. Piles of grass were his only cover in winter. He began working in a factory at the age of 13 and his four sisters and brothers died from cold and hunger. Now in his family of six, two children have finished middle school and are working and two are still in school. His wife is also working. Wang himself retired in 1965 and enjoys a comfortable old age on his pension.

The changes in Shanghai are profound, but they are only the first steps in a long journey. The Shanghai working class and revolutionary people, with a wealth of revolutionary tradition, are advancing on the high road of socialism.

3. Minority Nationalities

China is a unified multinational socialist country. More than fifty minority peoples occupying about 60 per cent of China's area make up about 6 per cent of the total population, the rest being Han. The minorities were oppressed by the Han for centuries. The Han looked down on them as barbarians and aborigines. Ruling powers in China recognized chieftains among them and collected taxes and tribute when they could catch them. Communists were the first to treat them as equals and to reach them with an ideology providing a place for them in the New China.

The general policy is to modernize minority areas with socialized organization, education, health care, and so on; but at the same time to preserve and protect distinctive cultural identities of the different nationalities, their languages, costumes, music, arts, and traditions. This requires training minority cadres in socialist ideology and modern technology, on the one hand, and educating the Han majority to appreciate and respect distinctive minority cultures, on the other. The Institute of Minority Nationalities in Peking, which we visited, symbolized this general policy.

In the Institute we met students in different costumes from all minority areas. They are there to learn Marxism-Leninism-Mao Tsetung Thought and science techniques to carry back to their villages as leaders and teachers. We also met Han students studying minority arts and music so they can go back to the Han area to teach Han children to appreciate minority cultures. In fact we have seen many performances of minority dances done by Han children in different cities, and quite a few minority songs have become national favorites. We also met professors and linguists who told us how they created written languages for some minority nationalities, who had not developed written languages of their own, so that now these minorities can publish their own newspapers and books.

A Mongolian student told us that he went through schools in Mongolian and only learned the Common language (based on the dialect of Peking, now used nationally) as the second language. The whole emphasis is to train minority cadres who will administer the autonomous regions themselves. When a Han specialist is needed in a minority area he or she is required to learn the minority language and customs.

There is another policy with regard to minorities which struck us as most enlightening. In a discussion with Chou En-lai on China's population control policy, he said that although birth control is the general policy, there is an exception—the exception being in the minority areas. The minority areas are sparsely populated and the population of the minorities had been kept down by the past oppression they suffered. Consequently, not only is population control not advocated in those areas, population growth is encouraged.

K.H.F.
K.T.F.

ABOUT NATIONAL MINORITIES*

What is the position of national minorities in China?

China is a single state of many nationalities. In addition to the Han people, who are the great majority, there are 54 minority nationalities. In the 1957 census their population was 38 million, about 6 percent of the total population. Ten of these nationalities had a population of a million or more. The other 44 range in size from several hundred to several hundred thousand.

While the number of the minority peoples is proportionately small, the areas inhabited mainly by them cover 50 to 60 percent of the whole country. Different nationalities often live together in the same place; in the majority of the counties in the country there are at least two or more nationalities. The greater portion of the minority peoples live in large or small compact communities of primarily their own people.

China's various nationalities have coexisted on her vast territory since ancient times, and together they created her history and culture. Over a long period in Chinese history, however, oppression of other nationalities was a part of the system of rule. The different nationalities within the country never had equal status. The Han rulers oppressed the people of other nationalities; when they held power over the country, rulers of nationalities which were a minority, such as the Mongols (Yuan dynasty, 1271-1368) and the Manchus (Ching dynasty, 1644-1911), oppressed the Hans. And, of course, the ruling class, whether of Han or other nationality, always oppressed and exploited the working people of their own nationalities too. As Chairman Mao said, *"In the final analysis, national struggle is a matter of class struggle."*

* From *China Reconstructs,* No. 10, December 1972.

Foreign imperialism invading China in the last hundred years worked in collusion with the reactionary ruling classes to oppress and exploit the people of all nationalities. This bound the ordinary people of the various nationalities together in a common struggle against imperialism and feudalism. After more than 20 years of armed struggle under the leadership of the Chinese Communist Party and Chairman Mao, the people overthrew the reactionary rule of imperialism, feudalism and bureaucrat-capitalism and founded the People's Republic of China.

The people's government has brought national oppression to an end and established equality and unity among the various nationalities. China has entered a new era in which the different nationalities help each other and advance together. All peoples have equal rights in deciding and administering state affairs and in working together to build their socialist country.

What kind of social and economic conditions exist among the minority nationalities?

Liberation found the minority nationalities at many stages of social development. Over 30 of them were basically under a feudal landlord economy. These included the Hui, Chuang, Uighur, Manchu, Korean, Tung, Yao, Pai and Tuchia nationalities and the majority of the people of the Mongolian nationality. Among some of these, elements of capitalist economy were found to exist.

The serf system prevailed among the Tais in the Hsishuang Panna region in Yunnan province and the Tibetans; the Yi people of Szechuan were still in the stage of slave society. Remnants of primitive communism existed in varying degrees among the Lisu, Wa, Chingpo, Tulung, Nu and Pulang nationalities in Yunnan province and the Olunchuns and Owenks in the northeast.

Economically the minority areas were generally more underdeveloped than the Han areas. In some of these cultivation was done by setting fire to a patch of scrub and sowing the seed in holes dug with a stick or a crude iron hoe. Production was extremely low.

After the founding of the new China, the Communist Party and the government put in a lot of effort giving leadership and assistance to the minority peoples in carrying out democratic reforms—which put an end to exploitation and oppression by feudal landlords or slave or serf owners—and socialist transformation, which accomplished the change from individual to socialist (collective or state) ownership of the means of production. Removal of the restraints of feudalism, slavery or primitive communism and establishment of the socialist system greatly emancipated the forces of production and opened up broad prospects for social and economic progress in the minority areas.

To accelerate economic and cultural development in the minority areas, since liberation the government has done the following:

(1) In planning for economic and cultural construction it gives special consideration to investments for minority areas so that these areas can make faster-than-average progress and catch up with the rest of the country.

(2) Every year it allocates necessary financial subsidies to the minority areas.

(3) It sees that the minority areas get sufficient material supplies such as industrial and agricultural products and machinery and equipment.

(4) It sends large numbers of cadres, technical personnel, young people and veteran workers to the minority areas to aid in local construction.

(5) It enables minority people in the frontier regions or where transport is difficult to buy what they need at reasonable prices and sell their local and special

products at fair prices through state trading teams which tour these areas.

With these forms of assistance modern industries— steel, coal, machinery, power, chemical, textile, transport and communications—were developed for the first time in many of the minority areas.

Free treatment by mobile medical teams dispatched by the government helps overcome the lack of health and medical care that once existed in the minority areas.

How is political equality guaranteed for the national minorities?

Equality among the nationalities is the basic principle for the unity of our state, for unity among the nationalities and for solving all matters centering around the national question. The Constitution of the People's Republic of China states that all Chinese citizens regardless of nationality or race enjoy equal rights. It prohibits discriminatory and oppressive acts against any nationality. While regarding both great-nation chauvinism and local nationalism as harmful to the unity of our state and unity among the nationalities, the Party and government give special attention to educating cadres and people of the Han nationality to overcome Han chauvinism.

To guarantee equal rights to the minority nationalities the following measures have been taken:

(1) More than 50 peoples have been identified and recognized as separate nationalities. This was done on the basis of extensive investigation and study in accordance with the wishes of the people of these nationalities. Through the ages scores of minority peoples were never legally recognized as such by the reactionary rulers. The anti-people clique of the Kuomintang that ruled China for 22 years before liberation denied that other nationalities existed in China, and

referred to all peoples excepting the Han nationality as "tribes".

Many people of minority nationalities, on their part, did not want to be known as such, hoping to avoid discrimination and oppression. The Chuangs, who are China's biggest minority, were recognized as a separate nationality only after liberation.

In 1951 the Central People's Government issued a directive prohibiting all forms of address and abolishing all place names and tablet inscriptions "of a nature discriminatory and insulting to the minority nationalities".

(2)　Work has been done to guarantee that all minority nationalities, regardless of the number of the people, the size of the area they inhabit or the stage of social development they were in before democratic reform, have the right to participate in the administration of state affairs. There have always been deputies to the National People's Congress who are members of minority nationalities.

(3)　Efforts are made to see that cadres from the minority nationalities are employed by Party organizations and government offices at every level in the minority areas. The number of minority cadres has increased rapidly since liberation. In the Kwangsi Chuang Autonomous Region in 1970 there were 78,000 cadres from the minority nationalities as against 900 in the early days after liberation. Many minority cadres hold important positions at every level in local Party and government organizations. Three of the seven secretaries of the Communist Party committee of the Tibet Autonomous Region are Tibetans. A number of Party members from the minority nationalities have been elected as members or alternate members of the Central Committee of the Chinese Communist Party. Yi people hold 51 percent of the leading positions in the Party committee of the Liangshan Yi Autonomous

Chou[1] and the nine county committees under it. They hold over 80 percent of such positions in Party organizations at the district, township and commune level.

What is national regional autonomy? Why was this way chosen for China?

National regional autonomy is a basic policy of the Chinese Communist Party for solving the nationalities question within the country. It was formulated by the Party through applying basic Marxist-Leninist principles on the national question according to historical conditions and the present situation in China. Any nationality, as long as it has a compact community large enough to form an administrative unit (autonomous region, *chou* or county), can establish an autonomous area with its own organs of self-government which can exercise autonomy in administering internal affairs.

The purpose of national regional autonomy is to guarantee political equality for the national minorities and to give special consideration to the characteristics of the minority areas so that the policies and principles of the Party and government can be implemented more effectively. It also aims to give full scope to the minority peoples' initiative in participation in state life and the building of socialism, and to accelerate socialist revolution and construction in the minority areas. It is a necessary measure for promoting solidarity among the nationalities, consolidating the unity of the country and strengthening the dictatorship of the proletariat.

The Constitution and national laws provide that there should be regional autonomy in areas where minority peoples live in compact groups and that such autonomous units are inseparable parts of the People's Republic of China. As local governments, these are part of the apparatus carrying out the dictatorship of the

[1] Autonomous *chou* is an administrative area below the province.

proletariat. On the other hand, under the unified leadership of the Central People's Government, in addition to exercising the usual powers and functions of local organs of state, such organs of self-government at all levels have the right to administer local finances within the limits of the authority prescribed by law. They may, in accordance with the political, economic and cultural characteristics of the nationalities in their locality, make regulations on the exercise of autonomy as well as specific regulations. Examples are apportionment of electoral representation based on special local conditions, regulations for organizing organs of self-government and for tax collection. Such regulations become valid when approved by the Standing Committee of the National People's Congress.

In performing their functions, organs of self-government of autonomous areas employ the spoken and written language or languages commonly used by the nationality or nationalities in the locality.

In actual practice the policy of national regional autonomy has proved itself suited to the historical conditions of China and the wishes of the national minorities. There are at present 5 autonomous regions (province level)—the Inner Mongolia Autonomous Region, the Sinkiang Uighur Autonomous Region, the Kwangsi Chuang Autonomous Region, the Ningsia Hui Autonomous Region and the Tibet Autonomous Region—29 autonomous *chou* and 69 autonomous counties.

What is done to see that the languages, customs, habits and religious beliefs of the minority nationalities are respected?

That these must be respected is written into the Constitution. All acts running counter to them are violations of law.

Under the discrimination and oppression of the reactionary Han ruling class before liberation, many minority nationalities were not able to develop writing for their languages. Some which had writing were not allowed to use it. In some areas the existing written language was not in general use. Those with no written language had to keep records by making marks on wood or tying knots in cords.

After liberation all nationalities have the freedom to use their own languages, both in speech and writing. In areas where people of a minority nationality live in a compact community or where a number of nationalities live together, the people's courts conduct hearings in the language commonly used in the locality. Judgments, notices and other documents are made public in that language. Citizens of all nationalities have the right to make accusations in their own languages.

The government publishes Marxist-Leninist classics, Chairman Mao's writings and other books, as well as newspapers and magazines in Mongolian, Tibetan, Uighur, Korean, Kazakh and other languages. It also promotes films, theater and music in the minority languages. Both the central and local broadcasting stations carry programs in minority languages.

In old China the reactionary Han rulers in many areas did not allow the minority peoples to celebrate their national festivals. For following their own customs or ways of life, such as wearing national dress, the minority peoples frequently suffered insults and discrimination. Today the customs of all nationalities are respected, and the people have the freedom to wear their national dress. The colorful national dress of the minority peoples adds a bright spot to the dramatic and musical stage. As for undesirable customs, it is for the different nationalities to reform these of their own accord as their people raise their level of political consciousness and scientific and cultural knowledge.

People of all nationalities enjoy freedom to believe in any religion, but also the freedom not to believe, and freedom to carry on propaganda for atheism. This is a fundamental right of the Chinese people of all nationalities.

What has the new China done to develop education for the national minorities?

Because of the policy of oppression and discrimination of the reactionary ruling classes through the ages, education among the national minorities was in a deplorable state. Most of the working people could not go to school. There were very few schools. In Tibet, for example, there was not one regular school even of the primary level. All the serfs were illiterate. The feudal hold of the monastery, a pillar of the serf system, kept the working people ignorant and backward.

After liberation measures were taken to develop education for the minority peoples. Special sections or personnel in the education departments in the central and local governments give attention to this work. In minority areas where the people live sparsely scattered, classes and schools are more numerous than they would be if in proportion to the population. Limitations on age are extended for the minority people. Some schools run special preparatory classes for minority students to help them catch up with the others and go on to higher studies.

To meet the need for teachers, in addition to sending Han teachers to assist in the development of minority education, special attention is given to schools and classes for training teachers from the minority nationalities.

Nationalities institutes, located in Peking and other cities, have been set up for training minority cadres. Universities and colleges have been established in the principal minority areas, Sinkiang, Inner Mongolia, Kwangsi, Yunnan, Kweichow, Chinghai, Ningsia and the Yenpien Korean Autonomous *Chou* in Kirin province. All higher institutes make it a point to seek out students of minority nationalities.

Primary and middle schools have been set up extensively in all the minority areas so that the majority of school-age children are in school. Tibet, for example, has a nationalities institute, a teachers' school, seven middle schools and 2,500 primary schools. In 1971 there were 30 times as many young people in school as in 1959, before the democratic reform.

HSISHUANG PANNA: A MULTI-NATIONAL AUTONOMOUS CHOU*

Open plains dotting the crenulated mountains of southern Yunnan Province where, when winter descends elsewhere, the sun shines warm, flowers burgeon in a riot of colour and the fragrance of ripe fruit floats in on the breeze—this is Hsishuang Panna, as exotic as the "Peacock's Tail" it is often compared to.

At the southwestern tip of China, the Hsishuang Panna Tai Autonomous *Chou* is more than 4,000 kilometres from Peking and touches on Burma in the southwest and Laos in the southeast. Over a dozen nationalities live here in harmony; among them are the Tais, Hanis, Hans, Pulangs, Lahus, Yaos, Miaos, Was and Chingpos. The most numerous of the half million population, the Tais make up 47 per cent of the people in the rural areas. A tropical and subtropical climate, fertile soil, plentiful rainfall and frostless days the year round make the area ideal for various crops.

Only 23 years ago, the people on these green plains were groaning under the feudal manorial system. A few minority peoples tucked away in the mountain regions were in an even more backward state of social progress—some areas had just entered feudal society; in others, vestiges of primitive and slave societies remained.

The entire area was liberated in 1950, and land re-

* From *Peking Review*, No. 3, 1973.

form in 1956 put an end to the feudal exploitation system. Then democratic reform and socialist transformation were carried out under the leadership of the Chinese Communist Party. The fundamental change in the social system brought a boom to production. With the overthrow of the reactionary rulers who pursued a policy of "divide and rule" to foment racial dissension and feuds, the people of the many nationalities here have become united under the guidance of the Party's nationalities policy and made notable achievements in tapping the area's rich resources.

As in other places in China where national minorities live in compact communities, national regional autonomy has been instituted in Hsishuang Panna. The Tai Autonomous *Chou,* with the three counties of Chinghung, Menghai and Mengla under it, was established in January 1953. Organs to exercise autonomy have also been set up in areas where the Hanis, Pulangs, Yaos and Chinos live in groups. All the nationalities are completely equal politically. Leading posts in grassroots units are held by the labouring people of the different nationalities in the locality.

"The City of the Dawn"

A shimmering streak, the Lantsang River runs through Hsishuang Panna from north to south. On its western bank is the *chou* capital Yunchinghung—"The City of the Dawn." It is a neat tree-lined city of some 20,000 people where hundreds of factories, shops, schools, research institutes and other buildings are sheltered under evergreen coconut, betel nut and flame trees. Highways radiate out to 90 per cent of the *chou's* people's communes, and passenger and cargo ships ply between it and other towns on the Lantsang River. In addition to a school for training national minority cadres, there are two middle schools, two primary schools and a kindergarten with a total enrolment of 1,700.

There is also a well-equipped general hospital with 170 beds.

All this would have been unimaginable to anyone who had been here before liberation. Twenty-three years ago, it was a rambling settlement of less than 500 people whose only public structures were an office building of the reactionary Kuomintang government and a dozen or so thatched huts serving as caravan inns. Rank weeds and scrub grew everywhere and mosquitoes flew in droves. A notorious malaria-ridden place, it had to make do with a tiny clinic staffed by two. A lone primary school catered to less than ten pupils. The changes which have transfigured Yunchinghung today are typical of many places in the *chou*.

Granary

Agricultural production has made great headway; Hsishuang Panna has become today the granary of southern Yunnan. The peasants of the many nationalities in the *chou* have all organized into people's communes, and they have relied on the strength of the collective, coupled with aid from the People's Government, to develop farming.

The situation was vastly different before liberation. With two-thirds of the *chou* in mountain regions, the people used to fell trees and burn them every winter and spring. When sowing time came, they dug holes in the burnt ground with sharp sticks and threw in the seeds. After autumn harvesting, they gathered up their scant belongings and moved to another place, where the process began anew. Thus they roamed year after year, destroying large tracts of forests and getting paltry yields in return. The lion's share of what they harvested was taken up by rent, taxes and various religious fees, leaving the tillers food grain for only four months of the year. Wild vegetables and game made up the diet for the remaining eight months.

Liberation brought an end to this nomadic life and the people settled down to farm in permanent abodes. Such a major change, however, was not effected without a struggle.

In a small Hani nationality hamlet of 200 people atop Taka Mountain in Mengla County, two Communist Party members, Haichieh and Yangerh, led 48 households to build up farmland for a new settled life. A canal had to be cut to bring water up the mountain.

Long propagated by the feudal manorial lords, the belief in mountain, tree and water "spirits," however, cluttered the minds of the people. The two Communists sought out an old poor peasant, Tsochia, who had learnt through first-hand experience that talk about spirits was nothing but humbug.

Once while Tsochia was planting rice his leg began to bleed, and then turned blue and became swollen. Many people said he must have offended the "water spirit," who was out to get revenge. In spite of the big to-do, it turned out Tsochia had only been bitten by a leech and was cured by a doctor very quickly.

Laughing at his own credulity, the old fellow went around reciting the incident to dispel superstition. Haichieh and Yangerh also used the incident to help open the villagers' eyes and spread scientific knowledge.

Gradually, the villagers got rid of superstition, smashed the village "altar to the spirits" and made serious efforts to improve their paddyfields. The state sent in much-needed farm implements and other equipment. Technicians of Han nationality came to help them survey the land, and veteran Tai peasants taught them how to grow paddy-rice. After four years of hard work, this mountain hamlet had opened up more than 400 *mu* of terraced fields on the slopes irrigated by the clear water of the canal they had built. A small hydroelectric station now brings electricity to the village where orchards and tea gardens had risen on the heights.

On the plains, which are mostly inhabited by the Tais, farming developed at a faster speed. The Tais are noted rice-growers, but their cultivation methods were crude. Elephants and cows were used for ploughing without the use of fertilizer or weeding on the land. This gave them only 200-300 *jin* of rice a *mu*. Since liberation, they have completed over 10,000 small or medium-sized water conservancy projects, and acreage planted to two crops a year has expanded swiftly. Seventy per cent of the paddyfields grow fine strains which have resulted in output rising around 50 per cent. Chemical fertilizers and farm machinery are now used in a number of communes.

To change the relatively backward state of production in the border region, the state set up an agro-technical research institute and centres to disseminate farming techniques. Working shoulder to shoulder with local leading cadres and the people, scientific-technical personnel have done quite a bit to change cultivation methods, popularize good seed strains and build up a diversified economy.

Huge Botanical Park

Covered with dense forests all the year, Hsishuang Panna is a huge botanical park fashioned by nature. Tea grows at 1,000 to 1,300 metres above sea level, while tropical and subtropical industrial plants thrive at 1,000 metres and lower.

A famous native product of Hsishuang Panna, *puerh* tea is grown here on 50 plantations covering an area of over 100,000 *mu,* many times more than before liberation. Output has mounted—in 1971, the autonomous *chou* sold 12 times as much *puerh* tea to the state as at the time of liberation.

The scrub which used to cover the hilly regions below 1,000 metres has given way to forests of economic value. Over 300 tropical and subtropical plants introduced to the area grow on an area of 40,000 *mu*. Large teak and oil palm groves and rubber plantations have sprung up where before liberation none or very few such trees were planted. Wild plants such as the lard fruit have been tamed, and the valuable betel nut, cinnamon, pepper, cinchona and about 100 other medicinal herbs have been extensively planted.

Widely used in industry, wild lac used to grow unpicked for lack of purchasers. Now production is on the upswing. Output of fibrous plants and plants yielding perfume essence has increased. Cane sugar output is more than ten times that before liberation. The amount of tropical and subtropical fruit, such as coconuts, mangoes, bananas, pineapples and pomelos, has risen anywhere from several to several score times.

Scientists and agro-technicians sent by the state have set up tropical botanical gardens, research institutes for tropical crops, experimental stations for growing medicinal herbs and tea and state farms and forests, where they carry out large-scale experiments and spread scientific know-how. They have also investigated the economic value of many wild plants and cultivated seed beds so as to provide the local people with seeds and saplings.

First Generation of Industrial Workers

For a place which could not even produce a metal screw 23 years ago, this autonomous *chou* now has 4,500 people working in industries turning out many types of machinery, power, chemical fertilizers and mining coal, preparing tea and sugar, and making drugs and paper.

Different farm implements for opening up and cultivating terraced fields are supplied to the mountain regions, while farm machinery and chemical fertilizers are sent in large amounts to the communes on the plains. In 1971, nearly 3,000 machines for cultivating, reaping, threshing and husking rice were produced for the rural areas.

Rubber, tea, sugar and paper are processed in the localities where they are produced. Besides a large tea plant in the *chou* where all production processes are mechanized, preliminary processing plants using new equipment and techniques have been set up in places where tea is grown. Sugar-cane and bamboo, which cover the hillsides, no longer go to waste. Two sugar refineries using mechanized processes each have a daily capacity of processing 400 tons of sugar-cane.

Thirty-seven state-run factories in the *chou* form its industrial backbone, around which communes and brigades have built a network of small enterprises on the strength of their collective economy. In Chinghung County, for instance, one of the state-run "backbone" enterprises is a newly completed power station with a generating capacity of 3,000 kw. More than a hundred smaller power stations run by the communes and brigades bring electric light to many border villages and supply power for operating light machinery. All the national minorities in the *chou* have their own production workers who are making rapid political progress; many have joined the Chinese Communist Party. Helped by experienced Han workers, they have quickly become adept at their jobs. More and more of them have taken up posts of responsibility in factories and other enterprises.

"Malaria Area" No More

Smallpox, cholera and other scourges which seriously menaced the Hsishuang Panna people have been eradicated. Epidemic spread of malaria has been checked.

The *chou* has a contingent of over 500 professional medical and health workers and 800 hospital beds. Every county has a hospital and centres for epidemic prevention and mother and child care. Commune clinics can handle ordinary surgery, including obstetrical and gynaecologic operations. Production brigades and teams have trained health workers from among their own members who are not divorced from production. The population is on the rise, health has improved and mortality among the infants has dropped. The rural population has increased 63 per cent since 1950.

The Communist Party and People's Government pay great attention to the health of the Hsishuang Panna people and allocate large sums yearly to improve medical and health conditions. Mobile medical teams frequently come from Peking or other big cities to help cure and prevent diseases. The local people have also launched many campaigns to clear away garbage heaps and cesspools. The incidence of malaria in formerly endemic areas has sunk to below one per thousand as against 50 per cent in the early post-liberation period.

Hsishuang Panna had once been known as the "Plains of Death": malaria stalked the land, taking ten out of a hundred lives. Not only did the people get no medical treatment whatever, the feudal rulers constantly spread superstition in order to have the whip hand. The fog hanging over the land, they asserted, was the breath of devils, and malaria victims had to offer prayers and sacrifices to them. Malaria and other epidemics were often used to persecute the labouring people—feudal rulers dubbed poor peasants they hated most as *"pipa* demons" who spread disease, and tortured and even burnt them alive.

Prosperity and Unity

Before liberation, there were only a few score privately owned shops in all Hsishuang Panna, selling 20-odd items of the barest necessities. Now there are over 200 state and co-operative stores and service trades with 4,000 workers and staff members, dealing in 3,000 articles. The total return from retail sales in 1971 was 12 times that of 1949.

The rising living standards of members of the Chinghung People's Commune in Chinghung County are typical. The commune has 3,951 households, 68 per cent of which now own bicycles, 39 per cent have wristwatches and most have bank savings. But a better life has not effaced memories of the wretched past. Many poor and lower-middle peasants have kept the ragged quilts and clothing left over from the old days as "family heirlooms" to educate their children.

There is a Tai saying that "all the bitter bamboo shoots under heaven spring from one root," meaning that the labouring people of all nationalities who suffered in the old society were brothers and sisters. The reactionary rulers of the past spared no effort to stir up feuds and hostility. Now harmony reigns among all the nationalities in the *chou,* and people often name their villages, bridges, canals and other things after their new unity which they are so proud of.

There is a multi-national commune in Mengla County called Tuanchieh (Unity) Commune which through joint efforts recently built the Tuanchieh Reservoir. Three hamlets in the commune used to water their fields from the same river. Two were of Tai people, the other was Yi. Feuds arose during the transplanting season when each wanted more water for its own use. The three hamlets got together in winter 1970 and decided to solve the water problem once and for all by building a reservoir on the upper reaches of the river. When the project was completed, they named it the "Nationalities' Unity Reservoir."

Great as the changes have been in Hsishuang Panna, still greater changes are taking place. A musical people, the Tais like to pour their hearts into song. One song goes:

"Why are peacock feathers so fine?
Because the brilliant sun on them shine.
Why are our days sweeter than wine?
Because of Chairman Mao's revolutionary line."

III. SOCIALIST ECONOMIC
DEVELOPMENT

1. General Principles

China is truly a *developing* country. In just twenty-five years China has transformed itself from a sick and backward economy with mass starvation, rampant inflation, and crippling unemployment to a thriving socialist economy with full employment, stable prices, and a well-fed and well-clothed population. China's economic self-reliance and stability is not only a model for the Third World but also an envy of the advanced capitalist countries facing the most severe post-war economic crisis. As Chou En-lai proudly pointed out to one of the editors, China is one country which is unaffected by the world capitalist economic crisis (such as inflation and energy crisis). How was this economic miracle of the century accomplished? The following selections will provide the basic answers.

During our visits to China we saw modern industrial complexes, many local industries, and some mechanized communes, but we were most impressed by the fact that the overwhelming majority of the population is still engaged in agriculture using traditional means—i.e., muscle power. China is mainly an agricultural country employing farming methods similar to those employed elsewhere in Asia or Africa. On the surface a scene of peasants tilling rice paddies with water buffaloes in China is no different from a similar scene in Southeast Asia or India, but where lies the difference in the results? If one looked closer he would see that the Chinese peasants are working in groups, i.e., collectively. The basic difference lies in the new human relationship established since 1949.

The economic miracle of China is the direct result of adopting the socialist way of development. Unlike a capitalist economy where production is carried out for private profits, the whole economic activity of China is organized to meet the needs of the people. Profit motive has been substituted by "serving the people" as the motive. Under socialism private ownership of the means of production is replaced by public ownership, and anarchy in production is replaced by planned economy. Land, factories, natural resources, etc. are all either owned by the whole state or owned collectively by all members of a community. Collective ownership, as typified by the communes throughout the countryside, refers to common ownership by all members who live and work in them. All major industries are state-owned. This is a higher form of ownership since the means of production are in the hands of the whole people instead of just a section of the people. In terms of income, a uniform wage scale has been established for workers in the state-owned enterprises, but peasants' income depends on the productivity of a commune, which varies from region to region. The eventual goal is to transform collective ownership into state ownership of all means of production.

The change in ownership, by itself, cannot explain the economic success of China. Learning from the mistakes of Soviet Russia, which developed heavy industry at the expense of agriculture, China adopted the policy of "taking agriculture as the foundation and industry as the leading factor" formulated by Mao as the general policy for developing her economy. Taking agriculture as the foundation means putting the development of agriculture in first place, to feed and clothe China's millions. "Industry as the leading factor" means China is committed to building an advanced industrial economy. Industry plays the leading role by providing the technology and machinery, electricity, chemical fertilizers, etc. needed for agriculture and its mechanization. In

China the development of industry is based on agriculture; the modernization of agriculture depends on the development of industry. The two are interdependent and promote each other.

K.H.F.
K.T.F.

THE GENERAL LINE FOR SOCIALIST CONSTRUCTION*

The General Line for Socialist Construction is expressed in the words, "go all out, aim high and achieve greater, faster, better and more economical results in building socialism".

The call "Go all out and aim high" is to arouse the revolutionary spirit of China's hundreds of millions of people and bring their enthusiasm and resourcefulness into full play. These are the wellsprings of the power by which any greater, faster, better and more economical results in building socialism will be achieved, because it is the masses who are the real heroes. The Party's fundamental starting point in any undertaking is its firm faith in the majority of the people—primarily in the majority of the workers and peasants, who constitute the basic masses. At the same time its policy is to give cadres and revolutionary intellectuals full opportunity to play an important role. It is through truly relying on the masses, maintaining independence and keeping the initiative in our own hands, persisting in self-reliance and hard struggle and doing everything diligently and thriftily that China's socialist construction will be moved forward at a faster pace.

The words "greater, faster, better and more economical results" expressed in the General Line define a many-sided requirement for socialist construction. In any endeavor in this field, all of these must be considered. Stress only on quality and lower cost would make inroads on quantity and speed. And in the long run better quality and lower cost could not really be achieved. On the other hand, if emphasis were laid only on quantity and speed, quality and cost would be affected and

* From *China Reconstructs,* April 1973.

even the aims of achieving quantity and speed could not be met.

The four aspects are interrelated, they promote and supplement one another, they are inseparable parts of a whole. This reflects the objective laws governing the building of socialism.

The new China came into existence in 1949 with a backward economy and a poor material base for development. The enemies of the working people were not reconciled to their defeat: the imperialists enforced a blockade on China; inside the country the landlords, rich peasants, counter-revolutionaries and other bad elements hoped for a restoration of capitalism. In such circumstances, it was imperative to end China's poverty and backwardness by developing a socialist economy at a high speed.

In the first few years after liberation the Communist Party led the people to carry out land reform and rehabilitate the national economy. From the year 1953 on, under the guidance of the Party, the socialist transformation of all sectors of the economy took place step by step. (Peasants and handicraft producers organized themselves into farm and handicraft cooperatives. Industrial and commercial concerns owned by national capitalists became jointly owned by both the state and private capital.) It was fundamentally completed in 1956 and socialist public ownership became the economic basis of our country.

The socialist consciousness of the people all over the land rose to a new high. They were eager for the rapid development of the national economy in order to build the country as quickly as possible into a strong socialist one with modern industry, modern agriculture and modern science and culture. It was in these circumstances that in 1958 Chairman Mao summed up China's experience in building socialism and formulated the General Line for Socialist Construction. It expressed the desires of the Party and people and was drawn up to benefit them in the broadest possible way.

The promulgation of the General Line for Socialist Construction has stimulated a vigorous development in all fields of construction.

CHINA'S GENERAL PRINCIPLE FOR DEVELOPING THE NATIONAL ECONOMY*

BY CHUNG LI-CHENG

Old China had a very backward economy. At the time of nationwide liberation in 1949, China's grain output was only 216,200 million *jin*. Industry lagged even farther behind. The output value of modern industry accounted for only about 10 per cent of the total output value of the national economy with steel production a mere 160,000 tons.

The primary problems to be solved after the birth of New China were feeding several hundred million people and developing industry at the quickest possible speed. Unless these two were well handled, New China could not be consolidated. Furthermore, under our socialist system the relations between industry and agriculture are not merely those between two branches of material production, they are in essence the relations between two important groups of the working people— the workers and peasants. Since the worker-peasant alliance is the foundation of the dictatorship of the proletariat, this relationship between industry and agriculture and between workers and peasants must be so managed that it will firm up the proletarian dictatorship. This is why we have always regarded the correct handling of the relationship between agriculture and industry as a question of the utmost importance in our socialist economic construction.

* From *Peking Review*, No. 33, August 17, 1973.

Agriculture Is the Foundation

Chairman Mao has long elaborated the dialectical relationship between industry and agriculture. In his *On the Correct Handling of Contradictions Among the People* published in 1957, Chairman Mao pointed out: *"In discussing our path to industrialization, I am here concerned principally with the relationship between the growth of heavy industry, light industry and agriculture. It must be affirmed that heavy industry is the core of China's economic construction. At the same time, full attention must be paid to the development of agriculture and light industry." "As China is a large agricultural country, with over 80 per cent of her population in the rural areas, industry must develop together with agriculture, for only thus can industry secure raw materials and a market, and only thus is it possible to accumulate fairly large funds for building a powerful heavy industry." "As agriculture and light industry develop, heavy industry, assured of its market and funds, will grow faster."*

Summing up the practical experience of China's First and Second Five-Year Plans and basing himself on the law of economic development that agriculture, light industry and heavy industry are interdependent and promote each other's growth, Chairman Mao put forward in 1962 the general principle for developing the national economy: *"Take agriculture as the foundation and industry as the leading factor."* He also pointed out the necessity of putting agriculture in the primary position and arranging the national economy in this order—agriculture, light industry and heavy industry.

Agriculture is the foundation of the national economy. This is objectively so and the common law governing the economic development of all types of society. Talking about the physiocrats, Marx said: *"An agricultural labour productivity exceeding the individual*

*requirements of the labourer is the basis of all socie-
ties."* No socialist economy existed in Marx's time. He
could only arrive at this most general and correct conclusion by examining the different modes of production in history, especially the capitalist mode of
production. Before the advent of socialism, in societies based on the private ownership of the means of
production this law operated blindly and on its own.
With public ownership of the means of production in
the socialist society, it is entirely possible for people
consciously to master and apply this law and develop
the socialist economy in a planned and proportional
way.

Everyone knows that rapid development of industry,
especially heavy industry, is a matter of great importance in building socialism in an economically backward country. But how can industry, especially heavy
industry, be boosted at a faster rate? There are two
methods. One is to develop heavy industry by limiting
the growth of agriculture and light industry. The other
is to give full play to the role of agriculture as the
foundation and allow a greater growth of agriculture
and light industry to develop heavy industry.

The first method which stresses heavy industry to
an inordinate extent develops it in an isolated and lop-
sided way. It robs agriculture and light industry of the
investments, equipment, material and labour force
necessary for their growth and keeps them far behind
heavy industry. This creates difficulties in market, labour force and funds, brings on shortages of grain and
other consumer goods, and causes dissatisfaction among
the people. Moreover, heavy industry cannot be really
developed this way. From a long-term view this method
actually slows down the development of heavy industry
and yields less satisfactory results.

The second method hinges development of heavy
industry upon agricultural growth and provides it with
a more secure basis for development, thereby helping
it develop with greater and better results. The reason

is clear. Only when agriculture develops can it provide the labour force, grain and industrial raw materials needed in industrial development, expand the market for industrial products, accumulate more funds for industry and promote the development of industry at a faster rate.

As a socialist country, China cannot build socialism by begging from the imperialists. Still less can we follow their example of plundering the colonies and semi-colonies for cheap farm produce, industrial raw materials and labour force and dumping industrial goods there at high prices to develop industry. Socialist economy can only be built on the basis of maintaining independence and keeping the initiative in one's own hands and relying on one's own efforts, and the funds for socialist industrialization can only come from internal accumulation. We stand for the expansion of international trade to exchange needed goods on a footing of equality and mutual benefit. In a big country like ours with a population of several hundred million, we can only depend on the supply of agricultural and sideline products from our own resources and sell our industrial products mainly on the domestic market, especially the broadest internal market in the rural areas inhabited by more than 80 per cent of the population. Therefore, giving agriculture the primary place in the national economy is not anybody's fancy or subjective arrangement, but is determined by the position agriculture occupies and the role it plays in the entire national economy. It is also decided by the objective need of our socialist country, which must develop its socialist economy independently.

Light industry occupies a very important position in the development of the entire national economy and has a very close bearing on the people's life. Production in a socialist country is not for profit, but for meeting the people's ever increasing needs. The development of light industry not only helps improve the people's livelihood, but can raise the peasants' income and further promote agricultural growth by using more farm and sideline products as raw materials for light industry which, built relatively easily, has a short production period and a quick turnover of funds. In addition, its growth can accumulate more funds for heavy industry and calls for the supply of larger amounts of raw materials, machinery and equipment from heavy industry, thereby helping the latter to expand. In this sense, therefore, without the development of light industry it is impossible to supply the urban and rural population with a rich variety of industrial goods for daily use or to develop heavy industry at a faster rate.

Industry Is the Leading Factor

Stressing the importance of agriculture and light industry does not mean at all that heavy industry is any the less important. Heavy industry which produces the means of production can provide agriculture with an ever-increasing amount of farm machinery, chemical fertilizer, insecticide, electric power and building materials so as to speed up agricultural modernization. This is an important aspect for industry to play the role of leading factor. The development of heavy industry can also provide modern technique and equipment for the various sectors of the national economy and put the entire national economy on a new material and technical basis. Without the development of heavy industry, it will be impossible to have a consolidated national defence, defend the fruits of victory of socialist revolution, attain the all-round development of socialist economy, fulfil our proletarian internationalist obligations and support the revolutionary struggle of the people the world over. Therefore, it is necessary to lay great stress on the development of heavy industry in socialist economic construction. To accelerate the growth of heavy industry, we should handle well the relationship between agriculture, light industry and heavy industry and build heavy industry on the solid basis of agricultural development.

Paying attention to the development of agriculture and light industry does not mean that they should get more investments, equipment and material than heavy industry. It means that they should get a proper proportion of the investments, equipment and material which should not be freely diverted to other uses. This is not merely because the core of China's economic construction is heavy industry, which has so many departments and needs more investments, equipment and material. It is also because agricultural units in our country, except for state farms, are collectively owned by the labouring peasants and the seed, fertilizer, labour force and other investments needed in farming are mainly solved by the collective peasants. Except for the handicrafts and small-sized industries run by the people's communes, however, industry is owned by the whole people and its funds are provided by the state. Therefore, a bigger amount must be given to industry in the distribution of funds and equipment so as to ensure its development. The growth of agriculture requires that the state industries supply it with huge amounts of farm machines and tools. But the most fundamental thing lies in conscientiously carrying out the line and policies of the Party and state for the rural areas and fully mobilizing the socialist enthusiasm of the peasants. Only when farm production develops and the collective public accumulation expands is it possible to realize agricultural mechanization.

Here an excellent model is the Tachai Brigade in Shansi Province, a national advanced unit in agriculture. Tachai was a poor mountain valley where drought occurred nine out of every ten years and the per-*mu* yields never exceeded 100 *jin*. Under the leadership of the Party after liberation, the Tachai peasants carried out land reform and agricultural collectivization. They worked arduously and skilfully and displayed the revolutionary spirit of self-reliance, and finally turned the poor mountain valley into fertile land with high and stable yields of more than 1,000 *jin* per *mu*. They are now striving for farm mechanization. Since Chairman Mao issued the call *"In agriculture, learn from Tachai"* in 1964, a nationwide mass movement to learn from Tachai has been surging forward. Going all out and aiming high, hundreds of millions of peasants are making a steady effort to fundamentally transform China's farm production conditions.

Rapid Farm and Industrial Growth

Guided by Chairman Mao's revolutionary line and acting on the general principle of *"taking agriculture as the foundation and industry as the leading factor,"* we have achieved steady increases in farm production. Agricultural development has enormously promoted the rapid growth of light industry, heavy industry and other sectors of the national economy. In 1971, the nation's total grain output reached 492,000 million *jin,* which more than doubled the figure in the early post-liberation days. Big increases were also reported in technical crops such as cotton and oil-bearing crops as well as in forestry, animal husbandry, sideline occupation and fisheries. There were serious natural disasters in 1972, but thanks to the consolidated collective economy of the people's communes, large-scale water conservancy construction and farmland capital construction over the past years and the tenacious struggle to combat adversities, we gathered in a good harvest of 480,000 million *jin* of grain, equivalent to the level of 1970 which was a year of rich harvest. Technical crops also grew rapidly, and cotton—a major raw material for light industry—has increased fivefold compared with the years immediately after liberation. Now grain and technical crops supplied by our agriculture are sufficient to satisfy, though only initially, what the people and industrial development require.

China's light industry has also attained vigorous development. Compared with 1949, output of important light industrial products in 1972, including cotton yarn, cotton cloth, paper, sugar, salt, cigarettes and leather, showed an increase of several to dozens of times. At the same time, we have also branched out into new industries which produce chemical fibre, plastics and its products, synthetic detergent, wrist watches, bicycles, sewing machines, cameras, optical glass and photo-sensitive materials. This has enabled our light industry to gradually add to a relatively complete list of products of different varieties and initially cope with the increasing needs of people's living and state construction.

The vigorous growth of agriculture and light industry spurs on the development of heavy industry. Output of steel reached 23 million tons in 1972, or more than 130 times the pre-liberation figure. Output of coal, electricity, various kinds of machines and chemical products have either more than doubled or even risen dozens of times. China's industry has taken a big step forward in building an independent and comprehensive industrial system. Aircraft, automobile, modern ship-building and electronics industries, which were non-existent in the past, have been built. The level of self-sufficiency in equipment and raw materials has been raised, while machines, equipment and steel products are basically self-supporting. Owing to the development of industry in the hinterland, its geographical distribution has been gradually rationalized.

Under the guidance of Chairman Mao's revolutionary line, China's national economy has gained some successes. But it is still backward compared with the level of the developed capitalist countries. Ours is still a developing country. However, we are determined and have the confidence to build China into a prosperous socialist industrial country in a not too long historical period and make a greater contribution to humanity.

PUBLIC OWNERSHIP OF THE MEANS OF PRODUCTION IN CHINA*

There are two forms of socialist public ownership of the means of production in China at the present stage. One is socialist ownership by the state (that is, ownership by the whole people); the other is socialist collective ownership by the labouring masses.

Under the system of socialist public ownership, the means of production are no longer used as capital, nor is labour power sold as a commodity. This system of ownership enables the working class and the entire labouring people to free themselves once and for all from oppression and exploitation. It eliminates capitalist competition and anarchy in production as well as the recurrent economic crises characteristic of capitalist society. Manpower, materials and funds can thus be put to the most effective use. In contrast to capitalist ownership, the aim of social production under socialist ownership is not for profit, but to meet the growing needs of the state and the people. China's achievements in socialist revolution and construction are eloquent proof of the superiority of socialist public ownership.

Socialist State Ownership

Socialist state ownership of the means of production is the most advanced system of ownership in human history. Its appearance marked mankind's advent into a completely new era. It is a form of public ownership in a state under the dictatorship of the proletariat which represents the proletariat and the entire labouring people in owning the means of production and social products. In China today, the socialist state owns all the mines, waterways, forests and other natural resources as well as part of the land. Railways, postal and telegraph offices and banks also belong to the state,

* From *Peking Review*, No. 51, December 22, 1973.

and the state runs factories, farms, shops and other enterprises and owns their products.

It is imperative that the proletariat, after seizing state power, should transform capitalist private ownership into socialist public ownership and build up its own economic foundations. Only thus can the proletarian dictatorship be consolidated. Historical experience has shown that, if the proletariat fails to bring about this change on the strength of its dictatorship immediately upon seizing power, the overthrown bourgeoisie will use its economic strength, in conjunction with armed counter-attacks, to try to subvert the proletarian dictatorship and regain its lost "paradise." In summing up the experience of the Paris Commune, the great teacher Lenin pointed out that one of the two mistakes which forfeited the Commune the fruit of its splendid victory was the failure to "expropriate the expropriators," to seize and put into the hands of the proletariat major enterprises, such as the banks, which formed the economic sinews of the nation.

Guided by Chairman Mao's revolutionary line since liberation, China relied on the state power under the dictatorship of the proletariat to confiscate bureaucrat capital, effecting its *"transfer to the people's republic led by the proletariat."* The bureaucrat-comprador bourgeoisie of old China, which had a myriad links with the feudal forces in the countryside, was suckled by and served the imperialists. Like the landlord class, it represented the most reactionary and most backward relations of production. In the 22 years of its rule (1927-49), the bureaucrat-comprador bourgeoisie headed by the four big family groups—Chiang Kai-shek, T.V. Soong, H.H. Kung and Chen Li-fu—amassed an enormous amount of capital valued at 10,000 to 20,000 million U.S. dollars. On the eve of nationwide liberation, bureaucrat capital owned 80 per cent of the fixed assets of China's industry and communications and transport, and monopolized the country's economic life-lines, but it was confiscated immediately after liberation. This eliminated the main part of China's capitalist economy. The economic lifelines henceforth came under the control of the socialist state.

National-capitalist industry used to occupy second place in China's modern industry, making up about 20 per cent of the total value of the fixed assets in industry and communications and transport. After bureaucrat capital was confiscated, the "redemption" method was used in carrying out the socialist transformation of national-capitalist industry and commerce. Step by step capitalist ownership was transformed into socialist state ownership—starting with the elementary form of state capitalism, that is, in industry, the private enterprises processed goods for the state and accepted state orders while the state purchased and marketed their entire output; in commerce, the elementary form of state capitalism consisted of designating private enterprises to purchase certain commodities or making them distributors on a commission basis. This developed into the higher form of state capitalism, that is, first turning individual enterprises into joint state-private enterprises and then bringing about this change throughout entire trades. While carrying out the socialist transformation of capitalist industry and commerce, planned economic construction on a big scale was undertaken, which expanded the socialist state sector of the economy and consolidated and strengthened socialist state ownership. This laid the main economic foundation for the proletarian dictatorship.

Modern industry and communications and transport, the nation's economic lifelines, also came under socialist state ownership. State-owned industry supplies large amounts of machinery and equipment, apparatuses, fuel and power to promote the technical transformation of various departments of the state-owned sector of the economy. It produces large numbers of tractors, harvesters and transport equipment as well as electric power to promote mechanized farming. It also provides technical equipment and capital for economic, cultural and national defence construction. The state-owned sector of the economy is a powerful material force speeding up socialist revolution and construction and consolidating the proletarian dictatorship.

The establishment of socialist state ownership sparked the swift development of the social productive forces. Total value of industrial output shot up in the two decades since liberation. In steel, for one, output rose as many as 130 times in the years 1949-71, from 158,000 tons to 21 million tons. Socialist revolution and construction, ceaselessly advancing, have already transformed China from a poor and backward country into a socialist country with initial prosperity.

Socialist Collective Ownership

Apart from state ownership, socialist public ownership takes the form of collective ownership in agriculture and handicrafts. After the proletarian seizure of state power, the question of whether the proletarian dictatorship can be consolidated hinges, in large measure, on the correct handling of the peasant question and on turning individual ownership by the peasants into collective ownership and the socialization of agriculture. *"Without socialization of agriculture, there can be no complete, consolidated socialism."* It is impossible for the dictatorship of the proletariat to rest for any length of time on two different economic foundations—that of socialist industry and individual small-peasant economy. As Lenin pointed out: *"Small production engenders capitalism and the bourgeoisie continuously, daily, hourly, spontaneously, and on a mass scale."*

Without transforming the small-peasant economy, the disintegration into the two extremes in the countryside will inevitably cause the mass of the peasants to become poor and bankrupt while a few well-to-do middle peasants will become rich peasants. If this should happen, the worker-peasant alliance which forms the foundation of the proletarian dictatorship will be in danger of splitting up. Without transforming the small-peasant economy, the scattered and backward individual agriculture will be unable to satisfy the increasing need of socialist industry and the cities for commodity grain and industrial raw materials, and socialist industrialization will not be able to proceed at full speed. Collectivization of agriculture—transformation of backward individual agriculture into large-scale, collectivized, mechanized socialist agriculture—is the only way to resolve the contradiction between socialist industrialization and a small-peasant economy. This is the road that must be taken in reinforcing the socialist position in the countryside, in building socialism, and in strengthening the worker-peasant alliance and consolidating the proletarian dictatorship.

After completing the anti-feudal land reform, the first step is to realize agricultural collectivization, the second is to achieve mechanization of agriculture on this basis—this is our Party's basic line in agriculture. Chairman Mao has pointed out: *"With conditions as they are in our country, co-operation must precede the use of big machinery (in capitalist countries agriculture develops in a capitalist way)."* Based on the universal Marxist law that any substantial development of the productive forces can only come after a change in the relations of production, this thesis of Chairman Mao's correctly handles the relationship between agricultural collectivization and mechanization in China. It has shattered the schemes of Liu Shao-chi and swindlers like him to obstruct and sabotage the agricultural co-operation movement through advocating "mechanization before co-operation." The road to developing socialist agriculture in China is "co-operation before mechanization." After the completion of land reform, it took only four years to complete in the main the socialist transformation of agriculture through the organization of mutual-aid teams, moving on to agricultural producers' co-operatives of an elementary type and then to those of an advanced type. This was achieved in accordance with the principle of voluntariness on the part of the peasants. Agricultural co-operation thus realized converted the ocean of individual ownership by the peasants into socialist collective ownership. Collectivization was a great spur to agricultural production, thus fully revealing the big part played by socialist relations of production in propelling the productive forces forward.

In 1958, under the guidance of the Party's general line of going all out, aiming high and achieving greater, faster, better and more economical results in building socialism and the impetus of the Big Leap Forward, agricultural producers' co-operatives of the advanced type amalgamated to form rural people's communes in order to meet the needs of water conservancy construction in agriculture and the development of rural productive forces. The rural people's communes are the basic units of China's socialist society in the rural areas; they are also basic rural units of state power. Throughout a fairly long historical period, they are collective economic organizations of socialist mutual aid and co-operation. The advance of agricultural producers' co-ops of the advanced type to rural people's communes is a major development in China's collective ownership.

As Chairman Mao has pointed out, what distinguishes the people's commune is its characteristic of being *"big and public."* Big, in that its scale is much bigger than the advanced co-ops. With more land, more people and more funds, the commune can use manpower and the means of production more rationally and go in for a more diversified economy, concentrating on one main line of production while engaging at the same time in industry and other side-lines. Public, in the sense that the degree of public ownership is higher than in the advanced co-ops.

The people's communes have expanded the scope of rural collective ownership and have raised it to a higher level. They are more favourable to promoting the development of the productive forces. Unified planning within a bigger scope can be undertaken and socialist co-operation organized on a larger scale according to the principles of voluntariness, mutual benefit and exchange of equal values. They can thus carry out agricultural capital construction such as water conservancy projects which would have been difficult for any single advanced co-operative to do in the past.

The collective ownership of the rural people's communes at the present stage is generally at three levels—commune, production brigade and production team. Neither collective ownership at the commune level nor at the production brigade level is basic at present. The basic form is collective ownership at the production team level, that is, the production teams are the basic accounting units. As conditions gradually ripen, the basic form of ownership at the production team level will advance to the basic form of ownership at the production brigade level and then to that at the commune level. Collective commune ownership will eventually advance to socialist state ownership. This, of course, will be a fairly long process of gradual development.

At the present stage, the rural people's commune members still have small plots of land for their own use and engage in some side-occupations at home. In the pastoral areas, commune herdsmen own a small number of livestock. The state protects the people's private ownership of remuneration from labour, bank savings, houses and other means of livelihood.

Although both socialist state ownership and collective ownership by the labouring masses are forms of socialist public ownership, they differ in the degree of public ownership. Property belonging to state-owned enterprises and to people's communes, therefore, cannot be transferred gratis; this also applies to the property of the different people's communes. The principle of commodity production and exchange of equal values is used in economic transactions between them.

2. Agriculture

HOW CHINA SOLVED ITS FOOD PROBLEM*

Food is an extremely important question in human existence. In old China, under the rule of imperialism, feudalism and bureaucrat-capitalism, it had never been solved. Former U.S. Secretary of State Acheson predicted on the eve of the founding of New China that China's several hundred millions were an "unbearable pressure" and it was unlikely that the Chinese Communist Party would be able to solve this problem of feeding them.

Almost a quarter of a century has gone by and what has happened? The Chinese people, under the leadership of the Chinese Communist Party and Chairman Mao, have solved this problem. An initial self-sufficiency in food has been attained. So much for Acheson and others.

Initial Self-Sufficiency

What sort of base did New China's grain production have to begin with?

China has always been an agricultural country but every year, from the middle of the last century right up to liberation in 1949, there was a severe grain shortage and the country had to import grain. In 1933, for example, 3 million tons were imported but still the labouring people of China were starving. In those days agricultural production was throttled by the harsh feudal system of land ownership, and chronic natural disasters coupled with endless years of war aggravated

* From *Peking Review*, No. 45, November 9, 1973.

the situation. The annual grain harvest in 1949 was only slightly above 110 million tons.

After the founding of New China the liberated Chinese people, following Chairman Mao's directive that *"revolution plus production can solve the problem of feeding the population,"* have carried out the land reform, introduced collectivization of agriculture (from mutual-aid teams to agricultural producers' co-operatives and to rural people's communes), implemented the general policy of "taking agriculture as the foundation and industry as the leading factor" for building up the national economy, set in motion throughout the countryside the mass movement "In agriculture, learn from Tachai," developed the farm machinery industry and popularized scientific farming. These important socialist revolutionary measures and production practices have brought in their wake a fairly substantial growth in grain production.

China produced 250 million tons of grain in 1971, a 120 per cent increase over that of 1949, and last year brought in a good harvest of 240 million tons after overcoming serious natural disasters.

The old practice of sending grain from the south to the north where production had never been able to fully meet the needs began to change a few years ago. Initial self-sufficiency in grain has been attained throughout the country. State, commune and peasant household grain reserves grow year by year. Some wheat is imported each year, but rice and other cereals are exported to balance the people's staple food.

Grain production over the past 20 years or more has risen by an average of nearly 4 per cent annually, keeping ahead of the population increase which averages about 2 per cent a year. Grain production in the last decade has progressively increased by an average of about 5 per cent a year. The Malthusian argument has been refuted by facts which have proved the great truth: *"Of all things in the world, people are the most*

*precious. Under the leadership of the Communist Party,
as long as there are people, every kind of miracle can
be performed."* (Mao Tsetung: *The Bankruptcy of
the Idealist Conception of History.*)

Revolutionary Impetus

How is it that New China has been able to solve the
problem of feeding its people? The basic reason is that
China, under the leadership of the Communist Party,
carried out the thoroughgoing democratic and socialist
revolutions and set up the socialist system with public
ownership of the means of production as its basis.

Shortly after the birth of New China a tremendous
revolution in land ownership was carried out throughout the Chinese countryside. Land reform already had
been carried out in some places following the establishment of anti-Japanese democratic power in revolutionary bases set up during the war of resistance to Japanese aggression.

In old China 70-80 per cent of the land in the rural
areas were concentrated in the hands of landlords and
rich peasants who together made up only 10 per cent
of the rural population, while the working peasants
who made up 90 per cent of the population in the countryside owned about 20-30 per cent of the land. Each
landlord or rich peasant on an average appropriated a
ton of grain a year for himself while the peasants were
constantly short of food.

The land reform confiscated the vast areas of land
owned by the landlords, so that over 300 million peasants with little or no land were able to share out 47
million hectares among them as well as a large number
of draught animals and farm implements. This put an
end to exploitation under the feudal system of land
ownership. Production rapidly picked up and developed.

After the land reform the peasants farmed by individual households. This small peasant economy was very unstable and could easily lead to polarization in the countryside. So the Chinese Communist Party led the peasants to embark on the agricultural co-operative movement in the countryside which step by step turned the individual peasant economy into a socialist collective economy.

At first mutual-aid teams based on the individual peasant economy were formed by the working peasants. This developed into agricultural co-operatives of an elementary type where peasants pooled their land and farm implements as shares. Earnings were divided among the members according to the amount of work done, and the land and implements contributed. Later these co-operatives developed into agricultural producers' co-operatives of an advanced type, which were larger and had more manpower at their disposal. By relying on their collective funds and manpower they could undertake small-scale capital construction on the farmland, develop production and bring in larger returns. No payment was made any longer for land or farm implements, since the peasants' major means of production were bought outright by the collective. By 1957 the nation's total grain output was 185 million tons, a 20 per cent increase over that of 1952, before agricultural co-operation started.

Ever expanding production enabled the peasants to see more and more clearly the superiority of collectivization and they became more determined than ever to follow the socialist road. With soaring enthusiasm in production coupled with eagerness to quickly pull agriculture out of its backward state, they began carrying out farm capital construction such as big water conservancy projects and soil improvement. But they were confronted with problems which the advanced co-operatives could not tackle. For instance, more manpower had to be employed and deployed for a variety of tasks in large-scale production and construction;

land and other means of production had to be rationally used on a wider scale for farming on large tracts of land and for specialized production.

In compliance with the desires of the masses, the people's communes—a brand-new form of organization —came into being under the leadership of the Party. They further expanded and improved the prevailing system of collective ownership in the rural areas, thus laying a solid foundation for the further development of agriculture. (For policies relating to the people's communes see "A Visit to the Tungting People's Commune" in *Peking Review*, Nos. 13-18 this year.)

Major Measures

To further develop grain production, the Chinese Communist Party and the People's Government laid down the general policy of "taking agriculture as the foundation and industry as the leading factor" for building up the national economy and the principle of "taking grain as the key link and ensuring an all-round development" for farm production. This gives first place to agriculture and puts grain production before everything else in farming.

Why is this so? The main reasons are: Grain is a must of the people's livelihood and is indispensable for industry, agriculture, commerce, education and all other undertakings. Moreover, the funds needed for socialist industrial construction are accumulated from industrial and agricultural production; farm and sideline products come from agriculture; and industrial products are sold in domestic markets. Only when agriculture makes headway can the development of industry be promoted. In addition, a certain amount of grain reserves is needed in case of natural calamities and surprise attacks by foreign aggressors.

With prominence given to agriculture, all departments of the state are required to give powerful support to farm production by providing it with manpower, materials, funds and technical assistance.

For industry, its support to agriculture lies mainly in supplying farm machinery, chemical fertilizers and insecticides. Whereas in pre-liberation days the farm machinery industry was practically non-existent, now most of the provinces, municipalities and autonomous regions in the country have their own tractor plants and small factories turning out power engines. And the small enterprises—iron and steel plants, chemical fertilizer plants, coal mines, cement works and hydro-power stations—which have mushroomed in all parts of the country are playing a big part in helping farm production. The output of small chemical fertilizer plants in 1971, for instance, accounted for more than half the nation's total.

As regards financial assistance, the state collects a low agricultural tax, without increasing it when production goes up and with tax exempted for those communes and brigades hit by natural calamities. As a result, agricultural tax paid by the peasants takes up an ever smaller proportion of their total income from farm production. It dropped from 12 per cent in 1953 to only 6 per cent in 1970. Apart from this, the state allocates huge funds every year for water conservancy works and the state bank provides a large amount of agricultural loans at low interest.

Since the founding of the People's Republic, the state has on many occasions raised the purchasing prices for farm and side-line products and reduced the prices of means of production for agriculture, while keeping the prices of daily necessities stable in the urban and rural areas. The implementation of such a price policy in support of farm production means that the masses have gained a total of 11,000 million yuan since 1966, the year the Great Proletarian Cultural Revolution began.

As a result of the efforts made by the whole Party and people, China has reaped bumper grain harvests in ten successive years since 1962.

Planned Supply

During the early days when New China was born, supplies of food grain were tight because of shortages. At that time, while paying close attention to grain production, the Communist Party and the People's Government made great efforts to regulate grain supplies so as to guarantee the people's livelihood. In 1953, the state banned all free grain markets and instituted planned purchase and supply of grain, putting it under unified management.

This was aimed at doing away with speculation, hoarding, market monopolization and other capitalist practices in the grain market, so as to rationally distribute grain and ensure the needs of the people.

When grain is purchased in a planned way, the interests of the state, the collective and the individual are taken into consideration. The state purchases at reasonable prices the surplus grain of the production teams after they have set aside enough grain for production (to be used as seeds and animal feed) and for the commune members' needs. The annual amount of state purchase is by and large the same. If the grain output increases, the state only purchases a little more from it; on the other hand, when output drops because of natural disasters, the state purchases less or even sells grain to the peasants.

Planned supply of grain by the state means overall planning and all-round considerations and rational distribution by taking into consideration the needs of the hundreds of millions of people in the land. In the cities and industrial and mining areas, for instance, food grain is supplied according to age and occupation (with differences in labour intensity) so as to ensure rational consumption. Peasants in areas mainly growing industrial crops are given the same amount of food grain as those in neighbouring grain-producing areas.

Today, everyone in China has enough to eat. Gone are the days when many people lived on the verge of starvation, or died of hunger.

Stable Grain Prices

Keeping commodity prices stable is one of the important principles in China's socialist economy. As grain is a must of the people's livelihood, to keep the grain prices stable, therefore, has a very close bearing not only on the people's livelihood but also on market prices in general. This is why the People's Government has adopted a series of measures to stabilize them.

In old China, with grain in the hands of the reactionary Kuomintang government and the landlords and capitalists, speculation and hoarding were rife. When grain was brought to market in autumn, the landlords and grain dealers did all they could to hold down the purchasing prices and hoarded it in large quantities. When there was a shortage of grain in spring, they raked in huge profits by raising grain prices.

After the birth of New China, the People's Government immediately brought the grain market under control by developing production and regulating grain supplies. By March 1950, or only six months after the founding of the People's Republic, grain prices which had been skyrocketing was brought under control. The prices became more stable in 1953 following the banning of free grain markets and the introduction of planned purchase and supply of grain by the state, thus ensuring the basic needs of the nation and ending the speculative activities which were harmful to the people.

The present prices of flour and rice, two main commodity grains in China, average 0.35 and 0.3 yuan per kilogramme respectively. (One yuan is equivalent to

0.526 U.S. dollar.) These prices have remained basically unchanged since 1953. This is also true of other grain prices.

All this has made a deep impression on people who know what life was like in old China.

In Kweichow Province, there is an 81-year-old man by the name of Chiao who began keeping notes of the fluctuating grain prices since 1908 in order to see when they would stop. His ledger shows that from 1913 to 1939 grain prices fluctuated constantly, and that from 1940 to 1949 they rose to over 200,000 times their former level. No more entries were made after 1950, for "from then on, prices have become stable and there was no need to make any entry," as the old man explained.

The People's Government has long abolished seasonal price differentials for grain. While keeping the selling prices of grain stable, the state has on many occasions raised the purchasing prices, with a greater margin of increase in areas where the economy is less developed or where the minority peoples live in a close-knit community. The loss thus entailed as well as transport and overhead expenses are all covered by the state. This has increased the peasants' income and the city people do not have to pay more for their food grain.

TACHAI—STANDARD BEARER IN AGRICULTURE

BY HSIN HUA-WEN

A Tremendous Change

The Tachai Production Brigade is an outstanding unit in China's agriculture. It is taking the road which our great leader Chairman Mao set forth to guide China in developing socialist agriculture.

Since Chairman Mao issued the great call in 1964 *"In agriculture, learn from Tachai"*, especially during the Great Proletarian Cultural Revolution, the Tachai Brigade, a village in the Taihang Mountains, has become well-known throughout the country. It frequently has tens of thousands of visitors—rural cadres and poor and lower-middle peasants from other parts of the country—who come to learn from its outstanding experience. It is also visited by friends from many other countries. The mass movement to learn from Tachai is spreading wider and deeper in the countryside—in mountain regions and on the plains, north and south, and in agricultural regions and livestock-raising areas. This has given a great impetus to the rapid growth of China's socialist agriculture.

The Tachai Production Brigade in the people's commune of the same name in Hsiyang County, Shansi Province, has 83 households with a population of 430.

In the old society, this small village in rock-strewn mountains was almost isolated from the outside world. Nine years out of ten it was affected by natural calamities and the village was in abject poverty. It worked only 800 *mu*[1] of farmland (60 per cent of it being owned by one landlord and three rich peasant households) which were divided into more than 4,700 strips spread out over harsh gullies, ridges and hill-slopes. The soil was poor and erosion was serious. Grain yield per *mu* was only 100 *jin*.[2] Nearly 80 per cent of the population were poor and lower-middle peasants. They worked as hired labourers for the landlord and rich peasants, suffering cruel oppression and exploitation. They were poverty-stricken and many were forced to sell their children.

Gone for ever is all this. The once bare mountains are now covered with green. The canal along the mountain ridges leads water up to irrigate the terraced fields

[1] One *mu* is roughly equal to one-sixth of an acre or one-fifteenth of a hectare.

[2] One *jin* is equal to 1.1023 pounds or half a kilogramme.

on the slopes; crops grow well in the gullies. Tachai is now flourishing.

Since liberation in 1949, the poor and lower-middle peasants, guided by Chairman Mao's proletarian revolutionary line, have taken the road of socialist collectivization. They have struggled against class enemies and the age-old concept of private ownership. They have made vigorous and successful efforts to transform the hills and gullies.

Bringing their collective strength into play, they built several hundred stone embankments for the terraced fields on the slopes and led water uphill for irrigation. They carried out scientific experiments and improved farming technique so that the land gave stable high yields. In 17 of the 18 years since the agricultural co-operative was set up in 1953, Tachai was hit by natural disasters of varying degrees but still managed to increase output every year. Forestry, animal husbandry and sideline production also made big progress. More than 40,000 fruit and other trees were planted on barren slopes. The number of draught animals increased from 10 to 90.

Making rapid progress in mechanization and semi-mechanization, Tachai now has electricity and machines for irrigation, processing of farm produce and crushing of fodder. Carts and aerial cableways have replaced shoulder poles and donkeys as means of transport. Several million *jin* of farmyard manure are carried uphill mostly by cableway for the terraced fields. Machines are used in building permanent farm works. With revolutionary enthusiasm to transform nature, the poor and lower-middle peasants of Tachai last winter and this spring used bulldozers to level nine hillocks, joined the small plots together and turned them into "man-made plains". Work done every year by farm machines accounts for 60 per cent of that done by the brigade's labour power.

The village has taken on a new look. Blocks of new

houses and stone-walled caves have replaced the earthen caves, and electric light and tap water are supplied to every household. The brigade has ample grain reserves and public accumulation fund and every household has bank deposits and its own grain reserves.

How is it that Tachai has been able to bring about such great and profound changes? Chen Yung-kuei, secretary of the brigade Party branch, said: "The fundamental reason is that people have changed their thinking. People can change the land, technique, output and village because they have changed their thinking. This change is the result of arming them with Marxism-Leninism-Mao Tsetung Thought."

Chairman Mao teaches: *"Once the correct ideas characteristic of the advanced class are grasped by the masses, these ideas turn into a material force which changes society and changes the world."*

Under the leadership of the Party branch, the several hundred poor and lower-middle peasants and other commune members of Tachai who have made such extraordinary and heroic achievements have paid attention always to giving first place to proletarian politics in their work and placed Mao Tsetung Thought in command of everything. They have fostered the spirit of self-reliance and hard work and the communist style of cherishing the state and the collective. Their lofty aim is to farm for the revolution. Their motto is to make revolution and go all out so as to make still greater contributions to the emancipation of mankind.

Forward Along the Socialist Road

The Tachai Brigade emerged as the standard bearer of China's socialist agriculture in a fierce struggle over more than two decades between the proletariat and the bourgeoisie and between the socialist and the capitalist road.

The local Party branch headed by Chen Yung-kuei

always works to arm the cadres and peasants with Mao Tsetung Thought and has led them in waging an unswerving struggle against the renegade, hidden traitor and scab Liu Shao-chi, his local agents and the unreformed landlords and rich peasants—a struggle which has been crowned with one victory after another.

The struggle dates back to the days shortly after land reform, when Chen Yung-kuei initiated a mutual-aid team of poor and lower-middle peasants in response to Chairman Mao's call *"Get organized!"* The mutual-aid team marked the first step taken by the Tachai peasants along the road of socialist collectivization.

Not taking their defeat lying down, the handful of landlords and rich peasants, bent on leading Tachai on to the capitalist road, instigated people to keep to individual farming and predicted that the mutual-aid team would fail. The poor and lower-middle peasants waged a tit-for-tat struggle and frustrated their sabotage.

Chen Yung-kuei's mutual-aid team was made up of the village's poorest people, four elderly poor peasants and five orphans of poor peasant origin. It reaped a good harvest the first year after its founding, its grain output per *mu* exceeding that of the peasants working on their own. This was a blow to the class enemy and an encouragement to the other peasants. Soon the team grew to 49 households.

The local poor and lower-middle peasants, following the socialist road indicated by the great leader Chairman Mao, planned in 1952 to set up an agricultural co-operative in which land belongs to the collective. But Liu Shao-chi and company branded their plan "utopian agrarian socialism", alleging that no agricultural co-operative could be established before farming was mechanized.

Under the influence of this counter-revolutionary revisionist line, it was not until the year 1953 that the county authorities reluctantly allowed Tachai to establish a co-operative with a maximum membership of 30 households, a figure far below the number of applicants.

The local Party branch headed by Chen Yung-kuei refused to obey, believing that the decision went against Chairman Mao's revolutionary line. An agricultural co-operative was finally established in conformity with the desire of the masses of poor and lower-middle peasants. The first year after its establishment, the co-operative registered a grain output of 240 *jin* per *mu*, 50 per cent higher than what the peasants working on their own got from their land.

In 1958, a people's commune was established in the locality and Tachai became one of its production brigades. Inspired by the general line for building socialism laid down by Chairman Mao, the Tachai peasants launched a mass campaign for remaking nature. With unbounded revolutionary zeal, they terraced mountain slopes into fields and adopted new farming techniques. Grain output went up constantly. The poor and lower-middle peasants and other commune members hailed this as a victory for the road of collectivization indicated by Chairman Mao.

Taking advantage of the grave natural calamities in 1961, Liu Shao-chi and company whipped up the evil wind of *sanzi yibao*[3] in a vain attempt to undermine collective economy and restore capitalism in the countryside. A capitalist-roader from the county came to the commune to which Tachai belonged, preaching a return to individual farming and the opening of free markets. He even instigated the class enemy to engage in profiteering of farm produce.

In this struggle, the Party branch acted on Chairman Mao's great teaching *"Only socialism can save China"* and his instructions on consolidating the collective economy. It encouraged the poor and lower-middle

---

[3] The extension of plots for private use and of free markets, the increase of small enterprises with sole responsibility for their own profits or losses, and the fixing of output quotas based on the household.

peasants to recall their suffering in the old society and contrast it with their happiness in the new. It energetically publicized the superiority of socialism, criticized capitalism and exposed the class enemy's schemes to disrupt the collective economy and restore capitalism. In so doing, it resolutely defended the cause of socialist collectivization.

Once a neighbouring brigade offered to buy Tachai's surplus hay at a high price. The Tachai Party branch lost no time in organizing the commune members to discuss "What should we do when other brigades have difficulties?" The poor and lower-middle peasants angrily denounced profiteering as they recalled how in the old society the landlords, rich peasants and speculators fleeced the poor people and forced them to sell their children by raising food prices in lean years. They declared they should not sell their surplus hay for profit. The brigade then unanimously decided to sell the hay to the neighbouring brigade at the state price. In addition, Tachai sold the state 240,000 *jin* of its surplus grain, exceeding the amount provided in the state plan. It also let some other brigades borrow grain from its reserves so as to help them consolidate and develop their socialist collective economy. This is just one instance of the communist style of the Tachai people who ardently love the country and the collective.

Chairman Mao in 1964 issued the great call *"In agriculture, learn from Tachai"*. This was an immense inspiration to Tachai's poor and lower-middle peasants. However, Liu Shao-chi and company bitterly hated Tachai, this standard bearer in firmly taking the socialist road. They spread the rumour that "Tachai is rotting" and sent a work team to "check up" on the work at Tachai in an attempt to negate the brigade as an advanced unit.

From the moment it came to Tachai, the work team worked hand in glove with the landlords and rich peasants. It resorted to frame-ups to attack the Tachai Party branch headed by Chen Yung-kuei and seized leadership from it. It tried by every means to find loopholes as pretexts to attack the Party branch by surveying the farmland and checking the grain accounts, the storage and the brigade members' income. The poor and lower-middle peasants, however, rallied closely round the Party branch and put up a tit-for-tat struggle against the work team. They cited numerous facts to refute the work team's fabrications. The head of the work team was dumbfounded when Chen Yung-kuei and the commune members asked him what line he was pursuing. Finally the team had to beat a retreat and cleared out crestfallen.

Through this struggle, the Tachai poor and lower-middle peasants raised still higher their consciousness of class struggle and the struggle between the two lines.

During the Great Proletarian Cultural Revolution, the Party branch of Tachai headed by Chen Yung-kuei led the masses in rebelling against the capitalist-roaders in the Hsiyang County Party Committee and criticized the counter-revolutionary revisionist line pushed by Liu Shao-chi and company. They are advancing valiantly along the revolutionary line indicated by Chairman Mao and making new contributions to building the new socialist countryside.

Build a New Socialist Countryside by Self-reliance

At the time when the peasants organized the co-operative, Tachai remained a backward mountain village with its 4,700 strips of land scattered over the gullies, ridges and mountain slopes. The co-operative had only a few draught animals and such simple farm tools as ploughs, picks, spades, shovels, baskets and shoulder poles. There were only 50 able-bodied men and women.

Although socialist collectivization had provided Tachai with the favourable conditions for changing its backwardness, the problem still arose: How could the poor soil be turned into fertile fields and the backward mountain village transformed into a thriving new socialist countryside in the shortest possible time? This question was submitted to the Party members and other peasants for discussion. Most people advocated relying on themselves while a few suggested asking the state for loans.

Chen Yung-kuei and the poor and lower-middle peasants said: "In making revolution we must rely on ourselves instead of others. The state is ours. If we all rely on the state, whom could the state rely on?" With their encouragement the commune members worked out a ten-year plan for remaking nature in accordance with Chairman Mao's teachings on *self-reliance and hard work*.

Under the leadership of the Party branch, a battle against nature began the very winter the co-operative was set up. Though working in piercing cold weather, the peasants were all wet with sweat. They quarried stones with hammers and chisels and in one and a half months succeeded in throwing up 20 stone embankments across a gully at different levels. With shoulder poles and baskets, they carried in fertile soil from elsewhere to create farmland behind the embankments. This initial success proved the might of self-reliance.

The Tachai poor and lower-middle peasants nurtured by Mao Tsetung Thought worked with revolutionary heroism like the Foolish Old Man who removed the mountains. They went on re-shaping the gullies the following winters. Typical of their revolutionary courage in remaking nature was the transformation of the village's longest gully called Langwochang (Wolf's Pad). It was one and a half kilometres long and about seven metres wide with steep gradients. In the winter of 1955, the peasants built 38 stone embankments along the gully and turned it into a flight of terraced fields with tens of thousands of cubic metres of fertile soil, but mountain torrents destroyed the embankments and washed away all the soil and crops the following summer. The peasants were undaunted. They rebuilt the embankments that winter, more solid than before. To guard against mountain torrents, they built a small reservoir in the upper part of the gully. But the embankments were destroyed again during a major summer storm in 1957.

The landlords and rich peasants then seized the opportunity to spread defeatism. "How can man vanquish nature?" they raved.

Chen Yung-kuei, who had worked as a farmhand for the landlords for 20 years in the old society, refuted the nonsense spread by the class enemies. He inspired the masses with the concept that the revolutionary people can change nature so long as they grasp objective laws and give play to their revolutionary drive. He led the poor and lower-middle peasants in conscientiously summing up experience and carefully analysing the reason for their failure. After enthusiastic discussion, the whole village, united as one, was determined to have a third go at Langwochang Gully in order to eliminate floods. They regarded this as a struggle against both nature and the class enemy.

The third battle was even more arduous. In order to reduce the onslaught of mountain floods, more embankments were built in curved rows with deep foundations and big boulders. The crevices were filled with mortar so as to reinforce the embankments. Despite biting winds in the dead of winter Chen Yung-kuei led the Communist Party members and cadres in doing the most difficult jobs. Chia Chin-tsai, an old Communist and poor peasant, went uphill early every morning to quarry, wielding a 19-kilogramme hammer. His hands often bled. Thanks to his efforts, one piece of rock after another, each weighing 300 kilogrammes, was moved.

Inspired by the exemplary deeds of the Communists and poor and lower-middle peasants, the other commune members, including women and school children, plunged into the battle with seething enthusiasm, many of them turning out by whole households. After 27 days of hard work, they completed the project, three days ahead of schedule. They constructed 44 embankments along the gully and collected tens of thousands of cubic metres of earth to build 44 terraced fields. Their work has withstood the tests of storms and mountain floods year after year and has now become the land which gives the highest yields in Tachai.

In the past ten years, they have constructed 228 embankments of various sizes in 250,000 workdays, and linked the 4,700 strips of land into 1,800 plots.

By adding soil, deep-ploughing and applying big amounts of organic fertilizer, they have covered each plot with fertile soil half a metre deep. This helps prevent drought and waterlogging and enables the land to give stable, high yields.

Educating the Peasants in Mao Tsetung Thought

The fundamental experience of Tachai as a national pace-setter in agriculture is that its Party branch always gives first place to educating the peasants in Mao Tsetung Thought. It firmly grasps the revolutionization of people's thinking so that the peasants break with the centuries-old concept of private ownership, develop the communist style of cherishing the state and the collective, and foster the idea of farming for the revolution.

This education by the brigade Party branch has brought up peasants of a new type.

Typical is the change in commune member Chao Hsiao-ho. In the old society, he had tended sheep for a landlord since childhood and was later sold to another county together with the sheep. He returned to Tachai after liberation. When Tachai set up its agricultural co-operative, he joined and has worked with enthusiasm and cherished the collective ever since. He drove a horse cart to the county-seat one day to fetch rolled steel for his team. On his return he found that he had inadvertently taken one extra piece. Should he make another trip to return it? Chao Hsiao-ho said: "The state has plenty of rolled steel. What are one or two pieces to it?" The Party branch took note and guided him in studying Chairman Mao's article "Serve the People". They patiently taught him that while it was important to cherish the collective, it was even more important to cherish the socialist state. Chao Hsiao-ho recognized his erroneous thinking and returned the piece of steel.

Nurtured by Mao Tsetung Thought, Chao Hsiao-ho has become a good commune member dedicated to the public interest. One autumn day when he drove some mules and horses to fetch the newly harvested maize, one mule lost its footing and was about to fall down a cliff. Chao Hsiao-ho risked danger to himself by leaping to the edge of the path to break the fall. The mule was saved but Chao Hsiao-ho was badly injured. After he recovered, he drove a horse cart for the brigade. The other cart drivers usually took a helper along but Chao Hsiao-ho often went alone. He said: "In making revolution you should make all-out efforts. If I'm afraid of hardship and death I won't live up to Chairman Mao's expectations."

The way the Tachai Party branch helped Chao Hsiao-ho shows how it constantly educates people in Mao Tsetung Thought and uses various methods to help people destroy self-interest and foster devotion to the public. It turns ordinary peasants into new socialist peasants who cherish the state and the collective, who always have the motherland in mind and the whole world in view and are conscious that they are farming for the revolution.

Tachai Brigade members have surplus grain but they consciously and deliberately eat buns made of maize with bran. This coarse meal of the poor people in the old society reminds them not to forget the old days or the many poor people in the world who have not yet emancipated themselves.

Young commune member Li Yu-lu paid no attention to economy as he became well off. To educate him and other young people, the Party branch called them to a meeting under a big willow tree where Chen Yung-kuei told them the family history of Li Yu-lu. People called this willow tree the poor man's tree because the landlord used to tie poor men to it and beat them. Li Yu-lu's mother went begging like other poor people in the old society. One day she picked up half an ear of maize on the road. The landlord accused her of stealing it from his field, tied her to this tree and beat her the whole night. She died as a result. Chen Yung-kuei told the young people never to forget the past and that millions of people in the world still live in misery. This was a profound education to Li Yu-lu and the other young people. Li Yu-lu changed a great deal. He has since worked with enthusiasm, lived a plain life and become an activist in the study of Chairman Mao's works.

In Tachai remain a few dilapidated cave dwellings beside rows of new housing, and a small plot of poor soil, which have been deliberately preserved to remind the young people of the old hard days.

Mao Tsetung Thought has helped broaden the minds of the Tachai people. They view everything they do as related to the country's socialist construction and the world revolution.

The Party branch always strives to educate people in Mao Tsetung Thought at key moments of class struggle, in daily life and work and in the face of natural calamities.

The people of Tachai were severely tried in 1963. There was a downpour lasting seven days and nights in August of that year. The ensuing disastrous mountain torrents destroyed more than 100 stone embankments, large tracts of terraced fields, a big part of the crops and 80 per cent of the housing.

As soon as he heard of this Chen Yung-kuei, who was then at a conference in the county town, rushed back to the village. He was distressed when the other brigade cadres informed him of the situation. But his long experience in struggle taught him that no difficulty was unsurmountable because Tachai had the wise leadership of the great leader Chairman Mao and the Communist Party, the strength of the collective and the revolutionary zeal of the poor and lower-middle peasants. He asked calmly: "What happened to the people?"

The commune members replied: "The people are all safe. So are the draught animals. Most of the grain has been rescued."

"We should congratulate ourselves," Chen Yung-kuei said. "If we had such a calamity in the old society, at least 100 people would have lost their lives and the rest would have to go begging elsewhere. Now, in a big disaster like this, not one life was lost, and no one had to leave the village to beg or sell his children. With people, we have everything. Chairman Mao says bad things can be turned into good things. The fields were destroyed; well, then, we'll create better ones. The houses collapsed; alright, we'll put up new ones. Let's build a more beautiful Tachai with our hands!" His words warmed everyone's heart.

The Party branch organized the cadres and peasants to study Chairman Mao's work "The Foolish Old Man Who Removed the Mountains" and his teachings on *self-reliance and hard work* and on *"Bad things can be turned into good things"*. The following question was discussed: Should they rely on state relief to tide over the difficulty caused by the natural calamity or depend on themselves, on the efforts of the collective, to rebuild the village? Which would be more beneficial to both the state and Tachai?

The commune members drew immense strength from Chairman Mao's teachings. Some of them pointed out that although there were difficulties for the time being, there were also favourable factors; for instance, the brigade had reserve grain and accumulation funds. Others said that difficulties have a dual character: They give people some hardships, but they serve to temper their revolutionary will, and this is especially important for young people.

They spent a few evenings in study and discussion, achieving consensus of opinions in the light of Mao Tsetung Thought. They summed up the advantages of self-reliance and put forward this slogan: "We will not accept relief money from the state, nor state relief grain, nor other material aid." The higher authorities had appropriated material and funds and sent a delegation to express sympathy. It asked Tachai to accept relief on four occasions, but each time it got the same answer: "Send it to fraternal brigades, we are able to tide things over on our own."

The brigade members—men and women, old and young—turned out to straighten up the flattened plants one by one. On plots where the crops had been washed away, they sowed vegetables. Then they divided up into several groups to repair the terraced fields, accumulate manure and make bricks. They worked in the fields by day and put up new housing in the evenings by the light of kerosene lamps, all going at it with vim and vigour.

Thanks to their unswerving struggle, they wrested an average per-*mu* grain yield of 740 *jin* from the 560 *mu* left after the flood. The brigade's total grain output, the food grain quota for its members and the grain it delivered to the state that year were no less than the previous year's.

Once the people are armed with Mao Tsetung Thought, their outlook changes and they have immense strength. The people of Tachai repaired all the damaged fields in two years, completing work originally scheduled to take five years, and built the fields to a still higher standard. In four years they fulfilled their ten-year construction plan for new housing. The brigade members now live in stone-lined cave dwellings and brick houses better than the old ones.

Tachai was hit by an extraordinarily heavy hailstorm in 1968 which severely damaged its 700 *mu* of autumn crops. Despite this the commune members wrested another excellent harvest that year.

Tempered by severe natural calamities, the Tachai people have a deeper understanding of the verity of people out to learn from other brigades. They say: "We can never stop on the road of revolution. The struggle to transform one's world outlook is unending. Looking back, we have taken a step forward, and looking forward, our achievements are always only the starting point for continuing the revolution."

MIDSTREAM COMMUNE GOES IN FOR MECHANIZATION

BY WEI CHIU

Midstream Island is a fifteen-square-kilometer island situated in the middle of the Yangtze River alongside Tantu county, Kiangsu province. The rolling waves that pound its shores splash back from a dyke that forms a 9-meter-high, 15-meter-wide (base width) ring around the island. The land is kept farmable by seven pumping stations along the dyke and 26 pumping stands inside, all run by the Midstream People's Commune, which pump out flood or rainwater when needed.

After our ferry landed, we looked down from the top of the dyke upon a busy midsummer harvest scene—humming threshers gobbling up sheaves of wheat and pouring forth the tawny grain, Dongfanghong tractors plowing up fields of stubble in preparation for rice transplanting.

Tractor and Pumping Stations

Descending the dyke, we came to a set of tile-roofed buildings which turned out to be the commune's main pumping station and its tractor station. The tractors were out working; a dozen large Chinese-made threshers stood in the sheds. The harvest was almost over and their task was finished, we learned. At the pumping station we found some mechanics working on seven large diesel engines. Among them was station head Yu Tao-sheng, his hands covered with grease.

A veteran mechanic at 36, Yu showed us around the station. "Our island is only a little over two meters higher than the river," he explained. "River water surging in and rain water accumulating were always a big problem. The commune invested over 100,000 yuan to build this main station, which has a capacity of 408 cubic meters per minute. In July 1969 a two-week downpour caused the worst flood in history. But we ran all the pumps in the commune round the clock for 17 days and saved the crops on our 1,100 hectares of land. We got a bumper harvest that year."

Yu Tao-sheng related how he had come to the island with his father when he was ten, during a famine year. Then the island had been cut up into nine parts by the river, and during a flood it became nothing but a sheet of water. Most years they harvested only a few dozen *jin* of grain from a *mu* of land. After paying rent to the landlord, from a year's backbreaking toil they had hardly enough left for two meals of porridge a day. In winter and spring before the new crop came in, they sometimes had to quiet their hunger with the roots of reeds.

After liberation in 1949, the peasants of Midstream Island decided to get organized as Chairman Mao had urged. After going through the stages of mutual-aid teams and cooperatives, in 1958 the whole island united in a single people's commune with some 2,000 households. With a bigger collective economy, the commune built dykes and water conservation projects and developed farming, forestry, animal husbandry, side occupations, fishery, and its own industry. As production improved the commune has accumulated 2,240,000 yuan, half of which was used for mechanization.

"Of course," said Yu, "we acquired our farm machinery gradually. When the commune was set up we had only one small diesel engine. Then the whole country was hit by three years of natural disasters in a row. We didn't have large pumps to fight the droughts and floods. Learning this, Liu Shao-chi's agents in the locality urged us to go back to individual farming, and to sell our farm and sideline products at high prices on the free market. That way, they said, we could accumulate more funds for machinery. But we knew that with each family working alone, *nobody* would be able to afford machinery. And with each family farming its small plot, even if we bought large machinery we could not use it. 'What are you up to, talking like this?' we said, and held our collective economy together as Chairman Mao advocates. We mechanized through our collective strength.

"Today we have 41 diesel engines used to run pumps, 18 tractors and dozens of other farm machines. Of course these are not enough to meet the needs of all our farm work, but almost all our pumping, plowing, sowing, threshing, transport and grain processing are done by machine."

Local Mechanics

Just getting the machines was not enough, said Yu. They needed people to operate and maintain them. Soon after the commune was formed it sent several groups of young people from poor families, like himself, across the river to training classes run by the county or by the Chenchiang special administrative region. After they returned to the commune they trained one batch of apprentices after another. Now the main pumping station and tractor station have over 70 mechanics. Many of them are adept at repairing a variety of farm machinery. Three to five mechanics have been trained for every production team.

Yu Tao-sheng took us to the tractor station's repair compound. The foundry workers were busy with last-minute preparations for casting pipe for pumps. Amid a shower of sparks two young women welders were making concave plates for threshers. In the machine shop several older workers were teaching young operators how to make parts for tractors.

Yu introduced us to Lo Chang-ken, one of the first group sent to study machinery.

"Those of us in the first group had had very little education," recalled the 39-year-old veteran mechanic. "Not like the young workers now who have all been to middle school. I had only two years of schooling and I didn't know whether or not I could do it. Then I thought of two things, and my mind was made up.

"Before liberation one year there were big floods on Midstream Island. A capitalist from the riverbank came over in a boat with a pump. Before starting to pump he first collected his fee—30 liters of wheat for every *mu*. We scraped together what little grain we had set aside for food and seed to pay him. He stowed the grain in the hold of his boat and slipped away in the middle of the night.

"The second event occurred in 1955 during the time of the co-ops. The state allocated us a pump through the supply and marketing station. None of us knew how to operate machinery, so it stood around for a while in the station and then they reallocated it.

"Before liberation we poor peasants were always being bullied and oppressed by the landlords and capitalists. After liberation we became our own masters, but this still wasn't enough. We realized that the fundamental way out for agriculture is to mechanize on the basis of collectivization, as Chairman Mao told us."

After a decade of going thoroughly into the principles of construction of various types of farm machinery, Lo not only knows how to operate and repair them, but can also do drafting and design. At the moment he was working on widening the cross-slide of an old lathe to enable it to process larger pump parts.

Veterans like Lo and Yu, with help from the younger workers, have made many technical innovations aiding mechanization. By converting 21 old coal-gas engines to diesel engines, they increased the commune's pumping power and saved buying over 60,000 yuan worth of new engines.

Liberates Manpower

Coming out of the repair compound we turned into a straight shady road leading to the offices of the commune revolutionary committee. There Sun Kuo-chu, secretary of the commune Communist Party committee, told us how Midstream Island had benefited from mechanization.

"Getting better harvests every year has meant a corresponding increase in the manpower needed for reaping, transport, threshing and storing. Work is so concentrated over the time of the summer harvest and sowing that we must put in at least 130,000 workdays in a period of about a month. But even if everybody turned out every day for a month, we would still have only 90,000 workdays. Either the harvest or the sowing would suffer. Now we can cut, thresh and put away 670 hectares of wheat in about a week and finish sowing at the same time.

"The commune never used to plant rice because of flood and drought. In the last few years, with pumps for irrigation and drainage, we have been able to grow one or two crops of rice on 670 hectares of wheat land after the harvest. Last year's per-hectare grain production was about double that before the commune was set up and over ten times that before liberation. When we were still in co-ops, every year we had to buy several hundred tons of food grain from the state. Now the commune sells the state an average of 2,400 tons a year. Cotton had never been grown on Midstream Island before, but now we produce almost 500 tons a year.

"Mechanization has freed our manpower. While concentrating on grain and cotton, the commune has been able to use a third of its manpower to plant 1,500,000 trees—pines, cypresses, Chinese toons and sweetgums—and for developing sericulture, pig raising and fish breeding. The value of output of the commune's industries is also growing rapidly. As production increases, the commune members' standard of living is also improving."

At his suggestion we took a turn around the island.

Flourishing Scene

On the same road as the revolutionary committee's offices are the commune's auditorium, department store, restaurant, hostel, bathhouse, post and telegraph office and bank. The latter has become quite important as Midstream Island's peasants, whose incomes doubled since the commune was formed, are saving more. The total has passed 200,000 yuan. A bit farther along are the commune-run shoe factory, tailor shop, farm tool plant and the mill that processes the members' grain, oil crops and fodder.

The hospital and middle school are nearby. The hospital, housed in several simple one-storey buildings, has 40 beds and a staff of 22. Its surgical department can take care of ordinary abdominal operations. All children of school age go to primary school and 95 percent of them go on to middle school.

The commune's well-being is in evidence everywhere —in the dense green rice shoots, the neat rows of village houses, the mulberry gardens growing luxuriantly, the pigs in the sties. The fish farm also raises mussels in a stream and cultivates pearls. Peaches and pears were bending the boughs in the orchard that covers large stretches of land. The commune produces over 80 tons of fruit a year.

Facing the orchard are a commune kindergarten and home of respect for the aged. Nine old people who have no relatives to take care of them live in the clean one-storey houses. Each could tell a tragic tale of how his or her family broke up and died off as a result of floods, famine and landlord exploitation.

The oldest is Mother Huang, 87. Her husband died in 1924 and her son in 1942. She cried her eyes blind, and was only able to keep herself alive by begging. Now all her food and clothing are supplied by the commune and there is someone charged with taking special care of her.

Mother Huang used to shudder at the very mention of rising water. But no more. And when she hears the whirring of the commune's large pump, a look of peace passes over her round face.

3. Industry

China is in the process of an industrial revolution. There are factories going up all over the place. It will be only a matter of time before China becomes a great industrial nation. However, China is approaching her industrialization very cautiously. Capitalist industrialization in the West caused untold suffering by uprooting the rural population and creating the twin monsters of urbanization and pollution. China now has the advantage of learning from the mistakes of capitalist industrialization. Under socialist public ownership, where production is carried out in a planned way to meet the needs of the people, the evils of capitalist industrialization can be consciously avoided.

First of all, China wants to industrialize without urbanization. Instead of moving the people to where the factories are, China brings factories to where the people are. New factories and industrial complexes are being built in the countryside in different parts of the country (again, for social and defense reasons). This is in line with one of the basic socialist commitments to bridge the gap between the city and the countryside.

Second, China pays special attention to environmental protection and pollution control so that industrialization does not bring more harm than good in the long run. All new factories are equipped with pollution control devices. We visited a new petrochemical complex near Peking where waste water from the factories is purified before it is discharged into the river. Scientists were using the purified water to raise goldfish and ducks to make sure it would not harm wildlife. Older factories are in the process of being equipped with pollution control devices. The lack of concern for the environment in the past was blamed on Liu Shao-Cho's revisionist policy of putting emphasis on meeting the production targets instead of the general welfare of the people.

Third, local industries run by the communes are springing up all over the countryside. These are primarily industries for meeting local needs and for utilizing local resources. For example, in Linhsien county where the famous Red Flag Canal is located, industry is developing on the basis of the great increase in farm production after the completion of the canal. With the canal came electricity and with electricity came industrialization. Before liberation, there was not a single factory in the country. Where there was one plant for repairing farm implements, there are now thirty-two country-run factories and mines, turning out iron, coal, cement, farm implements, electric pumps, insecticides, chemical fertilizer, cotton textiles, alcohol, shoes, and other products. We also visited a new factory making light bulbs and fluorescent lamps. The industrial revolution in China, above all, is occurring in the countryside.

Even in the large industrial centers in the cities, life in a factory is quite different from life in a capitalist factory. A factory is not just a place where you go to work but a community in itself. It is democratically run by an elected Revolutionary Committee which has jurisdiction over not only the factory but also workers' residential quarters, factory schools (including nursery school, primary school, high school), stores, hospital, militia, and everything else connected with the workers in the factory. The factories we saw are well landscaped with trees and flowers. We also saw fruit orchards and vegetable gardens on the factory grounds. Factories are encouraged to be as self-sufficient as possible.

With rational planning, there is every reason to believe that China will be able to avoid the pitfalls of industrialization. As an example, it was heartening to learn from Premier Chou En-lai that China has decided against developing private cars as the major means of transportation; instead they will stick to the bicycle— "It is good for your body and it doesn't pollute the air," as Chou put it.

K.H.F.
K.T.F.

THE WORKERS ARE THE MASTERS*

One hundred and two years ago in 1871, the proletarian poet Pottier wrote in *The Internationale:* *"We have been naught, we shall be all!"*

We found this lofty aim of the proletariat being realized in Shanghai, China's biggest industrial centre.

We were there just before May 1, International Labour Day. Interviewing workers and members of the leading body in a number of factories, we heard similar accounts of past want and privation, now gone for ever; of the dreaded shadow of unemployment, also a thing of the past; and of today's new life, spoken of in glowing terms.

Just what is the position of the workers today in the factories? "We are the masters in our own factory," was how it was often put to us. Facts substantiate it in terms of the system of ownership, leadership and management.

The Shanghai Watch Factory is one illustration.

Two Figures: 18 and 2,500,000

The very existence of this big modern factory is a tribute to the labour, ingenuity and struggle of the working class. In the spotlessly clean watch assembling workshop, worker-technician Wang Chia-teh related the story of the "Shanghai" wrist-watches' birth.

Shanghai before liberation was an international watch exposition with watches galore—every make and description from many countries. Not one, ironically enough, was made in China.

After liberation the demand soared as the working people began buying them. Fifty-eight craftsmen from 26 clock-making or watch repair shops were formed

* From *Peking Review,* No. 26, June 29, 1973.

into a team by the government to make China's first watches in 1955. With no blueprints to go by and only the most old-fashioned gear for making clocks and minor watch parts, they were sustained by an overriding desire to manufacture, for the first time, watches for their own country.

Wang Chia-teh was one of the 58. Recalling those days, he took us back to the narrow-walled repair shop where, stripped to the waist in the sultry heat of a Shanghai summer, he bent over to put the delicate mechanisms together. It was 72 hours later when he held up the first finished product with loving care. By October 1, New China's sixth birthday, Wang and his colleagues had a present ready—a first lot of 18 watches. One of these, incidentally, we saw on display in the factory reception room. Compared to the automatic calendar watches and other men's and women's watches the factory now makes, this first-born was not much to look at. Yet recalling the sweat and hopes that went into its labour pangs, we looked at it with great affection.

Of the 18 watches resulting from those initial endeavours, some developed the strange quirk of running smoothly on the table but stopping as soon as they were put on. The workers were undismayed. The first step had been taken, and they were sure to go on from there.

Preparatory to setting up the Shanghai Watch Factory, a working group went into operation the following year under the auspices of the municipal industrial department. The workshop was first housed in a run-down store, 50 metres square. Later they moved into an old apartment building (they did not get to the present site until 1960). The government allocated some equipment and personnel. After two years of trial-production, they got their final blueprints and technological process. Small-scale production then began.

The first "Shanghai" wrist-watches reached the market on July 1, 1958, the anniversary of the Party's founding. Wang and his mates, too excited to stay in bed, were up at the crack of dawn and strolled out into the streets. They were surprised to see groups of people waiting outside the shops to buy the new products, about which the papers had published news. Overwhelmed by this proof of the people's enthusiasm for Chinese-made watches, they promised themselves that they would, under the leadership of the Party and the state, help build a large watch factory.

They kept that promise. Output that first year, 1958, was 13,000; by 1972, the figure was 2.5 million. Quality was up to standard and customers flocked to buy them. The factory's staff had swelled to 3,650.

No Easy Road

The road was not an easy one. Behind those figures is a story of sharp struggle between the socialist and the capitalist lines. Vice-secretary Kung Chien-ping of the Party committee, the factory's leading organ, told us something about it.

There was a sharp clash of opinion on how the factory should develop when it was first set up in 1958. There were those who argued that big imports of machinery and equipment from abroad and setting up costly workshops and installations were imperative for operations requiring such precision. They submitted a plan—a sluggard's plan as it turned out—which set three years for designing, five for trial-production and ten for full production.

The whole thing smacked strongly of the influence of the revisionist line in running industry advocated by Liu Shao-chi and his followers. Most of the workers, on the other hand, had but one idea and one plan: There must be a "big leap." Throughout the country the year of the Big Leap had started, inspired by the general line formulated by Chairman Mao of *"going all out, aiming high and achieving greater, faster, better and more economical results in building socialism."* The erroneous line was thwarted. The factory went into production that very year. The next year, 1959, saw 74,-000 "Shanghai" watches being sold over shop counters.

The third year of the plant's infancy, 1960, was another year of trial. China's national economy was in temporary difficulties due to serious natural disasters and betrayal by the Soviet revisionist leading clique which withdrew all Soviet specialists and experts. Liu Shao-chi and his clique were clamouring for a drastic cut-down in industry, for retrogression, as it were, and "It'd better be a big one," they demanded. Could the watch factory survive? It not only did just that but made another leap: Production went up to 450,000 that year. This was the way the workers gave their answer.

Interference by Liu Shao-chi's revisionist line, however, had its effects in the next five years, 1961-65, and hampered the workers' initiative. Production still rose, but the rate was slow and the one-million mark remained beyond reach.

One of the effects of the erroneous line was that the factory leadership established an overly large administrative set-up and made many irrational rules and regulations. If a worker wanted to introduce an innovation, he had to go through a lot of red tape: five okays were needed before he could start—from the technicians in charge of the technological process in his own workshop and at the factory level, from his workshop head, from the head of the technical section and, finally, from the chief engineer. The machinery was graded: the few imported lathes, Class A, could only be repaired by technicians at the factory level; Chinese-made lathes, Class B, could only be repaired by workshop technicians; and only workers' self-made equipment, Class C, could be repaired by the workers. Once when a worker changed a screw on a new modern lathe, he was called upon by an irate technical department to make a self-criticism.

The Great Proletarian Cultural Revolution beginning in 1966 was a fierce blow to the revisionist line. The factory, too, thoroughly criticized its influences. The productive forces emancipated by the revolution greatly boosted output and improved quality.

Vice-secretary Kung said: "The energy and resourcefulness of the workers are inexhaustible. Do you know that our workers not only run the machines, they design and make some themselves? They've made about a third of our equipment. Actually, 88 per cent of our equipment is made in China. Our machines are pretty complicated. The smallest lathe is 30 cm. long and 10 cm. high, whereas the biggest is as tall as a two-storey building. Watch accessories are generally measured by 'the width of a silk thread'—one-hundredth of a millimetre. What does all this boil down to? It boils down to the fact that great things can be done so long as we follow Chairman Mao's instruction to *'whole-heartedly rely on the working class.'*"

Ownership by the Whole People

That the workers are "masters in their own factories" is borne out, first of all, by the fact that all the means of production in the watch factory, as in all large factories and plants in China, are owned by the socialist state. This form of ownership is ownership by the whole people, a form of public ownership in which the state under the proletarian dictatorship represents the proletariat and all other labouring people in owning the means of production and the products.

Lu Yung-chang, another vice-secretary of the Party committee, reeled off some basic facts. The factory buildings, equipment and installations as well as funds all belong to the state. The buildings, for instance, used to belong to one of Shanghai's many cigarette packing plants. As labour productivity went up, a greater quantity of cigarettes was being produced by each packing plant. In 1960, the government decided to stop one of the bigger plants and turn the buildings over to the watch factory. The cigarette packers did not lose their jobs—they were transferred to the watch factory, where they were helped to learn the ropes.

The watch factory is directly under the Shanghai Municipal Clock and Watch Company, which is in charge of all city factories making clocks and watches and their accessories, such as the jewels. Like similar companies in other lines, the Clock and Watch Company is under the industrial department of the municipal people's government (now the Shanghai Municipal Revolutionary Committee).

As a state enterprise, all watch factory activities are included in the state plan. Its annual production plan is drawn up after full discussion by the workers in the light of the needs of the state plan for developing the national economy. The state allocates all major raw and other materials. All products are sold by state commercial departments. Even the leading comrades of the factory itself, vice-secretary Lu informed us, have to buy their "Shanghai" watches in a shop, as the factory cannot sell any.

What about profits? Lu said with quiet humour: "Oh, yes, we make quite a lot—but the profit is essentially different from that of a capitalist enterprise. Every cent belongs to the state. The state treasury gets it all."

By increasing production, practising economy and reducing production costs, he said, the factory gets a sizable profit each year. This money, of course, is used by the state to expand socialist construction and raise the people's living standards.

Profits are certainly not the lever of production, Comrade Lu assured us. Though the automatic calendar watches, for example, are relatively high-priced and bring in greater profit, the factory does not produce many of them but largely makes ordinary watches considering the present purchasing power of the majority of the labouring people.

With wages gradually rising, 36 per cent of the watch factory workers took home bulkier pay envelopes last year. Welfare services are increasing. The money does not come from the profits, as the watch factory has no right to dispose of them on its own. These material betterments are by and large the same in all lines and come as a result of the state's unified plan for gradually raising the people's living standards on the basis of expanding production.

Naturally, no extra income or other benefits go to the leading personnel however much the profits. Pointing to an old sedan on the grounds, vice-secretary Lu told us: "That's a factory car, and it's mainly for the workers, in case of sudden illness or other emergencies. Sometimes we use it when meetings are called outside. We'll be criticized by the worker comrades for not being thrifty if we tend to use it more than necessary. We thank them heartily for such reminders, as *'building up our country through diligence and frugality'* is a policy laid down by Chairman Mao, and following it to the letter is a matter of great importance."

THE MASSES INNOVATE*

"Launch vigorous mass movements." "Go full steam ahead with the technical innovations and technical revolution." These directives of Chairman Mao form one of the basic principles for developing China's socialist industry. In the Shanghai factories we visited around May 1, International Labour Day, we witnessed some of the achievements brought about by the burgeoning mass movement for making technical innovations.

At the huge Shanghai No. 5 Steel Plant we saw a young woman worker at the controls of an overhead

* From *Peking Review*, No. 29, July 20, 1973.

travelling crane charging an electric furnace. We were told that until last year this crane which now handles a 30-ton load had a maximum load of only 20 tons. Improvements were made to keep in step with furnace capacity which had been enlarged from 12 to 18 tons.

"What equipment and accessories did you have to buy to do that?"

"None. We made all the changes ourselves," a worker told us. "Bigger charges, higher outputs."

In another workshop we were shown an automatic vacuum furnace for making various types of high-grade rolled steel. Its main components were also products of the mass technical innovation movement, designed and made by the workers and technicians themselves.

An integrated-circuit electronic digital computer in Futan University's mathematics department played *The East Is Red* and wrote out in English "Welcome, Welcome" as a greeting. Of course, this was nothing for a machine that does over 100,000 calculations per second. The computer was made by workers of a door handle factory in co-operation with a group of mathematicians.

At the Shanghai Watch Factory we were told that 13,000 watches were turned out in 1958 when the factory was set up. By 1972 it was making 2,500,000. Again technical innovations by the masses played a big part in expanding production and improving quality.

At the Shanghai Boiler Plant we saw a few old-fashioned pulley machine tools working side by side with modern ones. The clumsy, noisy machine tools of yesterday and the quiet efficient new machines made a sharp contrast, underlining the innovative power of the masses. Most of the new machines had been designed and made by the workers and technicians of the plant themselves, not bought from a machine tool factory.

The fruits of mass technical innovations were evident everywhere we went.

Bicycles and Zippers

Let's look at two very common articles—bicycles and zippers.

The popular "Fenghuang" (Phoenix) bicycle, with its trade mark of the fabled bird in gold, is the product of the 3,200-member Shanghai No. 3 Bicycle Factory which rose up from very humdrum origins. In its No. 4 workshop we saw an automatic painting line, one of the technical innovations introduced in the factory last year.

At one end we saw two middle-aged women workers fastening dull black frames, mudguards and parts to a conveyor and 90 minutes later, at the other end 170 metres away, glossy finished products which had been dipped into various chemical baths to remove rust and dirt and given three coats of paint being wheeled away by two husky young men.

Bicycle frames in this factory were not painted this way in the past. Shop director Chien Jung-chu told us that when the factory was set up in 1958 the frames were laboriously "laundered." He said that frames and parts were hand-dipped into tubs of chemicals and tubs of paint, a dirty, tiring and very inefficient process. Later, spraying was introduced. But this was no great improvement. Then in the early sixties workers introduced some mechanization, using cranes to dip batches of frames and parts. Operators had to go back and forth so that at the end of a day's work they had probably covered as much as seven kilometres. Loading and unloading were heavy work and smelly fumes made working in high summer temperatures almost unbearable.

Many improvements were introduced until an automatic painting line appeared last year. Whereas 16 hours were needed to coat a frame, it now takes 90 minutes and the work is lighter, more efficient and much more pleasant and healthier. One technician pointed out in passing that the automatic line employs a rather advanced technology to get a better finish.

This line was designed entirely by the shop's veteran workers and technicians and most of the equipment were made in the workshop. People were taken off production to design, make and install the equipment without interrupting normal production. Volunteer labour after working hours dug the foundations, did other earth-moving work and installed the line. The birth of the line was celebrated with drums and gongs on July 1, the Party's 51st birthday last year.

This automatic line is only one of some 12,000 big and small technical innovations adopted over the past 15 years, Kuo Sung-ting, the factory's Party committee secretary and revolutionary committee chairman, told us. Annual output rose nearly 12-fold without adding very many workers, and instead of only a single model the factory now turns out over 20 models of four types of bicycles.

The "Fenghuang" is one of the best bicycles China makes and has a ready market at home and abroad.

"No more teeth and finger work," was what people said when we were shown around the Huakuang Slide Fastener Factory.

The factory has 444 workers and staff, mostly women. One of the leading members of this small factory is the 38-year-old woman comrade and deputy secretary of the factory's Party general branch Yang Chin-fang who met us in her tiny office. From a drawer she took out a half-metre-long oblong length of metal jig weighing about three kilogrammes to show us how she had made zippers before liberation when she was an 11-year-old child labourer. There was a double row of teeth down the middle of the jig, one end of which she pressed against the table and the other against her chest. From the pile of tiny "teeth" on the table she picked a tooth up with pincers and fitted it on to the jig. If any teeth did not fit properly she used her own teeth to crush it into shape. This was what used to be known as "laying out teeth" and was the major operation in making zippers. After all the spaces had been fitted with teeth, the jig was taken to a bench and hammered to fix the teeth on to a cloth tab.

After liberation this workshop and other privately-owned industrial and commercial enterprises were gradually changed into socialist state enterprises. The workers' production enthusiasm shot up and competitions were held to earn the honour of being a "100-footer heroine," a designation for a worker who made 100 foot-long fasteners in an eight-hour day.

Only the most skilled working very hard managed to do this. When the big leap in socialist construction began in 1958, workers started making technical innovations and centred their efforts on solving this problem. A machine was built in 1959 to do this work and later during the Great Proletarian Cultural Revolution further technical innovations were introduced which more than doubled the speed of the process, from 1,400 r.p.m. to 2,800-3,200 r.p.m.

In the workshop we saw row upon row of these not very large machines drawing in the cloth tabs at one end and spewing out a continuous ribbon of zippers. There was one woman operator to every four machines and most had not been at it for very long.

"What's the footage for a skilled worker now?"

Comrade Yang smiled. "Not footage, but metres now," she corrected. "Each operator on an average turns out 4,400-4,600 metres in an eight-hour shift. Figuring a metre as roughly three feet, that makes all the operators skilled hands turning out more than 10,-000 feet of fasteners a day."

Technical innovations, large and small, were evident throughout the production process, from making teeth, polishing, cutting the zippers into lengths to quality checks. Though production has leapt, the number of workers has remained virtually unchanged. Annual output has shot up and some of the products are being sold abroad.

"The Innovator"

What was the force behind this extensive movement for technical innovations making for the continuous increase of productive forces? The answer is: Revolution.

Comrade Kuo Sung-ting, the Party committee secretary, offered some illustrations. Prior to liberation he was a worker in China's oldest bicycle factory, the Tungchang, started by a capitalist named Chu in 1897. Tungchang first sold only imported vehicles; it wasn't until later that it began to "manufacture" bicycles. Actually it merely assembled bicycles as nearly all the parts, from the frames to the rivets for fastening the trade mark, were imported. In 1948, shortly before liberation, the factory was turning out the grand total of 350 bicycles a year. In its day it was considered China's leading bicycle firm. Those were the days when the workers starved and were oppressed and it was impossible to develop a national industry using advanced technology as foreign imports pushed domestic products out of the market.

A leading comrade in one of the factory's workshops said he had been an apprentice in a small private workshop which had a small lathe. His job was to provide the power for the lathe by pedalling more than ten hours a day.

"I longed for electricity in those days as I pedalled and panted, but at the same time I dreaded its introduction since that would put me out of a job."

The working class became the leading class when the revolution triumphed and Shanghai was liberated. Living conditions gradually improved and labour enthusiasm soared. The workers began making technical innovations to improve working conditions and raise productivity. The privately-owned enterprises were gradually converted into socialist enterprises. In 1958 the industrial department of the Shanghai Municipal People's Government organized the Tungchang and 266 other small private workshops and shops (including individual street corner bicycle repairers) into the present state-owned Shanghai No. 3 Bicycle Factory on International Labour Day.

Socialist revolution freed the forces of production. As in the rest of the country, there was a great leap in the bicycle factory. As Chairman Mao said: *"Never before have the masses of the people been so inspired, so militant and so daring as at present."* The technical innovation tide rose.

Kuo introduced us to Comrade Ku Ho-lin. Known to his comrades as their factory's "innovator," he heads the technical team. He was sent by the factory to study at Peking's Tsinghua University a few years ago.

With only a year's schooling before liberation, Comrade Ku started work at 15 as an apprentice in a small privately-owned workshop. His three-year apprenticeship meant working more than ten hours a day without pay. All he got was his food. On top of his long hours he had to run errands, do the washing and cooking and housework in the boss' home and got kicked, cursed and beaten. In a fit of rage, the boss once threw boiling water at him. Comrade Ku's foot still carries the scars.

The workers' status changed with liberation. Ideologically, Comrade Ku's response was strong, especially when some leading comrades of the Shanghai Municipal Party Committee convened a meeting of workers to discuss technical innovations and he was invited to attend. "In the old society we workers were treated like dirt," he said at the meeting. "The Communist Party treats us workers as treasures. From the bottom of my heart

I want to do as much as possible for the Party, for the building of socialism."

He threw himself heart and soul into the technical innovation movement. In 1959, the second year of the factory's existence, he came up with an innovation that boosted his team's labour efficiency 19-fold. The Party committee of the factory called on all the workers to learn from him. In subsequent years he went ahead with his work, completing more than a hundred innovations in co-operation with his team-mates.

Even in the short time we spent at the factory we heard many stories about Comrade Ku. He frequently stayed behind after work to experiment, neglecting rest and meals at times. Preparing meals at home, he would sometimes knead models out of dough, or when washing up he would carve a prototype from soap. One time when he saw something wrong with a bicycle made in his factory in the street he stopped the cyclist. He gave the vehicle a thorough check and told the rider what was wrong before the latter went on his way. Comrade Ku's enthusiasm for innovations has earned him the nickname "the innovator."

Of course, technical innovations were not made solely as a result of overtime and sheer hard work. Comrade Ku went through a long and arduous study course. He had learnt draughting in a workers' technical class as well as taking on other subjects to increase his knowledge in his off-hours.

Far beyond one-man technical innovation efforts, his main contribution is in getting colleagues to join in. For example, when the factory was set up some conservative workers were ready to wait for new machinery from the state despite the call of the Party organization to go in for technical innovations.

Comrade Ku said: "The People's Liberation Army, with only millet plus rifles, beat hell out of Chiang Kai-shek's eight million U.S.-armed troops. We workers can surely transform the old equipment." After he was popularly accepted by the factory as an innovator, he said to comrades: "Just as one bit can't turn out an axle, one pair of hands can't build socialism. What can I do by myself? We all have to join in." His way of looking at things, his speech and actions moved many more workers to join him in making technical innovations.

SMALL VILLAGE BECOMES AN IRON AND STEEL BASE*

It was late New Year's Eve when we stepped onto the platform of the No. 9 blast furnace of the Ma-anshan Iron and Steel Company's No. 1 Smelting Plant. The last heat of 1972 was pouring out of the taphole, a fire-dragon racing through the trough into waiting ladle cars.

The telephone in the furnace office rang. Group leader Chao Chin-cheng picked it up and shouted in a hoarse voice, "Yes . . . No. 9. . . . Yes, our iron has been tapped."

It was one hour before midnight. The new shift watched the dancing flames in the furnace. Everyone was waiting for the first heat of 1973. Operator Tang Shao-yi used this time to tell me about the great changes that had taken place at Ma-anshan.

Once a Small Village

Ma-anshan city cannot be found on the maps of old China. It was only a small village of a few dozen families on the east bank of the Yangtze River in Anhwei province. When liberation came, the ruins of a few small blast furnaces left from the days of the Japanese invasion stood in solitude outside the village. The area was rich in iron ore. In 1953, the beginning of China's First Five-Year Plan, the people's government began to

---

* From *China Reconstructs,* April 1973.

build a small iron and steel base here. By the fall of 1958, the first small mines and blast furnaces had been built, including the one which later became the big No. 9 furnace.

"On the afternoon of September 20 that year," Tang said, "Chairman Mao came to visit us!" He pointed to the furnace ladder. "Chairman Mao climbed that ladder to the platform, shook hands with all of us, walked to the front, bent down and looked into the furnace through blue goggles. He asked us how much pig iron we could produce per day and with a smile calculated with us how much we could put out in a year."

To the leading staff members who were taking him around, Chairman Mao said, *"Conditions in Ma-anshan are very favorable. It can be developed as a medium-sized integrated iron and steel enterprise, because such an enterprise takes less time to develop."*

A great leap forward in China's economy came in 1958. The situation was excellent and on this basis Chairman Mao formulated the Party's general line: "Go all out, aim high, and achieve greater, faster, better and more economical results in building socialism."

As part of the unified national plan of the people's government, thousands of workers, engineers, peasants and staff people poured into Ma-anshan from all parts of China. In a little over a year, mines, mills and shops had mushroomed along the Yangtze River. When Chairman Mao came again a year later, Ma-anshan was already shaping up as an iron and steel base.

In the fourteen years since then, Ma-anshan has steadily rebuilt and expanded into a medium-sized iron and steel complex. The once almost-deserted village has become a steel city of over 200,000 people.

At the stroke of midnight, the No. 9 furnace began to spout the first heat of iron of 1973. As sparks leaped in all directions, the sweating workers warmly exchanged New Year's greetings with us.

On New Year's Day, the workers of Ma-anshan proudly announced that in 1972 they had surpassed all their iron ore, pig iron, steel and rolled steel targets. Steel was 14.47 percent higher, rolled steel was up 21 percent. Quality had improved and cost gone down.

What lies behind Ma-anshan's rapid development? During our visit, our eyes and ears told us that everyone —and their wives—had fought to apply the General Line for Socialist Construction. Initiative and creativity flourished. Taking Taching, the nation's oil center, as their model for building a socialist industry, they relied on themselves and their own hard work to solve all problems and overcome all obstacles.

Party leaders and revolutionary committees were often seen in the mines and shops studying concrete problems, working side-by-side with the men and listening attentively to their suggestions for faster, more efficient methods. When a new plant or mine was to be built or equipment improved, they set up "command headquarters" on the spot, mobilized and organized everyone and, as if going into battle, concentrated all energies to win.

The Battle to Open Mines

Beginning in 1969, mines were expanded and larger ones opened in the hills around Ma-anshan. Each one was conducted as a mass movement. Leaders, staff members, engineers and miners reviewed the difficulties and mistakes they had encountered in opening past mines.

A dozen small mines had been built by 1959. Then came three difficult years for China caused by bad weather and poor crops. Revisionist Liu Shao-chi and his followers took advantage of this to sabotage China's developing iron and steel industry and cut down the number of mines. In Ma-anshan this brought on a shortage of ore and sharply reduced iron and steel output. The bitter lesson was: open mines, push steel production upward, then open new mines, produce more steel, and so on. The men went ahead with new enthusiasm and energy.

The Nanshan mine was to be Ma-anshan's biggest. But the ore was deep at Tungshan, one of its three open cuts, and great quantities of earth had to be excavated to reach it. If the excavation was to be done fast so that mining could start, a long railroad had to be built quickly to haul out the earth.

Mine leaders assigned the job to a construction department and gave them three months to do it.

"Three months is too long!" the workers said. "To get at the ore quicker, we'll do it in half a month." Miners, staff members, engineers—and hundreds of wives and students—came to help cut the hills open, build roads, prepare the roadbed and lay ballast. The railroad was completed in twelve days, three days ahead of their promised half-month.

The Kushan mine, another Ma-anshan ore base, was covered with shifting sand dozens of meters deep. Ore could be removed only if the sand could be controlled—a tough problem which had prevented mining at Kushan for years. But the battle to open new iron mines had to be won. Using high head pumps, the workers lowered the water table in two years. This stabilized the sand and allowed large-scale exploitation to begin.

While the mass movement was opening mines rapidly, mechanization increased greatly. When we climbed to the largest Aoshan open-cut mine at Nanshan, we saw automatic drilling machines boring holes for explosives. Nearby, giant excavators were biting into the ore and dropping it into the cars of a waiting electric train. Women engineers hauled it straight to the dressing plant where the cars automatically dumped it into a pit. Mechanical devices then processed the rough ore into fine-quality powder.

The battle to open mines increased iron-ore production to five times that of 1966, made Ma-anshan self-sufficient in ore and doubled its output of iron and greatly increased that for steel.

Working for Technical Change

The rapid increase in production made new demands on Ma-anshan's equipment and technology. Always working on the basis of existing equipment and skills, the workers, staff members and engineers continually searched out latent potentialities. Unless absolutely necessary, they never asked the government for new equipment but found ways to improve old equipment and adopt new techniques. In this process, many technical innovators appeared.

One of the best known is Shih Ke-chi, a 40-year-old Communist, formerly a blast furnace inclined hoist operator, now the vice-superintendent of the mechanical power department of the No. 1 Steel Mill.

Before the cultural revolution, Shih and his co-workers had automated the hoist, one of the two major operations for charging the blast furnace. In 1968 he and other workers formed a technical innovation group to improve the other operation for charging—the loading and weighing of the scale car.

At night in the ice and cold of early 1969, light often came from the windows of a small room next to one of the blast furnaces. Shih Ke-chi and his group were reviewing their experience, analyzing their repeated failures and patiently carrying on new experiments and piling up data. Plant leaders often came to encourage them, and got other workers to look for materials and put up equipment for them.

In April they finally succeeded in making the operation of the scale car automatic. Then they worked out a unified electronic control system for the whole series of operations, making the charging of a medium-sized blast furnace fully automatic.

There are two open-hearth furnaces at the No. 1 Steel Mill. Ordinarily the molten steel flows through two spouts into two ladles. But here we saw three ladles. Why? Workers told us that two years ago a group of workers, leaders and engineers had been formed to handle problems of expansion. They increased the furnace's capacity by one-third but created a new problem—now the two ladles would not hold all the steel tapped. It was too difficult to make bigger ladles.

Finally the group hit on the idea of designing a special movable spout, easily connected with the old spouts, which would carry the surplus steel into a third ladle. The leaders approved the idea, and workers and the group built one in five days. No. 2 furnace followed suit.

These innovations were not exceptions at Ma-anshan. The company's converters, blooming and rolling mills, coking and sintering equipment, have constantly been improved and enlarged. In only three months, for example, No. 2 Steel Mill workers rebuilt their two Bessemers into top-blown oxygen converters, cutting down steel-making time and improving quality.

In the mass movement for technical innovations, younger workers did their part too, learning from veteran workers and mastering their skills through practice. Nearly all the young men and women workers in the machine repair department have gone to the department's night school to raise their political and technical levels. They invited old master workmen to teach them production skills and engineers to teach them technological theories. They took part in demonstrations of forging, riveting, welding and other skills. Under the guidance of veteran workers, they often exchange experience. In the past year, these young workers have put forward a hundred suggestions for technical transformation and carried out eighty smaller innovations.

Housewives Step Out

Ma-anshan's constant development of the mass movement method is reflected in a steady growth in the number of workers. Wives, too—by the thousands—have stepped out of their homes to add to the ranks. Nurseries, kindergartens and other institutions ran by the city, mills and mines have helped create conditions for freeing them from household chores.

We visited the Lunghushan mica and iron-oxide dressing plant of the Nanshan mine run by the miners' wives. Sun Chih-lan, head of the plant, told us that they had gone into production only last year. Mine leaders had sent two veteran workers to teach them how to separate micaschist from magnetite. In spite of the dilapidated buildings and machines converted from antiquated equipment, last year they sorted out 100 tons of mica, essential for making a corrosion-preventing lacquer, and 4,000 tons of magnetite.

Sun Chih-lan is also a leader in the wives' committee at the Nanshan mine. She told us that there are 1,200 wives living around the mine. Six years ago only 70 had taken on production jobs. Today the number has jumped to almost 800. Following their committee's overall plan, the wives have built ten small shops and make welding rods, parts for electric locomotives and cement railroad sleepers for the mines. They have supplied 310 types of spare parts in the last few years.

Wives have organized groups to grow vegetables and grain for the mines. They have set up nine nurseries. They have started service trades such as barbershops, tailorshops and shoe-repair shops.

Asked why the women took up work with such zest, Sun Chih-lan answered promptly, "We have two hands like anyone else. Why shouldn't we build socialism, too?"

4. Commerce and Finance

WHY PRICES ARE STABLE IN CHINA*

Life under the Kuomintang reactionaries before liberation in 1949 was a nightmare for the people. Inflation and skyrocketing prices made it impossible for them to make both ends meet. On pay-day, people could see crowds of workers' dependents waiting at the factory gates for their bread-winners to bring out the wages so that they could hurry off to buy grain. Otherwise, the slender pay would be worth much less that very day. Ordinary commodities were sold at the incredible prices of tens of thousands and even millions of "gold yuan" (reactionary Kuomintang government's currency). In the 12 years from July 1937 to May 1949 the Kuomintang government inflated its currency 140,000 million times and prices rose 8,500,000 million times. These astronomical figures were not fictitious but real in the old China.

After the founding of New China, the Party and the state promptly took steps to check the runaway prices. Beginning from March 1950 commodity prices in our country not only stopped rising but began to drop, and food-grain prices also began to be stabilized. Over the years, prices throughout the country have remained stable.

In Chinsha city, Kweichow Province, there is an old man named Chiao Kuei-chai who, from 1908 onward, had made a daily entry in a ledger of the continually rising price of grain. His ledger for the year 1948 showed the price of rice as follows: January, for one *tou* of rice, 112,000 yuan; March, 230,000 yuan; Au-

* From *Peking Review,* No. 40, October 6, 1972.

gust, 4,000,000 yuan. But after 1950, he felt there was no longer the need to make entries and so he gave the ledger to the People's Government. Now this ledger with more than 40 years of records of grain prices is kept in the Museum of Chinese Revolutionary History in Peking.

Prices of grain, cotton, edible oil, coal, table salt and other commodities have remained stable since liberation, and the prices of industrial products in daily use such as radio sets, plastic articles and enamelware have steadily dropped, while several big price-cuts have been made for medicines and medical equipment which are closely connected with people's health. The prices of medicines today are on the average only some 20 per cent those of 1950. An ampoule of penicillin, for instance, used to cost the equivalent of 50 *jin* of wheat flour at the time of liberation, but today costs only the equivalent of one *jin* of flour. The prices of some major agricultural means of production like chemical fertilizers, insecticides and diesel oil have also dropped by one-third to two-thirds compared with 1950.

The state has on many occasions raised purchasing prices for farm produce and subsidiary products so as to promote agricultural production and increase the peasants' incomes. Compared with 1950, purchasing prices for major agricultural and side-line products have increased 90 per cent. For example, the average purchasing price for 100 *jin* of six major food-grains was raised from 5.55 yuan in 1950 to 10.82 yuan (both in Renminbi) in 1971; for pigs, from 26.85 yuan per 100 *jin* in 1950 to 48.50 yuan in 1971. Selling prices, however, remain basically unchanged. The disparity, and management and handling costs are paid by the state so that the workers and urban dwellers' daily life is not affected.

The "scissors" differential between industrial and agricultural products left over from history has thus been greatly reduced through cutting the selling prices of industrial goods and raising the purchasing prices for farm produce. Parity rate in 1950 for industrial and agricultural products was reduced by more than 40 per cent in 1971. Before liberation peasants in some areas had to pay several dozen *jin* of grain for one *jin* of salt, and three or four eggs for one *liang* of kerosene for lighting lamps. Today, one *jin* of salt costs the equivalent of a little more than one *jin* of grain, and one egg can be exchanged for two *liang* of kerosene.

With increased incomes and no worries about prices going up, the people now put their spare money in the bank. Compared with 1952, total 1971 urban deposits increased 8-fold and rural deposits 101-fold.

Why is it possible to maintain price stability over such a long period? The basic guarantee for this is that, under the leadership of the Party and Chairman Mao, the Chinese people have overthrown imperialism, feudalism and bureaucrat-capitalism and set up their own state power. Guided by Chairman Mao's revolutionary line, China's socialist revolution and construction have won one victory after another. Specifically, the main reasons are as follows:

A Planned Economy

In China there is no capitalist competition or a state of anarchy in production. The national economy is developed in a planned and proportionate way. National industrial and agricultural production and the purchase and distribution of their main products all come within a unified state plan. Social purchasing power and the potential supply of commodities can be computed. The selling and the fixing and adjustment of prices of commodities are all carried out according to the state plan and not determined spontaneously by the law of value, as is the case in the capitalist society. Occasionally, owing to some unforeseen reasons, some imbalances between various economic departments and between supply and demand may occur, but these can be adjusted through planning and do not lead to fluctuations in prices.

Continuous Growth of Industrial and Farm Production

Stability of prices is impossible without an expanding production and a daily growing supply of products for the market.

Agriculture is the foundation of our national economy. Thanks to increased farm production after liberation, we have been able to grow more than enough food-grain although we have a large population. Bumper harvests have been reaped over the past ten years in succession. Total grain output in 1971 reached 492,000 million *jin,* over 270,000 million *jin* more than in the early post-liberation years. The peasants provide the state with an ever-increasing quantity of marketable grain to meet the requirements of industrial production and of the inhabitants in the cities. In old China, the peasants lived on chaff and vegetables for half the year, but now the state, people's communes and the peasants all have grain reserves which are constantly being augmented. At the same time, forestry, animal husbandry, side-line occupations and fishery have also made great strides, so that the quantity of non-staples such as meat, eggs and egg products, fish, poultry, vegetables and fruit supplied to the market is several times or over a dozen times larger than that before liberation.

On the basis of expanding farm production, light and heavy industries, too, have developed substantially. In old China even ordinary daily consumer goods such as kerosene and matches were wholly or partially imported from abroad. Since liberation China has built a relatively independent and complete modern industrial system.

In 1971 the output of cotton yarn, cotton cloth, paper, sugar, salt, cigarettes, leather, bulbs and other main consumer goods was several to dozens of times larger than that of 1949.

The continuous growth of industrial and agricultural production has provided the material basis for a flourishing market and long-term price stability in our country.

No Inflation

Each year the state appropriates vast sums of money for building factories and mines, expanding industrial and agricultural production, developing culture, education and health services, and improving the livelihood of the people. In addition, there are outlays for national defence, administration and other expenditures. Ninety per cent of the state revenue is derived from internal accumulations by state-owned enterprises and the other 10 per cent from the collective sector of the economy and other sources. Increases in revenue depend on increasing the socialist production, and not on increasing the taxes, incurring internal or external debts, or on printing and issuing paper money indiscriminately. The principle of balancing income and expenditure is strictly adhered to. There has been no deficit in our country's revenue and expenditure over a long period; instead, we have a small favourable balance.

Our country's Renminbi has remained stable over a long period and its prestige on the international market is growing steadily. As regards foreign trade and assistance to foreign nations, a number of countries and regions having intercourse with China has turned from using currency of other countries to using Renminbi in settling accounts. Issuance of currency in China is based on the requirements of national economic development and any increase in its circulation is proportionate to the increase of commodities in circulation. This has eliminated inflation and the resultant price fluctuations.

China has consistently upheld the policy of maintaining independence and keeping the initiative in our own hands and relying on our own efforts. We do not rely on internal debts, still less foreign debts. Immediately after the founding of the People's Republic of China, government bonds were issued for the purpose of rehabilitating the national economy. About the same time, especially during the War to Resist U.S. Aggression and Aid Korea (1950-53), we contracted some foreign debts. But these debts, internal or foreign, were all paid back in full many years ago. China is now a country without internal or external debts. Commotions on the international market and capitalist currency fluctuations do not affect us.

Socialist Commerce Prevails

Not long after the founding of New China, the Party and Government took firm measures to restrict and stamp out speculations by the capitalists. In 1956 the socialist transformation of capitalist industry and commerce was basically completed and a unified, socialist domestic market was formed. Socialist commerce controls all the major commodities on the market, regulates market conditions under a unified plan, exercises strict control over prices, sets rational price differences for different areas, for commodities of different quality and variety and for different seasons, conscientiously implements the policy of stabilizing prices and other economic policies, and continually strengthens its leadership and management with regard to rural fairs[1] while

[1] Rural fairs are country fairs where people's communes and individual peasants exchange products and help supply each other's wants. They are necessary complements of the state com-

restricting the growth of spontaneous capitalist forces.

As the national economy develops and the interflow of commodities progressively grows, purchases and sales by the commercial departments as well as their goods in stock register an all-round increase. Total volume of retail sales of commodities in 1971 was six times that of 1949. A nationwide commercial network has been set up in urban and rural areas to buy, distribute and supply commodities according to the state plan, thereby guaranteeing fulfilment of the needs of production and people's consumption.

The general policy *"To develop the economy and ensure supplies"* formulated by Chairman Mao for economic and financial work has been adhered to by the commercial departments. The task of commercial enterprises is to serve production and meet the needs of the people, and not purely for making profits. In China the prices of many commodities, especially those essential to production and the people's livelihood, are governed by the principle of securing only a small profit or merely paying for production costs. In the case of many commodities, such as grain, edible oil, meat, sugar and tea the prices are on the whole the same throughout the year. Prices of other commodities like medicines and chemical fertilizers are the same everywhere in the country. Some items' prices such as table salt and kerosene are no higher than the ceiling price even in the remote frontier regions. Transport costs over long distances from the source of supply to the consumers, margins and management costs are all defrayed by the state.

Practices by merchants in the old society and capitalist countries, such as buy cheap and sell dear, hoarding and procuring huge profits, are incompatible with China's socialist commerce.

---

mercial enterprises and supply and marketing co-ops; together they make up a unified socialist market.

MARKETS LIVELY IN CITY
AND COUNTRYSIDE*

While prices remain stable, the market in both city and countryside in China is livelier than ever as a result of the vigorous development of China's socialist industry and agriculture. Purchasing power increased and total sales of commodities in 1971 were 7.8 percent over 1970.

Good Supply

The supply of grain is sufficient so that everyone is guaranteed enough to eat, and a wide variety of non-staple foods is available in abundance. A continuous stream of meat, eggs, fruit and aquatic products flows into the cities. Consumption of meat and eggs has increased in the countryside. A good supply and wide variety of vegetables is available in the cities. In Peking consumption of vegetables averages 190 kilograms per capita annually. There are usually 30 to 50 varieties. Live fish and fresh vegetables are sold right through the winter. Fruit, tobacco, wines and liquors, tea and local and special products are widely available throughout the country.

The purchase of things like candies and cakes is now widespread among the working people, with sales continually rising. This is a sharp contrast to the past, when, before the liberation, working people rarely could buy such things. Before liberation the Harbin Food Shop on Huaihai Road in Shanghai never sold more than 15 or 20 kg. of these items a day, even in the busy season. Now over 500 kg. are sold in one night.

Textiles of all kinds are available in a wide variety of colors and designs, and quality is steadily improving.

* From *China Reconstructs*, April 1972.

During the first half of 1971, over 3,500 new colors and varieties were added to the Shanghai Bureau of Textile Industry's list of goods produced. There has been a substantial increase in sales of cotton and woolen textiles, synthetic fabrics, and satins and silks. In Tientsin sales of silk comforter covers and cotton sheets and towels were two to three times those in 1970, and the same was true for heavy fleece underwear and headkerchiefs.

The number of people in both town and countryside who bought bicycles, watches, radios and sewing machines in 1971 was well above that for the previous year. There was a good supply of aluminum, enamelware and plastic household utensils. Large city department stores generally stock 20,000 different items.

The year 1971 saw the supply of chemical fertilizer 13 percent over the previous year's, and a great increase in insecticides and power pumps for agriculture. In Shantung province in the first eight months of the year, over twice as many power pumps were sent to the countryside as during the same period of the previous year, while the amount of insecticide rose by over 90 percent. The rapid development of China's oil production has resulted in a sizable increase in kerosene for home use in the countryside and other petroleum products for use in agricultural production.

Prices Are Stable

The People's Republic of China has carried out policies aimed to keep prices stable ever since its founding in 1949. Prices for things needed in daily life have been stable for a long time. As production has developed, there have been repeated price cuts on some types of industrial goods. In 1969 the prices of medical supplies were reduced by 37 percent. The price of medicines is now only 20 percent of what it was in 1950. Prices of transistor radios were cut by a big margin in 1970.

Further cuts in prices of chemical fertilizer, insecticides, kerosene, diesel oil and lubricants were made in 1971.

At the same time the state has repeatedly raised prices paid to the producers for various kinds of farm and sideline products. The average purchase price for the main farm and sideline products has risen 90 percent in the past 20 years. Nineteen seventy-one saw another rise in prices paid for oil-bearing crops, sugarcane and some of the raw materials for Chinese medicine. Increased payments to producers in 1971 and savings as a result of price cuts augmented rural and urban purchasing power by ¥1,000,000,000.

The income of the agricultural producers, the rural commune members, has been greatly raised without increasing the burden on the consumers in the cities. Increased prices to the grain producer and the stabilization of prices to the consumer facilitate this. In addition, the state subsidizes the cost of shipping and storage of grain, and losses commercial units may take if they must sell under cost are subsidized by the state and not deducted from the price paid to the producer. This is only possible through unified socialist planning.

In the old society, one of the ways the landlords and profiteers exploited the peasants was to buy grain at low prices after the harvest and sell it at high prices when the peasants' granaries were empty, before the new crop was ripe. The debt for even a few bushels of grain in order to exist till harvest caused many families to lose everything they had, or even forced them to sell one of their children to keep the rest alive. In 1953 the state put an end to such seasonal variations in the price of grain. Both purchase price and price to the consumer remain the same the year round.

The purchase price of grain is also uniform throughout each province, municipality or autonomous region. This policy particularly benefits the mountain areas and remote regions which, because of distance, transport and other factors, in the past had to sell their grain at much lower prices. Also, despite the added cost of transport, things like medical supplies and books and periodicals sell at the same price all through the country. For other industrial goods, the regional difference in prices is much less than it was before the liberation.

Then peasants in some remote mountain regions had to trade up to 100 kg. of grain for 1 kg. of salt, and three eggs exchanged for less than 50 grams of kerosene. Now the price of a kilogram of salt is only a little more than that of a kilogram of grain and one egg exchanges for 100 grams of kerosene.

Commercial Units Aid Production

"Develop the economy and ensure supplies" is the general policy set by Chairman Mao for economic and financial work. In line with it, the workers in socialist China's commercial units are bringing a greater variety of commodities onto the market not only through their efforts at buying and selling but through their support to industrial and agricultural production. They do everything possible to guarantee the supply of materials for industry and agriculture regardless of whether they make or lose money.

Suggestions from representatives of commercial units often enable commune and team production plans to gear rationally with the local conditions for production and the national plan. Commercial workers also see that supplies of capital and consumer goods arrive when they are needed. In many areas commercial personnel help the communes and brigades repair farm tools and machinery, distribute improved varieties of seed, conduct experiments on fertilizers and insecticides that can be made with home methods, popularize advanced production techniques and help prevent and treat plant diseases and insect pests.

Commercial units are often the "eyes and ears" of the industrial departments, reporting to them the state of the market and customers' suggestions and needs. They also help industry solve problems of raw materials, technology and equipment. In some regions of the northwest and southwest where the base for light industry is relatively weak, commercial units help the industrial departments solve problems of materials and organize technological exchange. This has promoted the establishment of a number of light industries in these regions within a very short time, and has raised the quality of items for daily use and the degree of local self-sufficiency in them.

Now commercial units are also contributing to society through aiding in the repair of old, discarded items, and in the comprehensive utilization of raw materials. In 1971 Shanghai commercial units collected 388,000 tons of scrap iron for its industry, 48,000 tons of raw material for making paper and 160,000 tons of waste acids.

For better service to the workers and peasants, 24-hour stores and before-and-after-hours shops have been opened at docks, railroad stations and at busy corners in the cities. In the countryside and grasslands, in the past, peasants and herdsmen often had to walk a long way in order to buy things or sell their agricultural and sideline products. Additional stores, supply and marketing stations and mobile units enable them to do their buying and selling right near home.

A COUNTY BANK*

After nationwide liberation, the people's state power confiscated the bureaucrat-capitalists' banks and gradually transformed the small private banks to set up a unified socialist state bank—the People's Bank of China. Its offices are all over the country, with branches in every province, municipality, region and county, and

* From *Peking Review*, No. 22, 1973.

agencies and sub-agencies or saving centres in factories, mines and townships.

The branch bank in Fangshan County, on the south-western outskirts of Peking, is one of thousands of branches of the People's Bank.

We visited this county bank and from its business activities got a general idea of a socialist state bank and its role in the national economy.

This branch is not a small one, and is located on a rather quiet street in the county town of Fangshan. Neither tall nor imposing, the building does not have barred windows or the other open displays of money and power as was the case with banks in the old society. The main business office is in a large room in a one-storey building; an old-fashioned one-storey house at the back serves as the administration office and staff living quarters.

Li Hsin-lien, chairman of the revolutionary commit-tee of this branch, told us 240 people work in the bank and its 16 agencies and sub-agencies and 7 saving cen-tres, serving the county's 203 government offices, mass organizations, factories, mines and other enterprises and 31 people's communes with a total population of 560,000.

Pawnshops Before Liberation

Extreme poverty reigned in this county before libera-tion. There were two pawnshops and a few shops deal-ing in grain and groceries; they loaned money at usuri-ous interest to the working people who, exploited by landlords and capitalists, found it difficult to make ends meet. With nowhere else to go to get credit they turned to the pawnshops. In time of emergency, they pawned what clothing or other property they had for a loan.

Whatever they got from those dealers in human mis-ery was well under half the real value, and interest rates on a loan were outrageous. If what they pawned was not redeemed in the period of time set, their articles no longer belonged to them.

The family of Hou Chun-po who works in the Fangshan bank was no stranger to exploitation by usury and the pawnshops. When his father was sick in 1943, the family had no money for medical treatment. The mother tried everything possible to get a loan, at exorbitant interest. Unable to raise enough money this way, she pawned the only new garment she owned.

When her husband died she did not have the money to redeem the garment. Even worse, she was unable to pay back the money she had borrowed at high interest. The result was that Hou Chun-po's elder brother had to pay off the debt by going to work for the usurer. Because of the excessive interest, the amount of money that had been borrowed doubled in a year and so the family was still in debt right up to the time of liberation.

Fangshan was liberated in November 1948 and a people's bank set up the following year. Usury and pawnshops were done away with and the heavy burden on the Hou family was finally lifted. Hou Chun-po himself joined the bank later and is now vice-chairman of the revolutionary committee of its Choukoutien agency. Quite a number of people now working in the Fangshan branch had experiences similar to Hou's.

The working people of Fangshan County went in and out of the pawnshops in the old days to get a loan on their meagre possessions, today they walk heads high to the bank where they keep their savings. Although their lives have improved tremendously they still live frugally and put money they have saved in the bank to help accumulate funds for state socialist construction. About six kilometres from Fangshan township, Choukou village before liberation had 70 of its 300 households trying to find a living elsewhere. Today 70 per cent of the peasant households there have money in the bank. At the end of 1972 money deposits for the whole county were 26 times the amount in 1952.

This averages 18 yuan per person. Though small, the figure shows a world of difference from the working people's old days of starvation and want.

What the County Bank Does

The socialist state bank has many important functions. Li Hsin-lien showed us the office where more than 20 people were busy behind a long counter doing business with people from factories, villages and offices. Wooden signs on the counter read: "Industrial Credits," "Agricultural Credits," "Clearance," "Remittances," and so on.

Li said: "All our activities are centred on developing the national economy and getting greater, faster, better and more economical results in building socialism."

The bank's activities are wide-ranging and can be divided roughly into three main categories: credits, clearance and cash.

"Briefly," Li said, "by using capital and cash currency, the state bank stimulates industrial and agricultural production and the flow of commodities to make them better suited to the development of the national economy in a planned and proportionate way."

He continued: "The great revolutionary teachers Marx and Engels pointed out in the *Manifesto of the Communist Party* that after the proletariat has seized power *'centralization of credit in the hands of the state'* must be carried out through a state bank. China's socialist bank is the national credit centre, which means all loans must be made through this bank. No other departments are allowed to make loans or borrow among themselves.

"In old China all activities by the banks were done for profit, with the banks competing among themselves. Several self-styled 'national banks' were actually large banks manipulated by the reactionary Kuomintang chieftains, the four big families of Chiang, Soong, Kung

and Chen. They used the banks to fleece the people
on a huge scale. In those years of wild inflation and
soaring prices, the commercial capitalists and
bureaucrat-compradors hoarded and speculated with
the banks serving as centres for these nefarious practices.

"The banks were nationalized after the victory of the
Chinese people's revolution and things are very different today. Closely co-ordinated with industrial and agricultural production and commercial activities, the bank
determines who gets loans and how much, according
to the requirements of the national economic development plan. For example, funds are allocated each year
to the bank at Fangshan by the people's bank of Peking
municipality. All industrial, commercial, agricultural
and other units (these units are state or collectively
owned) within the county must apply to the bank or
its agencies and sub-agencies if they need loans. The
bank will, according to their state-set production plan,
work out and decide the amount each applicant needs
for production. All loans must be repaid within a set
time, plus a small amount of interest."

Comrade Chang who is in charge of industrial credits
explained how a loan is made. He talked about credit
for a certain oil refinery. According to the production
task set for the refinery by the state, the bank worked
out the quantity of fuel, raw materials, machinery and
spare parts required, and together with the refinery
fixed the amount of money required. The work of the
man issuing the loan was to go to the plant, get information about its production and sales of products and
help it do its economic accounting well and raise man-
agerial standards so that fulfilment of state production
plans is guaranteed and the plant is also aided to produce more goods with the minimum amount of money.

Chang gave us another example. A plant in Fangshan
making and repairing electric generators was given the
job in 1972 of making two large steam turbines. The
man from the bank's credit department went to the

plant and found there was not enough production equipment and funds. He saw to it that urgently needed funds were sent to the plant; on the other hand, he suggested and worked with the plant in clearing out its warehouse of idle machinery and materials which were sent to factories needing them more urgently. This solved the requirements of other factories and also helped the plant solve part of the question of funds needed for production, thereby reducing the amount it had to ask from the state. Last year this plant finished the two turbines ahead of time and met the state loan.

Speaking of the bank's second task, Li went on to explain the bank's function as a clearance centre, that is, all transactions of commodities and transfer of non-commodity funds by industrial and commercial enterprises, offices and mass organizations in China must be cleared through the People's Bank of China. The state bank through its several thousand branches all over the country has set up a clearance web. All factories, mines and other enterprises, offices and so on have an account in their nearest bank. Transfer of all materials and buying and selling of commodities are cleared through the bank. Even the tiniest sub-agencies in remote parts of the country can carry out transactions with other branches anywhere in the country.

For example, the Liuliho Cement Factory 15 kilometres outside Fangshan township sells its products to 14 provinces and cities. The bank's Liuliho agency sends bills for goods to the buyers' banks which, after checking with their clients, remit in good time payment to the Liuliho agency.

This way of doing things cuts down the volume of cash in circulation (otherwise each county would be called on to handle hundreds of millions of yuan a day) and speeds up turnover of funds. For example, the agency in Liuliho receives several hundred thousand yuan each day for the cement plant, thus guaranteeing the normal circulation of the plant's funds.

Because the state has clearly set down the production

quota and output value for each factory and because the bank is fully cognizant of the state plan and income and expenditure of any particular factory within the area, the bank can make suggestions or criticisms about usage of funds and see to it that the factory fulfils the state plan. This is one of the tasks given the bank by the state.

"Another very important function of the bank is that it is the national centre of cash activities," Li continued with his explanation of the bank's third task. Those who lived in the old society remember the Kuomintang government's wanton issuance of paper money which caused inflation and big currency devaluations and sky-rocketing prices. On top of this, the capitalists speculated, hoarded and wreaked havoc on the market. After liberation, the People's Government energetically developed production and simultaneously adopted a series of important economic measures, one of which was controlling cash. The state prescribed that cash in hand of all offices, mass organizations, army units and commercial and industrial enterprises must not exceed a fixed amount and that all temporarily idle cash must be banked. Apart from those made on a small scale, no transactions between them can be made with cash. These and other economic activities between them must be done through the bank. In this way, the state can adjust the circulation of cash in a planned way, economize on cash outlay, prevent commercial activities outside the plan and guarantee market supply and financial stability.

It was almost closing time and the bank was busier than ever as people from many nearby shops came to do business. A clerk from the foodstuffs shop, a cashier from the daily necessities shop and a worker from the grain store with work-clothes covered with flour, were there to deposit the cash for the sales that day. Li said that under socialism the aim of the bank and the enterprises was identical. The former keeps a watchful eye on production and makes things convenient for the masses while the enterprises and the masses look upon the bank as their own. People who have dealings with the bank every day consider it their "general accountant" or "general bookkeeper."

Rural Agency

As agriculture is the foundation of the national economy, the county banks all stress helping farm production. They play an active role in consolidating and developing the socialist collective economy of the rural people's communes.

To suppress usury and promote agricultural cooperation, the banks set up many credit co-operatives in the countryside in the early period after liberation. This is a form of collectively-owned mutual-aid organization among the masses as the funds come from the savings of the collective and the individual peasants. When the collective or individuals have any difficulty in production or in livelihood, they can borrow from these credit co-ops which are under the leadership of the state bank and supported by it. The credit co-ops are still an important force in developing rural financial work by the bank and in consolidating and developing the socialist collective economy. When the credit co-ops do not have enough funds, the bank lends them money at a very low interest rate. Surplus fund is transferred to the state bank which gives the credit co-ops a higher rate of interest than the credit co-ops demand for their loans. Of the 404 production brigades in Fangshan County, 401 have credit co-ops of which 70 per cent are self-sustaining in funds and have banked a sizable sum.

When we called at the Choukoutien agency we saw Hou Chun-po. He told us that in addition to banking activities its attention is centred on aiding agriculture. Following Chairman Mao's instruction that *"in the financial and economic field, the Party and government personnel at the county and district levels should devote nine-tenths of their energy to helping the peasants increase production,"* the agency issues loans to help peasants increase agricultural production and sends people to the villages to give specific help to production brigades and teams to implement the policy of "taking grain as the key link and ensuring an all-round development," improve production management, develop a many-sided economy, do a good job of economic accounting, cut down production costs and make the maximum use of limited funds.

The agency found that the Waching Brigade, one of 24 in the two communes within the area of the agency's activities, had relatively low grain yields and was not doing very well by way of side-lines and that it had had to borrow from the bank yearly. It had run up a debt of 110,000 yuan. Hou Chun-po and another comrade in charge of agricultural credits felt that giving it priority in loans every year was not the best method to help it. Rather, they should help this brigade learn from the Tachai Brigade, the national pacesetter in agriculture, emulate Tachai's spirit of self-reliance and hard work. They went to the Waching Brigade and together with the cadres and masses discussed ways of setting the brigade on its own feet. They helped to finance the brigade and its members in raising pigs, which greatly increased the sources of manure and the income of the collective and the individual members. As there was plenty of quartz rock in a hill near the village which had never been fully made use of before, the agency helped the brigade financially and in other ways to set up a workshop to process the quartz into sand which each year gave the brigade a return of more than 300,-000 yuan.

With the money earned from side-lines over the past three years, this brigade gradually repaid its debt and bought a tractor, thresher, winnower and other machines. The increase in machinery and manure brought a sharp rise in grain production.

5. Ecology

ECONOMIC DEVELOPMENT AND ENVIRONMENTAL PROTECTION*

BY FANG HSIN

The increasing amount of harmful industrial waste liquid, gas and residue in capitalist countries has resulted in serious pollution and damage to the environment, thus posing a threat to the health of the people. The question of economic development and environmental protection, therefore, has aroused widespread concern. With socialist construction surging ahead in China, it is important that we rely on the superiority of the socialist system to protect and continually improve our environment at the same time as we speedily develop our economy.

(I)

Man utilizes natural resources to create wealth through labour and develop the economy. In this process, he constantly transforms nature and improves the environment. But because of man's limited cognitive ability and knowledge of science and technology, economic development often brings harmful influences to the environment and hence to humanity. In explaining such influences, Engels cited the example of reclamation. In Mesopotamia, Greece and Asia Minor, people destroyed large tracts of forests to obtain cultivable land. They never dreamt that they were bringing, in succeeding ages, devastation to these areas by

* From *Peking Review*, No. 29, 1973.

removing, along with the forests, the collection centres and reservoirs of moisture. In the same way, the Italians in the Alps cut down the fir forests on the slopes, having no idea that by doing this they were striking at the roots of the dairy industry in their region; still less did they have any inkling they were thereby depriving their mountain springs of water, making it possible for these to pour still more furious floods on the plains during the rainy season.

There are, however, profound social causes for the serious pollution and destruction of the environment in capitalist societies. There, making money is of primary importance. Engels pointed out: *"As individual capitalists are engaged in production and exchange for the sake of the immediate profit, only the nearest, most immediate results can be taken into account in the first place."* Speaking of the malpractices of the Spanish planters, Engels penetratingly exposed the crime of the bourgeoisie in destroying the natural environment in order to get profits. Spanish planters burnt down whole forests on Cuba's mountain slopes in order to obtain sufficient fertilizer from the ashes for one generation of very highly profitable coffee trees. As a result, heavy tropical rainfalls afterwards washed away the unprotected top soil, leaving only bare rock.

Such uninhibited plunder of natural resources and destruction of environment increased along with the development of capitalist industry. In the mid-18th century, the industrial revolution took place; while the invention and popularity of the steam-engine released great productive forces previously unknown by society, it also gave rise to grave environmental pollution. Engels pointed out: *"The first requirement of the steam-engine, and a main requirement of almost all branches of production in modern industry, is relatively pure water. But the factory town transforms all water into stinking manure. However much therefore urban concentration is a basic condition of capitalist production, each individual industrial capitalist is constantly striving to get away from the large towns necessarily created by this concentration, and to transfer his plant to the countryside."* New pollution ensued, as Engels said, because *"modern capitalist industry is constantly bringing new large towns into being there by constant flight from the towns into the country."* This is the insuperable "vicious cycle" of capitalist society.

Monopoly-capitalists lust for maximum profits in capitalist countries today, and this results in even greater anarchy in production. Factories discharge industrial wastes and natural resources are exploited at will; cities develop even more abnormally and the environment suffers even worse pollution and harm, and the health of the masses of the labouring people is seriously endangered. All these facts, past and present, point to the conclusion that the pollution and destruction of the environment in these countries is a social phenomenon of capitalism and a manifestation of the sharpening contradiction between the private ownership of the means of production and the social character of production.

(II)

The socialist system is the most advanced social system in the history of mankind. Under socialism, public ownership of the means of production replaces private ownership and planned economy replaces anarchy in production. Industrial and agricultural production is arranged rationally; the abnormal development of the cities and urban concentration of population are avoided, so that urban construction is carried out in a planned and rational way and the masses can be mobilized and relied upon to protect the environment. In a word, the socialist system provides favourable conditions for protecting and improving the environment while swiftly expanding the economy. This does not mean, however, that the question of environmental protection does not exist under socialist conditions. On the contrary, we must pay great attention to it while developing the socialist economy.

China is a socialist country which *"proceeds in all cases from the interests of the people."* The basic object of developing the socialist economy is the people's welfare. An important principle in such development, therefore, is to protect the environment and eliminate industrial wastes. This is also the bounden duty of socialist enterprises. Otherwise, pollution and destruction of the environment will be harmful to the health of the workers and staff members and the people in general, and this will go against Chairman Mao's revolutionary line and the fundamental object of socialist economic development.

Economic development gives rise to the problem of environmental protection which, in turn, is an indispensable condition for carrying on normal production and developing the economy. If we allow the environment to be polluted and destroyed through lack of protection, it will endanger the people's health and the development of the socialist economy. Harmful industrial waste gas and liquid invading the farms hamper the growth of the crops, reduce yields or kill them altogether. Harmful waste liquid flowing into the rivers, lakes and seas endangers the growth of fish and other aquatic life and even causes them to die in large numbers. Industrial residue, if it is allowed to accumulate, will take up large tracts of land and farms, and if it is discharged into the rivers, will cause them to silt up and hampers navigation. Harmful waste liquid corrodes ships, pollutes water sources and spoils the water for residential or industrial use, thereby affecting the quality of industrial products. Besides, industrial waste gas corrodes workshops, pipes and other facilities.

Whether from the point of view of the object of socialist economic development or from the needs of developing the socialist economy itself, environmental protection is important and indispensable. Marxism holds that a problem should be observed from the relation between things and their development. Environmental protection must be carried out in order to develop the economy faster. Conversely, if environmental protection is neglected in the course of economic development, the people's health will be threatened and the economy will not be able to develop well. Experience has shown that pollution of the environment is rapid whereas its elimination takes a longer time. We must, therefore, lose no time in strengthening prevention work while seriously undertaking elimination of pollution. This will benefit our people and our future generations.

Chairman Mao has taught us: *"Marxist philosophy holds that the law of the unity of opposites is the fundamental law of the universe. This law operates universally, whether in the natural world, in human society, or in man's thinking. Between the opposites in a contradiction there is at once unity and struggle, and it is this that impels things to move and change."* Like all other things, the contradictions between economic development and environmental protection are constant and absolute and their unity is temporary and relative. Economic progress will give rise to new problems in environmental protection, and new problems in this field will arise and call for solution after the old ones have been solved. This is the dialectical relationship between economic development and environmental protection. We must have a correct understanding of it. Under the socialist system the ability to protect and improve the environment is decided, to a considerable extent, by the economic and technical level. Only when the economy develops at a faster pace can this ability be raised more rapidly. Therefore, we can only solve the problem of environmental protection by developing the economy, and not seek a good environment by slowing down economic development or by other negative methods.

(III)

Chairman Mao has pointed out: *"Socialism has freed not only the labouring people and the means of production from the old society, but also the vast realm of nature which could not be made use of in the old society."* To develop multi-purpose use under socialist conditions is an important means for both developing the economy and protecting and improving the environment.

Environmental pollution in modern times is mainly created by industrial waste gas, liquid and residue. In the absolute sense, however, there is no such thing as "waste." There are unused materials in the world but there are no materials which cannot be used. What is "waste" under a certain condition can be turned into a useful thing under another condition; what is "harmful" under a certain condition can be turned into a "beneficial" thing under another condition. The Chinese Government is embarking on, in a planned way, work to prevent and eliminate environmental pollution caused by industrial waste gas, liquid and residue. Some achievements in this respect have been made. For example, piled high and unused, the slag of an iron alloy plant used to be a harmful thing. By adopting multi-purpose use in the past few years, it has been turned into many products. This not only gets rid of the harmful effects of the slag, but provides industry with an excellent abrasion-resistant and corrosion-resistant material.

Multi-purpose use is also the inevitable road for concentrating on production in breadth and depth and developing industry with greater, faster, better and more economical results. Guided by Chairman Mao's revolutionary line and crossing the boundaries of trades, many enterprises in China are making big efforts in multi-purpose use. While maintaining one field as their main activity, they develop in a diversified manner. Instead of using resources once, for a single purpose and at a primary level, they make use of them many times, for a wider purpose and at a higher level. Thus, they tap a new and tremendous source of raw materials for socialist construction and open a new and broad field for economic development. For instance, substantial results were obtained by multi-purpose use in 1971 alone. Peking made use of more than 1.5 million tons of different kinds of solid waste. Shanghai extracted more than 6,500 tons of some 20 precious and rare metals from industrial waste residues, and recovered over a million tons of dyestuffs, waste acid, caustic soda, oil and fat and fertilizers from industrial waste liquids.

Mankind's ability to know and protect natural environment grows continuously with economic and scientific progress. History proves that many things, once regarded as waste, have become valuable today. Things which cannot be used today may become useful tomorrow. In the 19th century people produced soda from salt and sulphuric acid. The large amount of hydrochloric acid formed in the process of production was regarded as poisonous water and its disposal created pollution. Later this poisonous water became a basic raw material in the chemical industry.

At the turn of this century people used coal to develop the iron and steel industry, and tar produced in making coke was regarded as a waste. But it was later discovered that this is an important raw material for making dyestuffs, pharmaceuticals, synthetic rubber, synthetic fibre and synthetic plastics. In the course of our industrial development today, many things are disposed of as waste because we do not fully know them yet. Sometimes they create pollution and bring on arduous tasks in environmental protection. But we are fully convinced that with the development of production and science, these harmful things will certainly be turned into valuable things.

It is necessary to point out that to prevent any harmful effects we must seriously deal with industrial waste gas, liquid and residue which are very harmful and cannot be recovered and used for the time being because of technical and economic limitations. But in the people's interests, this is very necessary even if it calls for certain expenditures.

Chairman Mao has taught us: *"In the fields of the struggle for production and scientific experiment, mankind makes constant progress and nature undergoes constant change; they never remain at the same level. Therefore, man has constantly to sum up experience and go on discovering, inventing, creating and advancing. Ideas of stagnation, pessimism, inertia and complacency are all wrong."* Guided by Chairman Mao's revolutionary line and with the superior socialist system and hundreds of millions of industrious and ingenious working people, we will certainly create a society with a highly developed economy and a beautiful environment as long as we take the struggle between the two lines as the key link, carry out overall planning and rational geographical distribution and go in for multipurpose use to turn the harmful into the useful.

TURNING THE HARMFUL INTO THE BENEFICIAL*

BY CHI WEI

Every day large quantities of the "three wastes"— waste gas, liquid and residue—stream forth from industrial production. In capitalist countries, because the capitalists seek high profits and production is in a state of anarchy, these "wastes," which pollute the air and

* From *Peking Review*, No. 4, 1972.

poison the rivers, pose an increasingly serious menace to the people's health. This has become an insoluble social problem in the capitalist world.

"How is pollution dealt with in China"? Some foreign friends who have seen the effects of pollution are very concerned about this question.

In our country, the "three wastes" have done little harm to the people. This is because in a socialist country like ours which is *"proceeding in all cases from the interests of the people,"* we can rely on the superiority of the socialist system to take various measures to prevent pollution harming the people.

As early as 1956, Chairman Mao put forward the principle of developing multi-purpose use. To carry out this principle is not only the fundamental way of preventing the "three wastes" from becoming harmful in the course of developing industry, but it will promote the development of the national economy. During the Great Proletarian Cultural Revolution, we criticized Liu Shao-chi's counter-revolutionary revisionist line and the erroneous ideas resulting from the influence of the line which obstructed multi-purpose use. In recent years, a mass movement for multi-purpose use was launched on the industrial front. Relying on centralized Party leadership and the creative spirit of the masses, many cities and enterprises have gone in for large-scale multi-purpose use, eliminated the harmful and made effective use of the beneficial. From the "three wastes" they have recovered and extracted large quantities of raw materials for and products of metallurgical, chemical, light industry, textile and building departments. This has not only helped increase production but has improved urban and suburban sanitation and protected the people's health.

In the People's Interests

The aim of socialist industrial production is not profits but the prosperity of the country and the people's happiness. The capitalist practice of only seeking profit while ignoring the harm done to the people by the "three wastes" is alien to socialism.

We consider preventing the "three wastes" from harming the people and turning the harmful into the beneficial as an indispensable factor in industrial construction, from city planning, arranging and selecting factory sites to technological processes. A new industrial enterprise is not allowed to go into production if it lacks necessary measures to deal with the "three wastes" properly. Old enterprises which have not yet solved the problem of the "three wastes" are actively working on it.

Waste water containing phenol from the General Chemical Plant of the Anshan Iron and Steel Company, which is an old enterprise, used to damage crops and aquatic products and endanger people's health. Is it necessary to remove phenol from waste water? The masses of the workers and poor and lower-middle peasants said it was absolutely necessary and pledged to do so. The capitalist roaders said that they could not do it because it was a losing business.

During the Great Cultural Revolution, the plant's revolutionary committee organized all its staff members and workers to study Chairman Mao's teachings and mercilessly criticize the revisionist line, including trash like "making great efforts to do what is most profitable, less efforts to do what is less profitable and no efforts to do what is unprofitable" and "putting profits in command," advertised by Liu Shao-chi. They saw the question of whether or not to remove phenol as a question of "for whom?" which is a matter of principle, and one of whether or not they want to support agriculture and consolidate the worker-peasant alliance. After reaching unity in their thinking and pooling their collective wisdom and strength, they quickly made a device for removing phenol from waste water, thus turning the harmful into the beneficial.

Socialist enterprises are different from capitalist enterprises. The nature of the former determines that they cannot take into account the economic aspect only without considering the political aspect, or the interests of their own units without considering the needs of the whole. In carrying out multi-purpose use, workers in the Anhwei General Textile Printing and Dyeing Mill, after criticizing the erroneous views which regarded handling waste water as an extra burden and unprofitable, arrived at a clear understanding that socialist national economy is an integrated whole. Whether something is profitable or without profit must be judged from the interests of the whole. Something which may not be profitable for an enterprise can be profitable to the whole. In the revolutionary spirit of doing anything of benefit to the people, the workers worked in concert with commune members and agricultural college teachers and students to turn poisonous material into fertilizing silt by oxidating and dissolving microorganisms. After repeated experiments, they successfully carried out biochemical treatment of waste water from the printing and dyeing mill.

Utilizing Resources to the Greatest Extent

Apart from eliminating pollution, multi-purpose use is an important economic policy in China's socialist construction. The big efforts going into it will make it possible to utilize all resources to the fullest. The principle of multi-purpose use is applied in designing and building new factories as well as in the technical transformation of old factories. While mainly making one product, factories develop a diversified economy.

Multi-purpose use in China's largest industrial city Shanghai developed rapidly under the leadership of the revolutionary committees at various levels and a unified plan as well as by freely mobilizing the masses. Since there are many industrial districts in the city and factories in some districts are relatively concentrated, the city first concentrated efforts on the Peihsinching, Wusung, Taopu and Nanhsiang industrial districts where the "three wastes" were comparatively more. At the same time, it organized co-ordination between factories to speed up the battle against the "three wastes." The Shanghai Resin Factory and Liaoyuan Chemical Works and 27 other factories in the Peihsinching District jointly raised more than 200 suggestions on utilizing wastes. Up to now over 90 suggestions have been put to use and more than 200 tons of raw and other materials recovered. In producing chloromethyl methyl ether, the Shanghai Resin Factory needed a large amount of sulphuric acid and hydrochloric acid. Co-operating with the Liaoyuan Chemical Works, the resin factory now uses a certain kind of waste gas from the chemical works to produce chloromethyl methyl ether. As a result, not only is the waste gas used, but this saves more than 4,000 tons of sulphuric acid and hydrochloric acid for the state.

From practice people understand that multi-purpose use can be developed in a big way. Last year, the city's industrial departments got 1.4 million tons of different chemical materials out of waste liquid, the percentage of industrial residue used reached 70 and 20 to 30 kinds of valuable and rare metals were obtained from the "three wastes."

By relying on their own efforts and local methods and working hard for 40 days, the Hungchi Paper Mill in Hangchow's suburbs built a workshop producing 200 tons of ammonium humate a day by utilizing the waste liquid from paper making. Ammonium humate not only can be used as a fertilizer but as an insecticide which benefits nearby farmland.

After studying Chairman Mao's philosophical works, the masses of workers, peasants and soldiers have increased their knowledge, broadened their view and raised their ability of knowing and transforming the world. Workers in a chemical plant used to think that the "three wastes" could only be sent out into the atmosphere, got rid of by underground pipes or emptied into the seas. By studying materialist dialectics they came to know that the method of one dividing into two could also be applied to "waste materials" which could be transformed into valuable things under certain conditions. So they enthusiastically devoted themselves to multi-purpose use. Consciousness is transformed into matter. In the past few years, they have produced polycrystalline silicon, silicon oil, diodes and other products.

There is no limit to people's ability to know and transform the objective world. Thus there is no limit to utilizing the "three wastes." Using cotton seeds as its material, a plant used to treat the seed shells as fuel. Later, workers produced furfural from the shells, acetone from the gas emitted in making furfural, glucose out of the residue and glycerin, butanol, alcohol and *weiching* (a flavouring essence) out of the glucose residue. Indeed, there are no limits. They believe everything is valuable; there are only materials which have not been utilized, and there is no absolute waste which cannot be utilized. Continued scientific experiments have yielded important material from remaining "waste."

Broader Road

The principle of multi-purpose use is going deeper into people's minds and being translated into the actions of millions upon millions of people. Great attention has been or is being paid to multi-purpose use in every field, from the processing industry to mining and metallurgy, from heavy industry to light industry and from industry to trade.

The unfolding of multi-purpose use soon broke the old division of labour between different industrial segments and the demarcation line between different lines of endeavour and enterprises. A factory is divided into several, one raw material is used in many ways, a piece of machinery is used for many purposes, one worker is capable of many kinds of work apart from his specialization, and a factory can produce many things while engaging mainly in one product. All this gets better results from limited manpower, equipment and resources. Utilizing its own "three wastes," the Talien Steel Mill built by its own efforts ten small factories which turn out over 20 different products. The Peking Winery uses its "three wastes" to trial-produce hydrogen, chlorine gas, helium, polycrystalline silicon, adenosine triphosphate, 4-24 bacterial insecticide and a plant hormone, thereby combining light, chemical and electronics industries and products for supporting agriculture.

The multi-purpose use campaign has mobilized every possible force and promoted the development of local small industries. Many cities, counties and enterprises have organized retired workers, housewives and others not in the regular labour force to use "wastes" from the big plants as raw materials. Small factories run by neighbourhoods, schools, counties, cities or production teams were set up by self-reliance. Some small factories have turned out advanced products.

The masses in the Tangku District in Tientsin have set up dozens of small chemical works making scores of chemicals by utilizing the "three wastes" of the big plants. The muddy water from the Tientsin Soda Works was used by a small factory to produce calcium chloride; the waste in producing calcium chloride was used by another small factory to produce salt for industrial purposes; and the residue was utilized by still another small unit, a middle school-run factory, to produce sodium chloride which is used as a reagent. Everything was turned to good use.

Workers from trade departments in cities and towns

have gone to factories, neighbourhoods and villages in search of "wastes." They either processed it or supplied it to small factories as raw materials.

*   *   *

The principle of multi-purpose use correctly reflects the objective law of the development of production. Under the socialist system where the labouring people are the masters, mastering and using this law not only can end pollution, but also can expand production on a wide scale, creating ever more wealth for the state. At present, China's production technique is comparatively backward and multi-purpose use has just started. Under the guidance of Chairman Mao's revolutionary line, multi-purpose use will surely be developed on an ever wider scale.

TSITSIHAR SAVES ITS FISH*

BY LUNG CHIANG

Tsitsihar, with a population of one million, second-largest city in China's northeastern province Heilungkiang, is a fast-growing industrial center. Flowing through it is the Nunchiang River, which originates in the Greater Khingan Mountains and goes 1,379 kilometers southeast till it reaches the Sunghua River. Its clear waters abound in aquatic products, including fish of some 60 kinds. The river's catch accounts for half the output of the entire province.

In the past several years, however, the number of fish in the Nunchiang near Tsitsihar dropped markedly. In winter when the river froze over, large numbers of dead fish were found in the 400-kilometer stretch above and below Tsitsihar. The 1969 catch dropped to 17.9 percent of what it had been in 1960. What was the matter?

* From *China Reconstructs,* June 1972.

Polluted Water

The old city of Tsitsihar had practically no modern industry. Large-scale construction through three five-year-plan periods since the liberation built today's city —junction for transport routes from the Greater Khingan Mountains, the Hulunbuir Grassland and the plains of the Sunghua and Liao rivers—into an industrial center with modern factories manufacturing sugar, paper, food products, leather, medicine, chemicals and machinery.

It was found that industry was discharging a daily 250,000 tons of sewage and water containing chemicals into the Nunchiang River. Tsitsihar Municipal Party Committee and the city's revolutionary committee went into action. It sent investigation teams and increased support to city departments already treating waste water, liquids and residues.

In early 1968 more than 40 scientists and technicians from 14 research organizations in the country came to Tsitsihar and joined local workers, fishermen and technicians in surveying the Nunchiang River. In the bitter cold they covered 450 kilometers of the frozen river, visiting factories and villages along it and making detailed studies.

They found the following process taking place beneath the icebound surface: First the fish, swimming sluggishly, tried to lift their heads, then they lost their sense of balance and finally became unconscious and floated downstream. Dissection and laboratory tests of the fish revealed no unusual morbid changes. If unconscious fish were taken out and put in river water with plenty of oxygen, they quickly revived, indicating that the fish were dying from lack of oxygen in the water.

The survey also found that between December and April while the river was frozen, a yellow sticky mass grew at the bottom of the river, giving the water a rank smell.

Six months of investigation and laboratory tests proved it to be organic matter composed of an aquatic fungus. Its growth was promoted by the presence of large amounts of pulp, sugar-refining residue and nitrogenous substance. Water containing this yellow matter consumed 22.5 times as much oxygen as normal water. The decline in oxygen became more serious in winter when the yellow matter multiplied quickly and when the river froze over and did not take in oxygen from the air. Tests of the oxygen content in the river water made in January 1970 showed the following figures:

Tamin Bridge section (at Tsitsihar) 1.6 mg./liter

Fularchi Bridge section (below Tsitsihar) 0.8 mg./liter

Tailai Bridge section (below Tsitsihar) 0.4 mg./liter

Fish require 4 mg. of oxygen per liter of water for normal existence, and perish when the amount falls below this. In addition, the small amounts of such toxic matters as phenol, acid, soda, cyanogen and heavy metal ions in the water also hastened the death of fish.

Working Out a Plan

Once the cause of the death of fish was found, the Tsitsihar revolutionary committee formed a team of workers, cadres and scientists to seek measures to remedy the situation. The team solicited widely for ideas among the people. Industrial workers said the fundamental way to prevent pollution was for each factory to recover and treat its own wastes. Members of the Lungsha commune outside Tsitsihar suggested diverting and storing the industrial sewage water and purifying it for irrigating farm land. Fishermen asked that measures be taken to protect the aquatic resources.

These ideas helped the planners to establish clear principles to guide their work: Benefit to the people should be their point of departure; with future generations in mind, measures should be long-term ones and not mere expedients; and the problem should be considered from all sides so that while eliminating one hazard they would not be creating another. According to the principle of self-reliance, they worked out several plans and placed them before the masses for discussion. The final plan specified that factories manufacturing sugar and paper should recover the harmful matter in their own waste and use it as raw material for useful products, and that sewage and waste water free of harmful chemicals should be stored in reservoirs for irrigation. Tsitsihar medical workers urged that the plan include digging of deep wells to provide clean drinking water for the communes on the city's outskirts, as the chemical water stored in reservoirs might contaminate underground water. With these improvements the plan, approved by the Heilungkiang province revolutionary committee, was put into operation.

Wastes Become Useful

In 1970 the city's factories carried out mass campaigns to turn waste to use. Large amounts of chromium, oil, acid, soda, pulp and silver were recovered.

To manufacture by-products from its wastes, the Tsitsihar Sugar Refinery set up a number of new shops, operated mainly by wives of the plant's workers. From lime residue they produce 1,400 tons of low-cost, quality cement a year. From cinders they turn out two million bricks annually, which are being used to construct more shop buildings. They also make alcoholic spirits from the tailroots of sugar beets and distill alcohol from waste honey, the latter averaging one to two tons a day.

A sedimentation pool near the Tsitsihar Paper Mill's water-discharge outlet traps 150 tons of pulp a year, which is used to make packaging paper.

The Hua-an Machinery Plant has taken measures to recover practically all the harmful and toxic matter in its waste water. Since 1970 it has recovered more than 10 tons of chromic anhydride.

The Tsitsihar Electroplating Factory adopted a new process which did away with the use of toxic zinc cyanide. The cost is lower and products are of comparable quality. The factory's waste water, now free of zinc cyanide, is an excellent chemical fertilizer.

The Lungsha Waste Products Purchasing Station in 1970 extracted 70 kg. of silver from waste water from photo developing and the manufacture of mirrors.

Beginning in June 1970, under the leadership of the Tsitsihar Municipal Revolutionary Committee, the city's workers, peasants, armymen, students and neighborhood residents joined in the construction of a project to divert sewage for irrigation. Every day more than 5,000 people were at the work sites. In six months they built a reservoir with a capacity of 20 million cubic meters, dug a 6-kilometer channel and erected a 6-kilometer-long dam, with the workers from the auto plant taking on the most difficult section of the dam.

After the entire plan for treating wastes was put into operation, tests showed an improvement in the water in the 350-kilometer stretch of the Nunchiang below Tsitsihar. Tests for oxygen in the water in January 1971 showed a five to ten-fold rise over a year ago:

Tamin Bridge section 8.07 mg./liter

Fularchi Bridge section 9.03 mg./liter

Tailai Bridge section 9.47 mg./liter

Both the yellow mass and the rank smell had disappeared.

The number of fish in the river has been increasing since the winter of 1970. From mid-December 1970 to mid-January 1971 the catch at the Shihjenkou fishing ground totalled 150 tons, three times the figure for the same period of the previous year, before the water was treated. Fish weighing over 2 kg. are common catches again.

The 400 hectares of fields irrigated with sewage are yielding good crops. The Lungsha commune's Chienchin brigade got increases of 1,500 to 2,250 kg. per hectare. The commune's Aikuo brigade had never grown spring vegetables because its soil was too poor. Irrigation with sewage has improved the soil so much that the brigade now has a spring crop and is getting better yields of its summer vegetables.

Tsitsihar's leaders view decontaminating the Nunchiang River and keeping it clean as a long-term project for the benefit of the people. Not resting with the good results already achieved, in the hope of completely halting pollution they are now working on problems requiring long observation and study, such as learning which crops do not thrive well when irrigated with sewage, and purification of sewage water in the reservoir so that it will not affect the surrounding environment and underground water.

IV. LIBERATION OF EDUCATION AND PHILOSOPHY

1. Revolution in Education

One of the most significant results of the Cultural Revolution is the revolution in education. When the Communists took power in 1949 they inherited a vast, war-torn land. To reorganize and rebuild this vast country they needed all the help and co-operation they could get—including the national bourgeoisie and especially its intellectuals. The whole cultural field—especially the educational institutions—was staffed by these intellectuals. Even though the teaching materials were revised the whole educational structure and method remained essentially as before. Teachers emphasized book learning and students were concerned with making good grades. The higher educational institutions became the training ground for experts, specialists, and career seekers. What is even more alarming was the fact that young people of worker and peasant origin were systematically kept out of the university by entrance examinations which gave advantage to applicants of bourgeois and landlord origin.

The Cultural Revolution completely revamped the whole educational system. On all levels of education the emphasis is on uniting theory with practice, on learning through doing, and on raising the political consciousness of the students. The educational system is no longer a factory for the production of intellectual elites but a system to "enable everyone who gets an education to develop morally, intellectually, and physically and to become cultured, socialist-minded workers," as Mao prescribed. In contrast with the bourgeois educational system, with its departmentalization of knowledge and production of specialists, the new Chinese educational system aims at what Marx called "the all-round development of the individual," or "producing fully developed human beings."

Students throughout the educational system engage in labor—from kindergarten up to university. In a primary school we saw small children working in a school-run factory making chess sets. In a high school we visited students working in a radio factory. These are full-fledged factories producing goods to be sold on the market. With the whole young generation trained and disciplined by the labor process, China will not lack the human resources necessary for the great leap in industrialization.

Another important change brought about by the revolution in education is the new teacher-student relationship. In Old China the teacher-student relationship was patterned after the father-son relationship. There used to be a Confucian saying, "Master and disciple are like father and son. If you are his disciple for one day then he should be treated like your father for life." This authoritarian relationship has been under severe attack since the Cultural Revolution. As an old professor, Feng Yu-Lan, explained, "Why do the students come to the university? They study for the Revolution. The teachers teach for the Revolution and not for honor or fame as in the past. They have the same goal—they are both for the Revolution, for the building of socialism. From this point of view they are all comrades."

K.H.F.
K.T.F.

REVOLUTION IN EDUCATION: WHY THE UNIVERSITY ENROLLING SYSTEM SHOULD BE REFORMED*

BY CHU YEN

The course for pushing the revolution in higher education was charted by Chairman Mao's important directive of July 21, 1968 which, among other things, pointed out: *"Put proletarian politics in command and take the road of the Shanghai Machine Tools Plant in training technicians from among the workers. Students should be selected from among workers and peasants with practical experience, and they should return to production after a few years' study."*

Under the impact of the Great Proletarian Cultural Revolution and the movement to criticize revisionism and rectify style of work, the revolution in education, with the July 21 directive as its guideline, has made much headway in the past five years, setting in motion profound changes on the university campus. Institutes of higher learning began enrolling students again in 1970. Thousands of worker, peasant and soldier students have entered the university portals. Together with the revolutionary teachers, they applied Marxism-Leninism-Mao Tsetung Thought to the transformation of universities and pursued their studies along the road of being red and expert (politically and professionally qualified). The first group of students selected from among workers, peasants and soldiers have already graduated or will soon complete their courses this year. Meanwhile, a greater number of them are expected to be enrolled.

* From *Peking Review,* No. 38, 1973.

An Important Part of Educational Revolution

Reforming the enrolling system is an important part of the revolution in education. To select university students from among workers, peasants and soldiers and send them back to their midst after graduation has opened the way for the implementation of the principle that *"education must serve proletarian politics and be combined with productive labour."* This is of far-reaching significance to the building up of a new and mighty contingent of working-class intellectuals and the realization and consolidation of the all-round dictatorship of the proletariat over the bourgeoisie in the superstructure.

What sort of people the universities enrol and train directly mirrors the political orientation of education. Enrolment is a matter which exerts influence on a whole generation and has a bearing on which road should the young people be guided to take. Before the Great Cultural Revolution, when the revisionist line held sway in education, the old university entrance examination system served as an important check-post for bourgeois intellectuals to dominate the campus. Ostensibly paraded as "equality before marks," actually it was cultural autocracy of the bourgeoisie. The aim was to keep the university gates closed to workers, peasants and soldiers and their children. Working like a baton, this system herded the young people along the wrong road of "studying in order to become an official" and "giving first place to intellectual development" and encouraged them to climb the ladder of intellectual aristocracy. This entrance examination system and educational line ran counter to the needs of the socialist cause.

So when the Great Proletarian Cultural Revolution personally initiated and led by Chairman Mao began, action was first taken in the cultural and educational fields. And when this great revolution was on the rise, it was not by chance that the Red Guards, with the support of the workers, peasants and soldiers, lost no time in toppling the old entrance examination system. After Chairman Mao's July 21 directive had been made public, the universities initiated reforms in the enrolling system, and the long-cherished desire of millions upon millions of workers, peasants and soldiers was realized. Choosing university students from among workers, peasants and soldiers is a revolution in the history of education and an important achievement of the Great Proletarian Cultural Revolution.

Adherence to the reforms in the enrolling system is bound to meet with repeated struggles. One must take note of the fact that *"what is antiquated tries to reestablish itself and maintain its position within the newly acquired form."* To select students according to the July 21 directive, it is necessary to firmly put proletarian politics in command, give first place to political quality and attach due importance to practical experience. These are the premises, and it is necessary to supplement them with an appropriate test of the entrants' cultural level. Nevertheless, the way this test is conducted involves not only methods but the political line. It is imperative to make a sharp distinction between such a test of cultural level and the defunct university entrance examinations. Students are selected primarily on their political merits and practical experience. The cultural test is aimed merely to verify the practical experience of the entrants and their ability in using basic knowledge to analyse and solve practical problems. In so doing we can do a better job in choosing students on the basis of their moral, intellectual and physical qualities instead of testing how much of the middle school textbooks they can repeat by rote.

In this way, the educated youth will be encouraged to take a more active part in the three great revolutionary movements of class struggle, the struggle for production and scientific experiment and earnestly accept re-education by the workers, peasants and soldiers. This has been fully borne out by practice in the last few years. If the selection of students is decided solely on their cultural level which in turn is judged only by examinations of book knowledge alone, there is a great likelihood of misleading the young people on to the capitalist road of "studying behind closed doors" and divorcing themselves from workers and peasants. We must investigate and study by various means to find out the entrants' ideology and cultural level. We must never again take them by surprise at examinations nor judge by examination papers alone the wisdom, ability and political level of workers and peasants who are well-grounded in practical experience. Hasn't the old university entrance examination system from liberation up to 1966 given us enough lessons? What reason is there for not discarding this system which the bourgeoisie valued as a magic weapon? Did the imperial examinations of ancient times produce men of real learning and ability? Rather, it was quite often the case that those who did not make the grade at the preliminary examinations had some real knowledge and talent. Therefore, only by following Chairman Mao's directive and reforming the old examination system can we push the revolution in education forward and create favourable conditions for the healthy growth of the young people.

Relying on Workers, Peasants and Soldiers

Since the new system of enrolment entails selection of students from among workers, peasants and soldiers, we must firmly rely on the worker, peasant and soldier masses. In the days of feudalism the imperial examinations were in the sole charge of the "examiners." So were the university entrance examinations when education was under the domination of the revisionist line. The power of these "examiners" symbolized the dictatorship of the exploiting classes in the sphere of education. To invest the masses with the power of enrolling university students as is done today embodies working-class leadership and supervision by the worker and peasant masses in education. Here recommendation by the masses is basic, not something to be trifled with as mere formality. The masses know best who are up to the requirements to go to the university and who are not, and they are the best qualified to give recommendations. It is wrong for decisions to be taken by a few people behind the backs of the masses.

By doing a conscientious, good job in appraisal and recommendation out of a revolutionary sense of responsibility, the worker and peasant masses not only can pick outstanding youth for the universities according to the Party's policies, but can also give the young people an important ideological and political education. For this will enable all, the recommended and not recommended alike, to gain a clearer understanding of orientation, bring forth their vigour and vitality and advance along the road of integrating themselves with workers and peasants.

A Good Beginning

Practice in the past few years has borne out most conspicuously the superiority of selecting university students from among workers, peasants and soldiers. The new enrolment system has given impetus to the revolution in higher education and changed the face of the universities. This finds expression above all in political orientation. The new-type university students have all done several years' productive labour in factories or the rural areas and gained some practical experience. This is all to the good. But what is of primary importance is not that they have picked up some practical experience preparatory to taking up specialized studies but that learning from society and from workers and peasants they have raised their political consciousness, filled their minds with sound ideas and come to realize gradually the correct orientation of their growth. For those at the age of twenty or so, it is a matter of importance to the remoulding of their world outlook that their thinking, guided by the workers and poor and lower-middle peasants, is stamped with the brand of the workers and peasants. Thus they will see clearly they owe it to the working class and the poor and lower-middle peasants that they are given a university training. In this way, a more solid ideological foundation is laid for further solving the problem of for whom they study. Bearing in mind that "the workers, peasants and soldiers need us," the overwhelming majority of the graduates will return to the front line of the three great revolutionary movements full of vigour and vitality, and be one with the masses as before. The workers, peasants and soldiers say in their praise: "They look our way and do not turn their backs on us."

In sharp contrast to this, the old-type universities induced the young to keep aloof from workers and peasants. Some university students from worker or peasant families were so corrupted by bourgeois ideas that they were completely alienated from workers, peasants and soldiers. So goes one saying: "Bumpkins the first year and urbanized dandies the second, they cut ma and pa dead the third." Doesn't the comparison give us much food for thought?

Chairman Mao has always stressed: *"In the final analysis, the dividing line between revolutionary intellectuals and non-revolutionary or counter-revolutionary intellectuals is whether or not they are willing to integrate themselves with the workers and peasants and actually do so."* That the workers, peasants and soldiers welcome university graduates of the new type testifies to the complete correctness of Chairman Mao's orientation for the educational revolution.

Since worker, peasant and soldier students come from and return to the practice of the three great revolutionary movements, the object of higher education and the aim of training both differ from the past. This calls for a fundamental reform in the university syllabus. Once they set foot on the university campus, the worker, peasant and soldier students propel continuously the development of the educational revolution and effect changes, in an increasingly profound way, in the principles, contents and methods of teaching and even in the ranks of teachers.

A major problem in the reform is to employ the dialectical-materialist theory of knowledge and carry out the principle of *"uniting theory and practice"* so as to do away with the evil practice of divorcing theory from practice. Many teachers have come to understand that more often than not the way the worker, peasant and soldier students go about their studies differs from what is required by the old methods of teaching. This is because these students, having been in contact with practice, demand teaching to proceed from practice and by the method of enlightenment. Such being the case, the outmoded standards of teaching can no longer remain intact. In the past two or three years, the teachers and students, putting their heads together, have introduced bold reforms and begun to accumulate some valuable experience. This consists in energetically guiding the students to learn theory from practical experience, to apply the theory learnt and to concentrate efforts on cultivating the ability to analyse and solve problems. It requires teachers to help students give full play to their initiative and creativeness and organize and guide them to study by themselves. The purpose is to enable the students to make lively progress. Facts have proved that so long as the reform is carried out satisfactorily in this direction, the period of schooling can be shortened, courses made fewer and better and the quality of teaching improved, all adding up to better results.

Teaching Quality Improved

Some people are skeptical of workers, peasants and soldiers entering the university. Their doubts are focused on the quality of teaching and study, the quality of knowledge in particular. Basing themselves on mistaken viewpoints and wrong methods, these people judge new reforms by old concepts and evaluate new things with an old yardstick. Hence they cannot draw a correct conclusion.

We cannot talk about the quality of teaching apart from the political line. Political orientation is the first criterion of the quality of teaching. No matter how much one learns, it is useless if the orientation is wrong. What after all is knowledge in terms of cultural level? How do we judge whether one's knowledge is great or little, profound or shallow? These questions can only be answered correctly by the application of the dialectical-materialist theory of knowledge which puts practice in the first place and declares: *"The one and only purpose of the proletariat in knowing the world is to change it."*

Under the old educational system, however, students were confined within the school walls. For years many of them did not see how the workers worked and the peasants farmed, but recited and memorized rules and formulas year in and year out. The more they studied, the more foolish they became. When practical problems of class struggle and the struggle for production came up, their smattering of knowledge and great ignorance were there for all to see. Was there any "theoretical depth" to speak of?

We do not want to train bookworms but people who can play a useful part in socialist revolution and construction. As the students will leave the university after a few years' study, they are not expected to master all the knowledge which they can use all their lives. What is important is that they acquire a correct world outlook and methodology, master basic theoretical knowledge, learn how to use theoretical knowledge to analyse and solve problems and continue to increase this ability in the course of future practice. The worker, peasant and soldier students now pay greater attention to taking part in practical struggles from which they can draw new strength. Wherever they are they identify themselves with workers, peasants and soldiers, learn from the masses and put the knowledge they have learnt from books to good use. Many of them have already made gratifying achievements after taking up jobs again.

Our revolution in education is advancing, the ranks of teachers are being reformed and their level raised along with the deep-going development of this great revolution. Our teaching methods and materials are being steadily improved and perfected. In the course of practice, we have deepened our understanding of the laws of proletarian education. All this will surely serve to raise the quality of teaching constantly.

Profound changes have been brought about on the university campus since the admission of worker, peasant and soldier students in pursuance of Chairman Mao's July 21 directive. There have been wide repercussions in society, too. This is a very good thing. Fundamentally speaking, these repercussions mean dealing the bourgeoisie and the old forces of habit a big shock. This shows that, instead of taking over the educational system and ideology of the exploiting classes intact, we are carrying out a reform and making a revolution. The cause we have undertaken is *"the most radical rupture with traditional ideas."*

In China, the exploiting classes ran education for several thousand years and the revisionists for 17 years. By dint of the Great Proletarian Cultural Revolution, a fundamental revolution in education has just begun. Bourgeois influence is stubborn and the trial of strength between the two classes remains intense and long-drawn-out. If we fail to do our work well, a capitalist restoration is possible at any time. We must not take a casual attitude towards the struggle in this sphere, but must foster the revolutionary steadfastness of the proletariat, adhere to the philosophy of struggle, continue to make war on the old system and ideas and enthusiastically nurture and develop revolutionary newborn things.

NEW TYPE OF UNIVERSITY STUDENTS*

Tsinghua University at present carries out the principle of enrolling students from workers, peasants and soldiers with practical experience from all parts of the country. For the nation's institutes of higher learning to open their doors to workers, peasants and soldiers is a fundamental change brought on by the revolution in education.

This change means, among other things, the abolition of the old method which used to decide the fate of an applicant entirely according to marks. Such marks could at best only reflect book knowledge obtained through learning by rote, but could not show the applicant's all-round character in terms of political ideology, capabilities and actual scholastic standing. Many fine workers, peasants and soldiers were barred from higher learning as a result.

In general, present practice requires application by the worker, peasant or soldier concerned, plus the masses' recommendation and leadership approval and finally endorsement by the school. This method conforms with the wishes of China's hundreds of millions of labouring people. It puts into action the Party's mass line as it mobilizes the masses to select the students, and at the same time enables the school to gain all-round insight into the political, educational and other qualities of the applicant. The best elements of the labouring people can thus be chosen.

We recently went to Tsinghua to find out how this principle works in practice. In the northwestern suburbs of Peking, this well-known institute has 11 departments, including electronics engineering, chemical engineering, engineering mechanics, machine building and radio and communications.

In 1972, Tsinghua enrolled 2,000 new students— 2,800 in 1970—belonging to 11 different nationalities:

* From *Peking Review*, No. 9, 1973.

Han, Manchu, Mongolian, Hui, Tibetan, Chuang, Tung, Puyi, Korean, Uighur and Dahur. Coming from all parts of the country, the overwhelming majority of these worker, peasant and soldier students were from families of labouring people.

While at school, tuition, medical care, housing and other living expenses are provided by the state. Periodical medical check-ups are given to the students. Workers with five years or more production work behind them continue to get their regular pay.

We interviewed three of the newcomers to get their stories.

To Gain the Heights

Ma Fu-hsien, a foundry worker of 24, is an undergraduate in the mechanical engineering department.

From the Sian Grinding Wheel Machinery Plant, he had worked at the bench for seven years. During this time, he had on more than one occasion regretted his lack of scientific-technical knowledge. When at a mass meeting he learnt that the universities were open to enrolment, he immediately applied. The whole casting workshop backed him up. Recommendations were prompt and sincere. "He's a good worker," some said, "turning out first-rate products. He's no self-seeker; he always puts socialist construction of the motherland first." Old-timers praised him for being an energetic lad who was eager to learn and had become adept at his job in a very short time. Young workers commended him for his active part in the Great Proletarian Cultural Revolution.

Taking into consideration the opinion of the masses, the plant's revolutionary committee passed his application. The school checked on his educational level and found it adequate.

Asked why he wanted to go to university, he said: "We workers have a big job to master advanced techniques to build up socialism fast. I'm young, I want to learn and do my part."

At first, Ma found the going rather difficult, especially in mathematics. In one class, the students were asked to do 20 problems on the spot. Ma had barely plodded through half when the others had already handed in their papers. Yet he refused help, saying: "I've got to learn myself, not rely on others." Gradually, by dint of hard study, he began catching up.

Did he still have any difficulty? "Naturally," the young man replied. "But then, to a revolutionary, every difficulty is a challenge to be conquered." He went on to quote the great teacher Marx: " *'There is no royal road to science, and only those who do not dread the fatiguing climb of its steep paths have a chance of gaining its luminous summits.'* "

A New Battlefront

In the architecture and civil engineering department, one class majoring in underground construction is made up entirely of P.L.A. fighters, all recruits in and around 1968. Former platoon leader Chen Sung-ching from Fukien Province heads the class as chairman of the class committee. After Chen had enlisted in the P.L.A. in April 1968 while he was in senior middle school, his company had been sent to dig tunnels in the mountains. This was excellent tempering for him.

Once when there was a cave-in the squad leader and several other soldiers were seriously injured trying to put in the props. Without the slightest hesitation, Chen and some other comrades carried on while the injured were speedily taken to safety. Another time, the company took on construction of an awe-inspiring "underground dragon," so called because of the 7,000-metre difficult tunnelling through the mountains. Work in one place was retarded by the sudden emergence of ground water. Though it was at the height of winter

Chen took the lead in jumping into the icy pool to work. The project was finished on time. Cited many times by the unit leadership and much praised by his comrades-in-arms, he was admitted into the Communist Party two years after he had joined the P.L.A.

When Chen's unit was notified that Tsinghua was enrolling students, he was chosen to go and study there. This got the hearty backing of the whole company, and the school found him qualified. On the eve of departure, his commanding officer told him: "For a fighter to go to school is like being transferred from one battlefront to another. We hope you'll continue to display the spirit of not fearing hardship and being brave in battle, and come out victorious in this new campaign." Chen has always kept these words in mind.

When the term started, the school authorities gave the newcomers a briefing on the struggle between the two lines on the educational front. Before the Great Cultural Revolution started, they were told, Liu Shao-chi and political swindlers like him opposed Chairman Mao's policy that *"education must serve proletarian politics and be combined with productive labour."* Instead, they pushed a revisionist line which tried to turn students into bourgeois intellectuals, who would be indifferent to the revolution and eager for personal gain, and into "specialists" and "scholars" divorced from proletarian politics, from the labouring people and from practice in production. Under this line, the Party's class line in enrolling students was nullified, restrictions were put on admitting workers, peasants and soldiers, and those who did enter were often discriminated against. Some were dismissed on the pretext that they had "no future."

Hearing all this was a profound education to Chen, who said: "It's the victory of Chairman Mao's revolutionary line that has enabled us to come to university. I'll study hard, so that I can do my best in building up the socialist motherland."

From the Labouring People

We met Chin Yu-tzu who is of Korean nationality in the student dormitories of the electric power engineering department. A lively girl of 24, she majors in high-tension power transmission. We asked what she had thought about going to university. "I thought of Chairman Mao's love and concern for the national minorities," she answered. "You know, over ten Korean youth from my county were admitted into universities last year."

Chin Yu-tzu comes from a poor-peasant family in the suburbs of Shenyang in northeast China. Her father is a Communist, her elder brothers and sisters are workers, and other younger ones are in school. Everything is going well for the family. In the old society, however, the family had toiled for generations for the landlords as hired hands. It was as much as they could do to keep alive, let alone get schooling. After liberation she went to school. During the Great Proletarian Cultural Revolution, she was in senior middle school. An excellent representative of the Red Guards, she became vice-chairman of the school's revolutionary committee.

In 1968, she responded to Chairman Mao's call for *"young people with education to go to the countryside to be re-educated by the poor and lower-middle peasants."* With her family's consent, she requested and was sent to a mountainous region where conditions were difficult. Together with 300 schoolmates, she settled down in the Hungmiaotzu Commune in Hsinpin County, 500 *li* from home. She took an active part in the three great revolutionary movements—class struggle, the struggle for production and scientific experiment, and was elected to the commune's revolutionary committee the second year.

Last April, the news came that the universities were enrolling worker-peasant-soldier students. The commune members all thought Chin Yu-tzu the best choice. She, however, hesitated. "It makes me very happy to know that Chairman Mao is always thinking of the poor and lower-middle peasants," she said. "I want very much to raise my scientific and cultural level so as to be able to work better for the Party and people. But I've come to love the mountains and all of you so much, that I hate to leave. . . ." At the insistence of the peasants, she finally applied. A few days later, she was working at a reservoir site when she was notified to go to the county town to have her qualifications checked by the school people and get a medical check-up. She passed.

The day she left for Peking, the commune members gave her a big send-off at the railway station, beating drums and gongs. Granddad An Ying who was over 60 clasped her hands and said with tears in his eyes: "You're going off to university in Peking, where Chairman Mao is. This is a great honour for our commune. Wherever you are, don't forget you've come from the labouring people. . . ."

Chin Yu-tzu took with her to Tsinghua the old work clothes she had worn in the commune. "Under the old educational system," she said, "students were taught to look down upon labour and workers and peasants. Now that we—workers and peasants—have entered university, we must never take that road. We mustn't become separated from labour and the labouring people."

True to her words, she not only studies her subjects and works by Marx, Engels, Lenin and Stalin and Chairman Mao's works diligently, but volunteers for all sorts of manual work, such as sweeping the stairs and corridors in her spare time. Last summer vacation she stayed at school to join in a spell of physical labour. She has never forgotten that she is from the labouring people.

We came away from Tsinghua with our minds full of fresh impressions. These fine young men and women with practical experience, who had come from the forefront of class struggle, the struggle for production and scientific experiment, certainly know what they are studying for: they are studying for the revolution, and nothing can stop them.

TAKING ALL SOCIETY AS THEIR FACTORY*

Having gone through the Great Proletarian Cultural Revolution, Peking University is developing into a new-type socialist university. It has 17 departments embracing over 60 specialties and a teaching staff of more than 2,000. Since August 1970, it has enrolled some 4,000 students from among young workers, peasants and soldiers with practical experience all over the country. This is something unheard of in the old-type universities.

The liberal arts in Peking University, which is located in the northwestern suburbs of the capital, include Chinese, history, philosophy, political economy, international politics, law and library science departments. Chairman Mao has pointed out: *"The liberal arts should take all society as their factory."* Like the science and engineering colleges which have their own factories or establish contacts with local plants to enable teachers and students to link study with actual production, the liberal arts teachers and students, apart from class work, devote some time every year to taking part in class struggle and productive labour in factories, people's communes, P.L.A. units and shops and making social investigations, stressing theoretical study based on practice. Good results have thus been obtained in educational revolution.

Prior to the Great Cultural Revolution, Chairman Mao time and again called on the liberal arts teachers and students to go among the workers and peasants and learn how to make revolution by taking part in class struggle. He clearly pointed out: *"Education must*

* From *Peking Review*, No. 5, 1973.

serve proletarian politics and be combined with productive labour." However, Liu Shao-chi and his agents in the field of education pushed a revisionist line in a futile bid to lead teachers and students astray, making them divorce themselves from proletarian politics, the worker and peasant masses and productive labour.

Profound Changes

Repudiation of this counter-revolutionary revisionist line in education during the Cultural Revolution has enabled the students and teachers in the college of liberal arts to embark on the road of taking all society as their factory, thereby drastically changing the teaching system.

Since two years ago, they have incorporated their study in and out of the university. While attending classes, students concentrate their time and energy in systematically studying the basic knowledge of the various subjects they major in. Together with their teachers, they are out in society four months a year, applying what they have learnt to practice. In this way, the old bookish way of study has been done away with and the students' ability to use Marxist theory to analyse and solve problems has been raised.

In 1971, the students in the Chinese department specializing in literature and their teachers went to a production brigade in Miyun County on Peking's outskirts to do some investigation work. The heroic deeds of Liu Mao-ching, the brigade's late Party branch secretary who had led the peasants in building a socialist new countryside, inspired them to do creative writing. While tutoring students in such writing, the teachers lectured on the relevant parts of such courses as the Marxist theory of literature and art, writing methods, analysis of classical and modern literary works and grammar and rhetoric, and organized the students to conscientiously study Chairman Mao's *Talks at the Yenan Forum on Literature and Art* and other works.

The result was the students wrote a collection of revolutionary stories.

In co-operation with the Peking Historical Relics Administration, teachers and students in archaeology under the history department unearthed a Western Chou Dynasty (c. 1066-771 B.C.) village and discovered 3,000-year-old houses, kitchen ranges, pottery and other things. This initial training in field excavation helped extend their knowledge of what had been learnt in the classroom.

The Ming Tombs in Changping County on Peking's northwestern outskirts, where thirteen Ming emperors are buried, became lecture rooms on the history of the Ming Dynasty (1368-1644 A.D.) and Ching Dynasty (1644-1911 A.D.). Teachers and students read historical data, visited the luxurious underground mausoleum of a Ming emperor and his wife, and investigated the family histories of the peasants living in the locality for generations. What they found spoke volumes for the harsh exploitation and oppression of the peasants by the feudal rulers and the former's resistance and struggle. This was very conducive to grasping Marxist historical materialism and using the theory of class struggle to study historical problems and criticize the idealist concept of history.

From Abstract Concepts to Weapons of Struggle

Before the Great Cultural Revolution began, the philosophy department did not regard philosophy as a subject in which the students study theory to carry out class struggle and serve proletarian politics. Instead, it confined philosophy to textbooks and the classroom and asked the students to learn only some philosophical concepts from books. The situation has now fundamentally changed.

In conjunction with the study of the basic theories of historical materialism, 150 teachers and students of the philosophy department in the third year not long ago spent one and a half months carrying out social investigations in several factories, shops and schools and among the inhabitants in the capital's western district. They put the stress on investigating the management system of industrial enterprises, class struggle in commercial departments, education among children and youngsters, and other questions. In the course of which the students raised many practical and theoretical questions, such as the law of class struggle in the period of socialism, the features and law of struggle between the proletariat and the bourgeoisie in influencing and winning over the younger generation. With the teachers' guidance, they read and studied hard and strove to use the Marxist stand, viewpoint and method to answer these questions. In addition to over 60 fact-finding reports and study notes by individuals, they joined efforts to write more than 30 investigation reports.

To gain a deeper understanding of the Marxist theory of knowledge, a group of teachers and students from the same department visited the Yungting Machinery Plant where experienced workers had through collective efforts created a new-type drill bit. Their aim was to analyse, in the light of this technical innovation, such reactionary fallacies as idealist apriorism spread by Liu Shao-chi and other political swindlers and to find out typical examples of workers' applying the materialist theory of reflection in practice. On the basis of investigations, the students carried out mass revolutionary criticism together with the workers. Meanwhile, they earnestly restudied *Theses on Feuerbach, Ludwig Feuerbach and the End of Classical German Philosophy,* some chapters of *Anti-Duhring* and *Materialism and Empirio-Criticism* and other works by Marx, Engels, Lenin and Stalin and Chairman Mao's works like *On Practice* and *Where Do Man's Correct Ideas Come From?*

Teachers gave on-the-spot lectures on the basic viewpoints of the Marxist theory of knowledge. Before they came to the plant, some students had had some muddled ideas about the origin of man's knowledge and talent. During discussions and criticism meetings, the workers repudiated idealist apriorism which had been advertised by Liu Shao-chi and other political swindlers together with fatalism spread by the exploiting classes in the old society, pinpointing the fact that idealist apriorism was nothing but mental shackles used by the reactionary ruling classes for enslaving the people. Recounting her own experience of knowing nothing about technique at first and becoming a master of her line, a woman lathe operator explained that talent came only from practice. All this was a profound education for the students.

Lively Pedagogic Activities

When studying the road of development for socialist agriculture, the students in the political-economy department read Engels' *The Peasant Question in France and Germany,* Lenin's *On Co-operation* and Chairman Mao's works on agricultural co-operation. Afterwards the teachers took them to several people's communes with different characteristics to carry out social surveys. While in Hsipu Production Brigade (see *Peking Review,* No. 51, 1972) of the Chienming People's Commune in Hopei Province's Tsunhua County, a brigade commended by Chairman Mao during the movement for agricultural co-operation, they learnt about the entire course of agricultural collectivization from old poor peasants and cadres. When the co-operative which later developed into the present brigade had been set up, it was very poor and owned only three-fourths of a donkey, the sole draught animal shared by a number of peasant households of which one-fourth did not join the co-op. Today farming in this brigade is being mechanized. After reading and collecting a large amount of data coupled with serious study of Marxist works in the course of investigation, the teachers and students gained a deeper understanding of the Marxist-Leninist theory of co-operation.

Some teachers and students in the international politics department had their lessons on Lenin's *Imperialism, the Highest Stage of Capitalism* in the Mentoukou Coal-Mine, the iron-smelting mill of the Shoutu Iron and Steel Company and the Shihchingshan Power Plant on Peking's western outskirts. All had been victims of imperialist plunder. While extensively investigating the history of savage imperialist plunder, the teachers and students held forums with veteran workers who accused the imperialists of barbarous exploitation and raised many questions on the current international class struggle. This was an impetus to the teachers and students in their theoretical study and research work. With the help of the teachers, the students extensively read relevant material and at the same time studied Lenin's work. As a result, they arrived at a deep understanding of Lenin's thesis that export of capital is a major characteristic of imperialism. These lively pedagogic activities enabled the students to write four fact-finding reports, including "Plunder of the Mentoukou Coal-Mine by the Imperialist Powers," "An Investigation on Imperialist Capital Export in the Shihchingshan Tube Casting Mill" and "Imperialist Control and Plunder of the Shihchingshan Power Plant."

Taking all society as their factory has brought marked improvement in the quality of teaching to the liberal arts. Speaking of his own experience, a young philosophy teacher said: "I studied philosophy for five years in the old Peking University. When I wrote year-end and graduate theses, I often copied abstract concepts and philosophical jargon. Now with only a little over a year's study, students have begun to use Marxist theory to criticize the bourgeoisie and write articles with clear-cut views and rich contents. This is a striking contrast between the two lines in education and the results produced."

2. Reform of Intellectuals

An old worker summarized the essence of the Cultural Revolution for us as follows, "For thousands of years the practice has been that those who do mental work rule over the rest, and those who labor with their hands are ruled over. Chairman Mao has lead us to thoroughly reverse the reversal of history."

The historical division between mental work and manual work and the oppression of the former against the latter is one of the basic obstacles to general human emancipation which Communists are committed to overcome. The long-term policy for solving this division is, on the one hand, to educate the masses to do mental work, to think, to discuss politics and to philosophize; and, on the other hand, to re-educate the intellectuals to respect manual work and to participate in manual work.

"Intellectuals" includes all those who work with their brains instead of their hands. The term includes teachers, party functionaries, doctors, etc. In fact it is synonymous with "white-collar workers" in the West. We visited a "May 7" Cadre School and talked with many intellectuals and our impression is that the Cultural Revolution has indeed been "a revolution that touches people to their very soul," as Mao puts it. It is not that China needed the muscle power of the intellectuals but that participation in manual work and working and living with the workers and peasants was an experience the intellectuals needed to change their world outlook.

"The brain should rule over the brawn" is an old established Confucian precept. Intellectuals looked down on workers and regarded physical work as demeaning to their persons. We remember how some

Chinese students in the United States couldn't bring themselves to tell their relatives at home that they had to work as waiters or dishwashers to support themselves. It is not difficult to imagine the traumatic experience some old professors, for example, had to go through during the Cultural Revolution when they were sent down to work in the fields alongside the peasants. Nor is it difficult to understand why some committed suicide. But those we met who have withstood the test looked healthy and happy and are changed persons. Each had their own story to tell but they all emphasized the change in their world outlook, in their feelings and emotions about things.

We met Hsieh Ping-Hsin, a very famous modern Chinese poet and novelist, in Peking. A petite woman in her seventies, she looked as healthy as a peasant woman in her fifties. Among the many personal experiences she related, one thing stood out as an especially good illustration of the change in feelings she talked about. She said that during her long literary life she always considered the butterfly a symbol of freedom. When she first went to the countryside she could not understand why the peasants didn't share her romantic notion of the butterfly. But then she saw the vegetable garden she was tending eaten away by caterpillars and those caterpillars finally turn into butterflies. She now hates butterflies!

K.H.F.
K.T.F.

THE "MAY 7" CADRE SCHOOL*

A new thing born in the Great Cultural Revolution, "May 7" cadre schools are all over China. Every province, municipality and autonomous region as well as many special administrative regions, counties and cities, all have this type of school. More than a hundred belong to the departments under the Central Committee of the Chinese Communist Party and the State Council.

Those who have been sent to the school include veteran cadres who went through the Long March, the War of Resistance Against Japan or the War of Liberation; cadres who joined the revolution after liberation; those who went from their homes to schools and from there to government offices and who were lacking in practical experience; and young cadres who had been Red Guards. While at cadre school, they get their regular wages and the same welfare facilities as when they are on the job. The term generally is for a year or so, the least six months, the most two to three years.

Versatile Activities

Regardless of seniority or how high a post held, everyone is an ordinary student, a "May 7" fighter. At the Chingkou "May 7" Cadre School in Kirin Province, the former director of the agriculture bureau becomes a pig-breeder, the former secretary of the city Party committee a carpenter, a department head a cart driver and a county head a cook.

Students' lives are many-sided. They do productive manual labour as well as study. They criticize the bourgeoisie and do mass work. The school also organizes militia training and cultural and sports activities. Some

* From *Peking Review*, No. 19, 1972.

schools set aside time for students to study their vocations or raise their general educational level.

The "May 7" cadre school is a school for training cadres at their posts in rotation.

How does the school accomplish its tasks? How do students study? It can be generalized as follows:

Studying Marxist-Leninist Works. In the light of the revolutionary struggle and their ideology, the students study the works of Marx, Engels, Lenin and Stalin and Chairman Mao's works to raise their level of Marxism and their consciousness of the struggle between the two lines, thereby raising their ability to distinguish between genuine and sham Marxists.

The students at the Huangho "May 7" Cadre School in Honan spend half a day studying and the other half doing manual labour. In the busy farming season, they work during the day, studying in the morning or evening. Last year they studied the *Manifesto of the Communist Party, Critique of the Gotha Programme* and *The State and Revolution* as well as *On Practice* and *On Contradiction.* They pay special attention to linking theory with practice and often organize group discussions and criticism meetings.

Participating in Class Struggle. Students at cadre schools take part in class struggle and in criticizing the bourgeoisie to temper themselves. They often link their work and ideological problems with their mass criticism of swindlers like Liu Shao-chi, of the theory of the dying out of class struggle, the bourgeois theory of human nature, the theory of productive forces, idealist apriorism, the theory that doing manual labour is a punishment and the theory of going to school in order to get an official post. Some cadre schools carry out various political movements in step with the movements in the units they belong to. Some have sent students to rural people's communes to take part in or help local people carry out a political campaign like attacking active counter-revolutionaries, campaigns against embezzlement and theft, extravagance and waste and speculation.

Taking Part in Productive Labour. Cadre schools devote themselves mainly to agricultural production. Where conditions allow, they branch out into forestry, animal husbandry, side-occupations and fisheries. At the same time they go in for small industries, such as machine-repairing, manufacturing of chemical fertilizers, insecticides, paper- and brick-making, and sugar-refining.

Every cadre school has cultivated land—much was once wasteland—ranging from hundreds to thousands of *mu,* parts of which are reclaimed tracts along sea coasts or lakeshores and on barren hillsides and alkaline slopes. Inner Mongolia's Ikh Chao League cadre school converted much sandy land into fertile fields by covering the sand with layers of mud.

"Plain living and hard struggle" and *"self-reliance"* is the motto of all the cadre schools.

The object of students taking part in industrial or agricultural productive labour is not only to create material wealth for the country but mainly to better their ideology and to transform their subjective world as they transform the objective world.

Cadres of the General Office of the Chinese Communist Party's Central Committee turned the building of their school into a process of edifying their thought. Instead of choosing a ready-made site, they preferred to build it from scratch. They turned 5,000 *mu* of lakeshore and other wasteland into fields, and built dormitories and factories on their own. They dug canals, wading knee-deep in mud. They went into icy streams to get sand and braved eye-stinging smoke to burn limestone in the kilns. They fought floods to save people's lives and property. They met all these trials head-on to gain the revolutionary spirit of "fearing neither hardship nor death."

Going Among Workers and Peasants. Students often leave their schools for short stays in nearby people's communes or factories. Living, eating and working alongside workers or peasants, they learn from them and carry out social investigations among them at the same time. They also do mass work, such as organizing workers and peasants to study philosophy, helping them get some general education and aiding local Party organizations carry out Party rectification and Party building. All these activities aim at raising their ideological level and reforming their world outlook.

Transforming Man

Cadres come to the schools in turns. They go back to their original posts after "graduation," or are transferred to new work. Practice has shown that their stay at cadre schools, brief as it is, is excellent training. The great majority of students come out of the schools changed in outlook in more ways than one.

One artist at the Kuantang Cadre School in Hunan Province who had joined revolutionary work straight from school had not liked to draw peasants because he considered their weatherbeaten faces no objects for art. After entering the cadre school, he had a chance to live and eat with peasants, and made some social investigations into their lives. He found out the tragic histories of many peasant families in the old society under the exploitation of the landlord class. His sentiments changed, and he began to have a great compassion for the once-downtrodden peasants. He said: "Before, I looked at things according to bourgeois aesthetic standards; the more I drew, the farther from the labouring people I got. Now, the more I draw peasants, the closer I feel to them."

Lin Hsiang-wei, vice-director and chief engineer at a designing institute in Hunan, had designed a highway bridge which wasted tons of bricks because he wanted it fancy. The workers criticized him, without convincing him he was wrong. After going to the Kuantang Cadre School, he happened to be working at a brick-kiln. A rush assignment in summer had him drenched in sweat and covered with dirt in the sweltering heat day after day. Only then did he fully realize what it meant to make one brick. He said with genuine feeling: "It's only after you've taken part in labour that you get to feel akin to the workers and peasants." During a fierce rain-storm, Lin ran to the kiln and covered up the clay molds, though he got soaking wet. He often expresses his determination to continue to make revolution and thoroughly transform his old ideas, to become an intel-lectual welcomed by the workers, peasants and soldiers.

Veteran cadres with much revolutionary experience also gain a great deal from going to cadre school. It puts them back in the war years and helps them get rid of bureaucratic airs and the inactivity that crept up on them in peace time. It rejuvenates them.

Fang Fu-chin, a veteran of the 25,000-*li* Long March of the Chinese Red Army in 1934-35, was one of the first to enrol at the Meitsun Cadre School under the Kwangchow Railway Bureau. Once there, he was re-minded of the militant life he used to lead in the Ching-kang Mountains, Yenan and Nanniwan in the early days of the revolution. Invigorated, he joined the rank and file in climbing mountains to fell trees, and went wherever the difficulties were greatest. Out of consider-ation for his years, comrades often told him to take a rest. He refused, saying: "You may replace me in la-bour, but that'll never transform my ideology."

Yang Li-feng is a new cadre from a poor peasant family. She entered college in 1960 wearing a pair of simple cloth shoes her mother had made for her. Under the influence of the revisionist line in education, she developed the bourgeois idea of wanting to get up in the world. So she put the cloth shoes at the bottom of a chest. When schoolmates asked her to tell them her family history, she refused, ashamed of past poverty.

At the Hsiushuihotzu People's Commune in Faku County, Liaoning Province, Yang took part in peasant activities to recall past bitterness and praise the new life. She told commune members how her feelings had changed after going to college. The peasants helped her, saying: "You must understand that you've not only forgotten your family's bitter past, but that of your class. You've not only put away the cloth shoes, but the true qualities of the labouring people." Enlightened, Yang plunged into productive labour with renewed zeal and wore her cloth shoes again.

After coming out of cadre schools, most cadres are full of life, keep in close touch with the masses and have a good style in their work and way of living. The masses of workers, peasants and soldiers welcome their progress made in this period of "studying once again." They say: "We have full confidence in cadres who can work both at the top and down at the grass roots, and who keep close to the people."

Origin of Cadre Schools

"May 7" cadre schools were set up in all parts of the country according to Chairman Mao's May 7, 1966 Directive.[1]

[1] This directive pointed out that the *"army should be a great school. . . . In this school, our army should study politics and military affairs, raise its educational level, and also engage in agriculture and side-occupations and run small or medium-sized factories. . . . Our army should also do mass work. . . . Also our army should always be ready to participate in the struggles to criticize and repudiate the bourgeoisie in the cultural revolution."* It also called on people in other fields to *"learn other things"* while mainly engaging in their own work. *"They should also learn industrial production, agricultural production and*

In 1968, when the Proletarian Cultural Revolution was developing in depth, the question of how to carry forward the cadres' ideological revolutionization and revolutionize government institutions was discussed on a wide scale. In October that year Chairman Mao issued the call: *"Going down to do manual labour gives vast numbers of cadres an excellent opportunity to study once again; this should be done by all cadres except those who are old, weak, ill or disabled. Cadres at their posts should also go down in turn to do manual labour."*

Cadres at every level all over the country enthusiastically responded to this call and asked to go to the most difficult places to do manual labour and to *"study once again."* The "May 7" cadre schools were set up to meet these needs, and in the single month of October alone new ones appeared almost every day.

The guiding thought of these cadre schools which upholds the system of cadre participation in collective productive labour was pointed out by Chairman Mao and the Party Central Committee long before 1968.

Cadres doing productive labour is the fine tradition of the Chinese Workers' and Peasants' Red Army, the Eighth Route Army and the New Fourth Army, as today it is the tradition of the People's Liberation Army. In an army of the people, officers and soldiers help the masses in manual labour wherever they are. After liberation, cadres in government and Party organizations have learnt to carry forward this tradition. The system of cadre participation in collective productive labour for fixed periods has been in effect since 1958, and cadres have been taking turns in going to the countryside or factories.

In 1964, after summing up the experience of revolu-

---

military affairs. They also should criticize and repudiate the bourgeoisie." They must study "politics and raise their educational level." "Those working in . . . Party and government organizations should do the same."

tionary struggle in China and studying the positive and negative experiences in the international communist movement, Chairman Mao pointed out: *"By taking part in collective productive labour, the cadres maintain extensive, constant and close ties with the working people. This is a major measure of fundamental importance for a socialist system; it helps to overcome bureaucracy and to prevent revisionism and dogmatism."*

WHAT I LEARNED FROM THE WORKERS AND PEASANTS*

BY TSIEN LING-HI

I am an intellectual from the old society and have been teaching science for thirty years. You might say that my position at the Talien Polytechnic Institute—where I have been for most of these twenty-two years that the country has been under the leadership of the Communist Party and People's Government—was an ideal job for me. I have had good working conditions and have been accorded honors, both politically and professionally.

Yet, for quite a long time, though I had all these opportunities to be useful, I still kept running along rather like an automobile without a steering wheel. Consciously or unconsciously I was under the influence of the old ideas—I viewed my knowledge as my private possession to be used for my own good, and behind closed doors pursued purely theoretical research whether or not it had any relation to practical needs or problems. The fact is that I hadn't completely solved the fundamental problem: knowledge, research—for whom?

The Great Proletarian Cultural Revolution gave me quite a jolt. I learned a lot from the revolutionary criti-

* From *China Reconstructs,* June 1972.

cism of such ideas by the masses. Reviewing my past experience, I realized that the reason why my work had fallen short of the needs of the new society was because I had not taken the road for intellectuals pointed out by Chairman Mao; I had not got close to the workers and peasants. I decided I had to change, I would go out among them, breathe some fresh air.

In 1967 I asked for a few months to work in the Miaoling production brigade near our institute. The commune members were very glad to see me. "All those years you've been working in that big building and we've never seen you," they said. "This is a good start." They encouraged me. I lived with a peasant family, worked with the brigade members. They taught me about the farm work and told me of the class struggle in the countryside. I joined in their political study sessions and discussions on how to build the new socialist countryside in answer to Chairman Mao's call for agriculture to learn from Tachai. I found that when they worked hard from early morning till after dark it was not for personal fame or profit but for the revolution. In the past when I had engaged in scientific research, I had always put first promoting my own school of thought in my special field, and my own fame and gain —not what the cause of the proletariat needed. When I compared myself with these people I found there was a great difference in our thinking. I resolved to get rid of the idea of viewing knowledge as one's private possession and to use my technology to serve the people.

The members of the Miaoling brigade wanted to use the sewage from our school to irrigate their hillside fields. I worked with them on drafting a plan for the system, walking with them all over the mountains surveying. It was hard for me because my legs and back are not good, but when I saw how eager the commune members were to change their mountains, it gave me new strength. In three months of hard work their irrigation plan was realized. I was so happy to see the sewage water flowing into the wheat fields that I scooped up a handful and smelled it, causing the commune members to smile understandingly.

Gradually I came to have a common language with the peasants and they often came to talk things over with me. In the spring of 1971 one production team asked me to design them a bridge with an eight-meter span. To tell the truth, in the past I would have thought such a small project beneath me, and, furthermore, the commune members would never have sought me out about it. Now things were different. They trusted me, and I accepted their request with pleasure.

Utilizing the hours after work, I very quickly drafted a plan requiring 800 kilograms of steel reinforcing rods. I thought this about as economical as possible. But after looking at it the commune members asked that I cut the reinforcing rods down to 500 kilograms. I went home and studied the draft from every angle and finally added a pier which would cut down on the steel. I thought that certainly they would approve of this, but then some people raised a new request—"Old Tsien, could you look at it again? Would it be possible to build the bridge without any steel?" Their question stumped me. Of course it is possible to build a bridge without steel, but I wondered whether it could be done with the brigade's construction conditions and equipment. I consulted with stonemasons and bricklayers and learned from them, and also did some investigation in the Luta city department of architecture and design. At last I produced a plan for an arched cement bridge that could stand the weight of a tractor and could be built without steel rods or wooden supports. Using local materials, the commune members completed it in a very short time.

Reviewing the whole process afterwards, I didn't feel comfortable about it. If the commune members had adopted the first draft it would have meant a waste and an economic loss to the state. This once again showed me that even though one wants subjectively to serve the laboring people, he cannot do it well unless he has a real understanding of their life and the way they feel. I saw that through this process of laboring with them I had really come to feel the way they did and be concerned about the things they were.

One day in April 1971 the teachers and students of our institute went to a production brigade in the Lingshui commune to plant trees. When we finished I did not go right back to the school, but, even though it was raining, walked a few kilometers over the mountains to see a reservoir the commune members were constructing.

I learned that they had quite a few unsolved problems. The plan for the project had been made without taking local conditions into consideration. The dam was higher than necessary and this would waste a lot of labor. Judging from the pace of construction thus far, the project could not be finished before the flood season. The people were busy with spring sowing, so they could not afford to transfer a lot of labor power to the dam to speed work on it. Yet, if it were not finished in time, the uncompleted dam might be destroyed by floods. The commune members were very worried.

I went to the office of the brigade and suggested that perhaps the plan could be revised to cut down the height of the dam from 11 meters to 9 meters. Then it could be finished ahead of the flood season. The secretary of the Party branch was very happy with my proposal. "Good, now you're thinking the way we are," he said. "We had the same idea, but haven't carried it out because we couldn't agree on the final plan." He called a meeting of the Party committee, and after talking it over they agreed to revise the original design. A new target date was set for the construction. With hard work, the commune members finished the reservoir project in two months, in time for the flood season.

That year there were extraordinarily heavy rains, but the dam stood firm. The peasants were overjoyed. This matter may seem like something beyond my line of duty, yet it was just at this time, as I got out of my narrow circle of individualism and plunged into the revolutionary work of serving the people, that I began to realize the breadth of life and the far-reaching opportunities for my own future.

Of course, before the cultural revolution I had also had occasion to go to the factories and villages. But then I went in a car. I was the "professor", the "expert". I never thought there was any way in which the workers and peasants could re-educate me. Instead, I looked down on everyone and was always making criticisms. I never thought of myself as one who should learn from them. In this respect, one incident taught me a great deal.

When our institute was in the midst of the educational revolution in 1969, I went to a shipyard with a group studying reform of teaching in order to find ways to carry out Chairman Mao's directive that education must be combined with productive labor. One day I went with a worker to repair a machine. During the course of the work he was called away on other business. This is not difficult, I thought, if I go on the way he's been doing it, I'll have no trouble. But things were not so simple as I had imagined. I dismantled and cleaned one part of it, but after I put it back together, the machine wouldn't move. In fact, a part that originally should have been stationary had become loose. This was clearly a problem of mechanics, but neither my strength nor my book-learning was of any use.

I couldn't rest that night. I was afraid that people would make a big to-do about the matter and the great professor who couldn't do this little job would become the laughing stock of the plant. The next morning I told the worker what had happened. He had another look at the machine, did the job again methodically and soon the machine was turning smoothly. I felt that maybe a self-criticism was in order, but instead of blaming me, the worker told me in detail what I had done wrong in the operation. He pointed out that I had used too much force when putting in the fixing pins so that the part was in too tight. And then I had neglected to give it a few taps to loosen it a bit. His direct, sincere words brought home to me the idea that theory divorced from practice was one of my serious shortcomings.

This incident also showed me that I should learn from the working class not only politically, but also in the professional sphere—that I must get rid of the ideas fettering my mind such as placing theoretical work above all else and thinking that book knowledge could solve everything. It showed me that only if I conscientiously learned from these workers with practical experience would I ever have the kind of knowledge that could serve the people.

In May 1970 I was sent by our institute to help unravel a knotty problem in the shipbuilding industry. When I got there I found it was something with which I was completely unfamiliar. I cudgelled my brains all one night but still couldn't figure out where to start. I thought that perhaps I wouldn't be able to do the job. The next day when I went among the workers to investigate, while they told me about the situation they gave encouragement. "Don't worry if it's something new to you. We'll do it together," they said.

I talked with workers and other personnel engaged in building, maintenance, salvage and shipping and from their practical experience collected a lot of data. Then, with the workers and members of the group responsible for solving the problem, I carefully analyzed it and discovered some pattern to it. We found that good conditions existed for our design work to break with foreign conventions on this point and develop our own way.

During this period I frequently lived, worked and studied with the workers, told them what was on my mind and really made an effort to learn their revolutionary thinking and good ways of working. They were happy to have me and often helped me by pointing out my ideological faults or weak points. This kind of contact with them in practical work enabled me to learn many things I could not get from books. It also led me to a gradual understanding of the technology of the problem we were to solve, so that I could work out an initial plan for it. In three months of hard work we unravelled the knot in production. In the process I had a good tempering in practical work and another opportunity to see from my own experience the benefits of getting close to the workers and peasants.

A MAJOR MEASURE OF FUNDAMENTAL IMPORTANCE*

In 1964 Chairman Mao issued an important directive: "*It is necessary to maintain the system of cadre participation in collective productive labour. The cadres of our Party and state are ordinary workers and not overlords sitting on the backs of the people. By taking part in collective productive labour, the cadres maintain extensive, constant and close ties with the working people. This is a major measure of fundamental importance for a socialist system; it helps to overcome bureaucracy and to prevent revisionism and dogmatism.*"

With this directive in effect, collective productive labour has become a common practice for the cadres in China. This is especially true of Hsiyang County, Shansi Province, where the Tachai Brigade, the national pace-

* From *Peking Review*, No. 25, 1973.

setter in agriculture, is located. Here cadres at all four levels—county, commune, brigade and team—have persisted in this practice for the past decade. In recent years they have done so even more conscientiously and have become a cadre force with a high ideological consciousness, displaying the outstanding qualities of the labouring people. Since 1967 the mass learn-from-Tachai movement to "rearrange mountains and rivers" has been gaining momentum in the county. The stony, hilly area, slashed by ravines and ridges, has been built up into farmland, agricultural production has developed swiftly and the standard of living has risen markedly. Total grain output in 1969 was double that of 1966, and in 1971, nearly triple. Last year, despite a severe drought rarely seen over the past 100 years, total grain output was 76 per cent higher than in 1966.

The people of Hsiyang have put it well: A great change has come over Hsiyang since we started to learn from Tachai six years ago. First of all, we followed Chairman Mao's revolutionary line; second, the 200,-000 people of the county struggled hard; and third, the cadres worked together with the masses continuously and without stint.

Hsiyang's "One, Two, Three" System

No cadre in Hsiyang is exempt from collective productive labour and one who cannot work well is not a good cadre. It is almost impossible to distinguish between county, commune, brigade and team cadres or between cadres and rank-and-file peasants. They look the same, covered in dust on fine days and spattered with mud on wet.

Cadres participate in labour according to a "one, two, three" system. This means that county cadres must do manual labour at least one hundred days a year, commune cadres two hundred and brigade or team cadres three hundred.

How is it carried out? Take the case of Comrade Chen Yung-kuei, who is a very busy man. He is the Party branch secretary of the Tachai Brigade and secretary of the county Party committee. He is also a secretary of the Shansi provincial Party committee and a Member of the Central Committee of the Chinese Communist Party. But nothing keeps him from taking part in manual labour or maintaining close links with the masses. He has no office in the county town. Attending conferences at the regional and provincial levels or in Peking may take him away from the brigade, he does the studying and planning of work mostly in the brigade during the evenings. He draws on his experience in revolution and production in the Tachai Brigade for reference in directing work in other places.

Comrade Chen Yung-kuei's example guides the other 11 members of the Hsiyang County Party committee's standing committee. They spend about 100 days each working and living with the peasants at the grass-roots level every year. By summing up the experience gained there, they are better equipped to direct the work of the whole county. You can never find more than one-third of the cadres sitting behind desks at the same time in the county Party and government offices, for two-thirds of them are always down at the grassroots directing production as they take part in physical labour. Last year they averaged 106 days per person in collective productive labour.

Cadres of factories, mines and other enterprises run by the county spend half a day at office work, half at manual labour. They rotate for stints in the villages to help with sowing, harvesting and other farming tasks.

Working and living at the grass-roots level for most part of the year, the 306 commune cadres in the county averaged 215 days in physical labour last year.

The schedule for production brigade and team cadres consists mainly of physical labour in the day and administrative work in the evening. Brigade cadres last year averaged 310 days of physical labour each, and team cadres, 332.

Good Results

The cadres of Hsiyang County, particularly those at the county and commune level, have cultivated the fine style of forming close ties with the masses while participating in physical labour. They work with the peasants in the fields and, after work, study together with them. Brigade and team cadres do field work as a matter of course and earn work-points the same as the other peasants. Commune members say: "Today's cadres work like we do and think like we do."

Real knowledge is born of practice and correct thinking comes from practice. The cadres of Hsiyang have acquired a deep understanding of this through participation in collective productive labour. In the same way, they have cultivated "the five abilities": to see problems in work; to know what can be done and how to do it well by personally taking part in farm and other work; in ideological-political work, to get the message through to the peasant masses in relation to specific production task; to listen directly to what the peasant masses say; and to acquire the wisdom, sentiments and skills of the working people. These five abilities make them better organizers and leaders of revolution and production in the villages.

In the Santu Commune there is a ravine which used to cause great havoc. For years the peasants had wanted to remove this menace but were unable to. The cadres had also wanted to take measures to combat the menace but had hesitated to do so. Last year cadres from the commune went and worked with the peasants of several teams and, together with them, criticized and repudiated the reactionary view held by Liu Shao-chi and other political swindlers that history is created by a handful of "geniuses." In the course of this, all established in their minds the Marxist-Leninist view that it is the masses who are the real heroes. Thus ideologically armed, the cadres determined to organize the masses to conquer the Santu ravine. A plan was drawn up. Last October they organized a force of 2,000 and deployed them along an 11-kilometre front to reclaim farmland. Chao Huai-jui, secretary of the commune Party committee, led all the cadres to set up their offices at the work-site. With the cadres taking the lead, the masses worked unstintingly and the project was completed in 50 days instead of the planned four months. They moved more than 1.7 million cubic metres of earth and rock and hacked out a culvert 11,000 metres long. Thus they turned 11 kilometres of rock-strewn river bank into more than 30 hectares of flat farmland. Waging this campaign to conquer the Santu ravine has enriched their experience in leading production work. Since the winter of last year, the commune cadres and peasants have joined their efforts to build seven reservoirs and 16 water-retention basins to turn more than 200 hectares of land into irrigated farmland. This campaign has deepened the cadres' understanding of the power of the masses and strengthened the masses' confidence in the leadership of the cadres.

System Upheld Through Struggle

The system of cadres taking part in collective productive labour has become a common practice for cadres in Hsiyang County. This is the result of the struggle between the two lines—unswervingly upholding the Marxist-Leninist line and struggling against the revisionist line—and between proletarian and bourgeois ideology. As early as 1956, shortly after agricultural producers' co-operatives were formed, the Party committee of Hsiyang County organized cadres to take part in collective productive labour as an important political measure. The county Party committee paid great heed to this, so that by 1960 it had gradually become a common practice.

After 1960, however, this practice met with interference from Liu Shao-chi's revisionist line. Liu Shao-chi and his gang spread decadent ideas of the exploiting classes such as "joining the Party to become an official" and "physical labour is punishment." A fierce struggle raged throughout the county over the issue of cadre participation in collective productive labour. Comrade Chen Yung-kuei and other cadres of the Tachai Brigade stood at the forefront of the struggle, maintaining that such a system was a guarantee against divorcing oneself from physical labour, from practice and from the masses and a guarantee for maintaining the fine qualities of the working people. They stood firm against the revisionist tendency and resolutely led the masses in taking the socialist road. In 1963 the Tachai Brigade emerged with flying colours by offsetting the effects of torrential rains and beating a path of developing socialist agriculture through self-reliance and hard struggle. The following year Chairman Mao issued a call to the whole nation: *"In agriculture, learn from Tachai."* Other cadres in Hsiyang County learnt from Tachai's cadres, emulating the revolutionary spirit they had displayed in sharing weal and woe with the masses, overcoming natural disasters and advancing continuously along the socialist path.

In 1967, during the Great Proletarian Cultural Revolution, the Revolutionary Committee of Hsiyang County was founded. Summing up the lessons of the struggle between the two lines, it reaffirmed the decision that cadres at all four levels—county, commune, brigade and team—must take part in collective productive labour. In March this year the county Party committee organized a study class for the Party secretaries of 90 advanced brigades to sum up experience and overcome shortcomings so as to develop agriculture faster. The participants all agreed on the three most basic experiences: conscientious implementation of Chairman Mao's revolutionary line and upholding the spirit of the general line of going all out, aiming high and achieving greater, faster, better and more economical results in building socialism; faith in the masses and reliance on them and carrying out energetic mass movements; and lastly, regular participation in collective productive labour by cadres. The Party committee endorsed these three points and acting on the opinions of the members passed a "resolution on maintaining the system of cadre participation in collective productive labour."

3. The Movement to Criticize
Lin Piao and Confucius

In 1927 Mao singled out "the four thick ropes binding the Chinese people—namely, political authority, clan authority, religious authority and male authority," as the objects of the revolution. The philosophical foundation upholding these authorities was Confucianism. Confucian ideology shaped the Chinese mind as firmly as Christianity shaped the Western mind. The visible ropes have been cut, but the invisible ropes, which, as Marx puts it, "weighs like a nightmare on the brains of the living," are not so easily cut. For the socialist revolution to succeed China must thoroughly expunge Confucianism from the brains of the people.

Every progressive movement in modern China attacked Confucianism. One of the first acts of the leader of the great nineteenth-century Taiping peasant revolution was to smash the statue of Confucius which he had worshiped in his youth. The May 4th Movement earlier in this century raised the slogan of "Smashing the Confucian Shop." But old ideas die hard. They crop up sometimes in the most unexpected places—such as in the writings of Liu Shao-Chi and sayings of Lin Piao. All conservatives and reactionaries in Chinese history used Confucius to consolidate their rule over the people. Chiang Kai-shek, who is known to Americans as a converted Christian, officially designated Confucius as "the sage" and advertised himself in China as a Confucian.

What makes Mao a great revolutionary leader is his ability to attack the roots of the problem. The Lin Piao affair, in terms of numbers was a minor conspiracy involving only a handful of people. Ordinary leaders would consider the matter closed once the conspiracy was uncovered. But, for Mao, it was a signal for a major movement to push forward the ideological revolution. The fact that persons high up in the revolutionary ranks, such as Lin Piao and Liu Shao-Chi, still harbored Confucian ideas (and of course they were not the only ones) showed the need for a vigorous campaign to get rid of the remnants of Confucianism. The timeliness and necessity of the mass movement to criticize Confucius can be illustrated by an example. During our first visit to China in 1972 we asked a high official in Peking, "Why do we only see women taking care of children in child care centers and kindergartens? Don't you think men should take part in child care also?" He answered, "Well, women are better with kids. They are more gentle and patient. You know the Old Chinese saying—'Father should be stern and Mother lenient.'" The Confucian saying embodies precisely the male chauvinist outlook which is one of the Confucian ideas under attack by women in China.

"The Communist revolution is the most radical rupture with traditional property relations; no wonder that its development involves the most radical rupture with traditional ideas," proclaimed Marx and Engels in *The Communist Manifesto*. Confucianism is the sum total of the traditional ideas of China, it represents the past of China. Mao Tsetung Thought is the sum total of the experience of the Chinese revolution; it represents the future of China. During the transitional period the two-line struggle in ideology will continue until the future triumphs over the past, until full communism is established.

K.H.F.
K.T.F.

LIN PIAO AND THE DOCTRINE OF CON-
FUCIUS AND MENCIUS*

Inspired by the spirit of the Tenth National Congress of the Communist Party of China, the movement to criticize Lin Piao and Confucius is developing in depth. Lenin pointed out that in the acute struggle between the proletariat and the exploiting classes, *"the more varied the exploiters' attempts to uphold the old, the sooner will the proletariat learn to ferret out its enemies from their last nook and corner, to pull up the roots of their domination."* The current vigorous struggle to criticize Confucius is a component part of the criticism of Lin Piao and is precisely a battle to pull up the roots of Lin Piao's counter-revolutionary revisionist line. Lin Piao's hide-out was flooded with the trash of Confucian ideology and stank of putrid Confucianism. More and more facts show that the reactionary doctrine of Confucius and Mencius was an important source of Lin Piao's revisionism. Lin Piao and company resorted to this reactionary doctrine for restoring capitalism politically, tampering ideologically with the Party's theoretical basis, mustering ranks of counter-revolutionaries organizationally by recruiting deserters and renegades for a diehard clique, tactically playing counter-revolutionary double-dealing tricks and engaging in intrigues and conspiracies. Once Lin Piao's disguise was stripped off, he was exposed for what he was —an out-and-out devout disciple of Confucius.

Lin Piao Followed Confucius in Advocating "Self-Restraint and Restoration of the Rites" in His Attempt to Restore Capitalism

Lin Piao's political line was a counter-revolutionary revisionist line, an ultra-Rightist line of restoration and

* From *Peking Review,* No. 7, 1974.

retrogression. In his own words, it was "restraining oneself and restoring the rites." In less than three months, between October 1969 and January 1970, Lin Piao and his diehard conspirator wrote four scrolls reading: "Of all things, this is the most important: to restrain oneself and restore the rites." "Restraining oneself and restoring the rites" was the reactionary programme Confucius put forward in order to restore the slave system. In regarding "restraining oneself and restoring the rites" as the most important of all his affairs, Lin Piao revealed his impatience and wolfish ambition to subvert the dictatorship of the proletariat and restore capitalism.

The latter part of the Spring and Autumn Period (770-476 B.C.) was a period of tremendous social changes in Chinese history, one of transition from the slave system to feudalism. At that time China was in great disorder. The slaves frequently rose in rebellion. The newly emerging landlords vigorously advocated reforms and waged struggles to seize power from the slave-owners. All this brought the old slave-owning order of "rule of rites" to the brink of total collapse. Taking the stand of the declining slave-owning class, Confucius slandered the excellent situation in which "the rites were lost and music was ruined" as "absence of right principles throughout the country" and put forward his reactionary political programme of "restraining oneself and restoring the rites." By "restoring the rites," he meant suppression of the slave uprisings, opposition to the reform line of the Legalist school representing the newly rising landlord class, and the pulling of society backward. He wanted to restore the rule of the slave-owning society of the Western Chou Dynasty (c. 1066-771 B.C.) in accordance with the rites of the Chou Dynasty and the dictatorship of the slave-owners in line with the principle that "ceremonies, music and punitive military expeditions proceed from the son of heaven." He meant to "revive states that were extinct, restore families whose line of succession had been broken, and call to office those who had fallen into obscurity," and to reinstate the overthrown regime of slave-owners and the slave-owning aristocrats who had been deprived of their privileged status, so as to seize back power from the newly rising landlord class. In a nutshell, Confucius' "restoration of the rites" meant restoration of the old order. Lin Piao also attempted a restoration. They had the same counter-revolutionary nature and political needs. That was why Lin Piao grasped at "restraining oneself and restoring the rites" and considered it "most important." His counter-revolutionary coup d'etat and *Outline of Project "571"* are the best explanations of his clamours for the "restoration of the rites."

Lin Piao's "restoring the rites" meant subverting the dictatorship of the proletariat. Lin Piao and his gang rabidly hated this dictatorship and the Great Proletarian Cultural Revolution. They slandered the dictatorship of the proletariat which protects the people and suppresses their enemies as "enforcing the laws of Chin Shih Huang," and attacked continuing the revolution under the dictatorship of the proletariat as "creating contradictions." They did their utmost to smear and negate the tremendous achievements of the Great Proletarian Cultural Revolution and wantonly vilified the new things that have emerged during the Great Cultural Revolution. They slandered the excellent situation and the thriving socialist cause since the start of the Great Cultural Revolution as "crisis-ridden" and "stagnant," and described our state of the dictatorship of the proletariat as dark and dreary. In short, in their eyes, nothing in socialist New China was in keeping with their "rites." Like Confucius, they were all reactionaries who extolled the past to negate the present and advocated retrogression.

Lin Piao's "restoring the rites" was a bid to usurp supreme power in the Party and the state and restore the dictatorship of the landlords and comprador-bourgeoisie. In October 1969, when Lin Piao wrote "restraining oneself and restoring the rites" on a scroll, he echoed Mencius and counselled his sworn followers that "this is most urgent." What did "most urgent" mean in fact? Let's look at the following:

In the winter of 1969, Lin Piao hung on the wall near his bed a scroll in his handwriting: "No ruler of a dynasty can surpass King Wen of Chou. . . ." He styled himself a "sovereign" and alluded himself to "King Wen." He was impatient to realize his dream of becoming an emperor.

In 1970 Lin Piao resisted Chairman Mao's instructions again and again and produced his anti-Party political programme, clamouring that "if the state has no head, there will be no right titles and words will not be proper." He was desperately anxious to become "head of the state," and conspired to usurp Party leadership and seize state power. Following that, he launched an abortive counter-revolutionary coup d'etat at the Second Plenary Session of the Party's Ninth Central Committee.

In 1971 Lin Piao and company concocted a plan for a counter-revolutionary armed coup d'etat entitled *Outline of Project "571."* They were impatient to "seize political power throughout the country" and launched the coup in September that year.

These facts prove that the prime purpose of the Lin Piao anti-Party clique's "restoring the rites" was to seize supreme power of the Party and the state. This was the "most urgent" of their counter-revolutionary strategies.

The class content of Lin Piao's "restoring the rites" was to establish in China a feudal-comprador-fascist dynasty of the Lin family. Confucius shouted that he wanted to "revive states that were extinct, restore families whose line of succession had been broken, and call to office those who had fallen into obscurity." Internally, Lin Piao picked up this Confucian rubbish, carried out counter-revolutionary activities for a restoration, and rabidly shouted that they wanted to "give political liberation to all" enemies of the dictatorship of the proletariat in an attempt to reinstate the landlord and capitalist classes, which were overthrown by our Party, army and people under the leadership of Chairman Mao, and restore capitalism. If that should happen, big and small despotic landlords as Huang Shih-jen and the Tyrant of the South (villains in the modern revolutionary ballets *The White-Haired Girl* and the *Red Detachment of Women* respectively—translator) would once again ride roughshod over the people, and the renegade, enemy agent and traitor Wang Ming and others like him would swaggeringly come back to power and become "guests of honour" of the Lin dynasty. And, thousands upon thousands of revolutionaries would fall victim to the counter-revolutionary butcher's knife, while millions upon millions of workers and peasants would once again be plunged into misery. Internationally, Lin Piao and company acted according to the motto they had taken over from Mencius—"the small states regarded the large as masters"—and engaged in capitulationist, traitorous, counter-revolutionary activities, trying to seek the patronage of Soviet revisionist social-imperialism and alignment with imperialism, revisionism and reaction against China, against communism and against revolution. If the plot of Lin Piao, the "super spy," had succeeded, the beautiful land of China would have been trampled upon by the tanks of Soviet revisionism, the social-imperialist gangsters would have run amuck in China, and the Chinese people would have been subjugated and enslaved.

In a word, by picking up and waving the tattered banner of Confucius' "restraining oneself and restoring the rites," Lin Piao attempted to change fundamentally the Party's basic line and China's socialist system, subvert the dictatorship of the proletariat and restore capitalism. However, all this was no more than an idiot's daydream.

Chairman Mao has said: *"'Lifting a rock only to drop it on one's own feet' is a Chinese folk saying to describe the behaviour of certain fools. The reactionaries in all countries are fools of this kind."* And Lin Piao was a reactionary of this kind. He intended to ascend the throne as a vassal-king under the "nuclear umbrella" of his master—Soviet revisionism, but crashed to death in the desert. Holding the broken banner of "restraining oneself and restoring the rites," he traversed the road *"Make trouble, fail, make trouble again, fail again . . . till their doom,"* came to a dead end and went to meet Confucius.

Using the Reactionary Philosophy of Confucius and Mencius in Opposing Dialectical and Historical Materialism

In an attempt to restore capitalism, Lin Piao had not only a counter-revolutionary political line but a counter-revolutionary ideological line that served it. The reactionary philosophy of Confucius and Mencius was a major source of this ideological line. Lin Piao opposed materialism with the Confucian theory of "heaven's will" and theory of "innate genius," opposed materialist dialectics with the doctrine of the mean, opposed the Marxist theory of classes with the Confucian concept of "virtue, benevolence and righteousness, loyalty and forbearance," and launched an all-out attack on dialectical and historical materialism.

Confucius preached the "heaven's will," alleging that there was a supreme god called *tien* (heaven) who created man and all things on earth and controlled everything in nature and the world of man. His will was irresistible. The slave-owners, like King Wen of the Chou Dynasty, had the power to rule the people because they had a heavenly mandate. Likewise, Duke

Chou[1] and Confucius had heavenly mandates so that they possessed "virtue" and became "sages" to "enlighten" the people. This religious and theological idealist theory was invented solely for the purpose of preserving the dictatorship of the slave-owners. From this reactionary theory of "heaven's will" Confucius derived his apriorism that some people were "born with knowledge" and his idealist conception of history that heroes were the makers of history. Lin Piao seized the idealist trash of Confucious as treasures in his bid to usurp power and restore capitalism. He wrote a scroll with the words "The heavenly horse flies through the skies, free and alone" and hung it in the centre of the wall by the head of his bed, comparing himself to a heavenly horse, describing himself as a dragon-like and exceptionally endowed person, a superman and a genius that heaven had sent to the world of man. In an inscription he wrote to his diehard conspirator, he described the "virtues," which he and his band claimed to have, as "qualities from Heaven." Isn't this the same as Confucius' statement that "Heaven endows me with virtue"? For many years, Lin Piao and his diehard conspirators tried in a hundred and one ways by lies and sophistry to palm off the theory of "innate genius" as Marxism. But this is futile. "Qualities from Heaven," these characters in his own handwriting, showed that his theory of "innate genius" was a replica of Confucius' theory of "heaven's will." In clinging to the theory of "innate genius" which was his anti-Party theoretical programme, he was trying to prove that he was a supreme ruler with a mandate "from Heaven."

Lin Piao argued that *"chung yung"* [the doctrine

[1] Duke Chou whose name was Tan was a younger brother of King Wu who founded the Western Chou Dynasty. After the death of King Wu, Duke Chou became the regent as King Cheng was still too young. He instituted the rules and systems upholding the dictatorship of the slave-owners of the Chou Dynasty.

of the mean] was "rational." This exposed his true nature—opposing the revolution and dialectics. By *"chung yung"* Confucius and Mencius meant that everything should be done according to the "rites"; being neither excessive nor deficient was *"chung,"* and maintaining normalcy and constancy was *"yung."* In a word, the doctrine of the mean required that everything should be done according to the old rules of the slave system and the least deviation or change was impermissible. This is a metaphysical theory that reactionary classes use to defend the old system and oppose any changes. Lin Piao lauded this theory to the skies and said it was "rational." Proceeding from this "rationality," Lin Piao viciously cursed that the struggle by the proletarian revolutionary line against the revisionist line "has been excessive" and "entirely leftist," "has gone to the extreme," "has been carried out to extreme" and "has created a mess." What a heap of labels! This, however, cannot in any way tarnish the brilliance of Chairman Mao's revolutionary line. It only serves to show that what Lin Piao upheld was an ultra-Rightist line aimed at preserving the old system and order and turning back the wheel of history. When talking about "being excessive," Lin Piao was opposing the revolution with the Confucian doctrine of the mean. Chairman Mao refuted this fallacy long ago, pointing out that *a revolution is not a dinner party,"* and that *"proper limits have to be exceeded in order to right a wrong, or else the wrong cannot be righted."* Lin Piao cried about "creating a mess." Well, it is only the order of the bourgeoisie and revisionism that has been disrupted. Without disrupting that order, we cannot destroy the old world and create the new. Does it scare the bunch of you that your order is disrupted? Well, this is just the beginning, and much remains to be done before eliminating all exploiting classes in the world. The world outlook of the proletariat is materialist dialectics which *"is in its essence critical and revolutionary"*

(Marx: "Afterword to the Second German Edition of *Capital*"). Whether we foster new things to defeat old ones or use every means to prevent the old things from dying is a major issue in the struggle between the two lines. Theoretically, this struggle is bound to appear as one between materialist dialectics and metaphysics. Lin Piao used Confucius and Mencius' doctrine of the mean to oppose dialectics. This is an ideological root cause for his pushing an ultra-Rightist line.

Lin Piao said that the "virtue, benevolence and righteousness, loyalty and forbearance" advocated by Confucianism were the principles for "human relations," that this was "historical materialism." He also said that "loyalty, which means treating people with benevolence and love, and forbearance, which means tolerance and forgiveness—these are Confucian principles." He talked about "benevolence and love," entirely removing the class character, and talked about "human relations" while negating class antagonism. He thus used the reactionary theory of human nature of Confucius and Mencius to tamper with and negate the theory of class of historical materialism.

The theory of human nature as preached by the Confucian school is a hypocritical idealist theory. It advocates an apriorist and supra-class human nature. Confucius alleged that "benevolence" meant "to love all men," and Mencius said that man was born in possession of "benevolence" and that "man is born good." Did they love all men irrespective of classes? Not in the least. When the State of Cheng[2] killed all the rebelling slaves, did not Confucius commend the slaughter and say "excellent"? Did not Mencius theorize the exploitation of and rule over the slaves and labourers as "a universal principle"? Neither did they love the newly emerging landlord class. As soon as he took office as

[2] A state under the slave system in the Spring and Autumn Period, Cheng was in the southern part of the present Honan Province.

acting prime minister of the State of Lu,[3] Confucius killed Shaocheng Mou, a representative of the reformers. Confucius promptly expelled his disciple Jan Chiu, broke off their relation of teacher and student, and instigated his other disciples to attack him because he served the newly emerging landlord class. These proved that the "human love" irrespective of classes, "benevolence" by birth and other notions advocated by Confucius and Mencius were all trash aimed to fool the people. In fact those they loved were the handful of slave-owners of the exploiting classes and the reactionary slave system. While talking about "benevolence and love," Lin Piao in his plan for a counter-revolutionary armed coup d'etat, the *Outline of Project "571,"* viciously plotted to "devour" the proletariat at a mouthful, to assassinate the great leader of the proletariat, overthrow the working people who are now masters of the country, and institute a fascist dictatorship. Those they loved were actually the handful of class enemies whom we have overthrown. This is Lin Piao's "human nature," also the human nature of the landlord and capitalist classes. A chieftain of the Chiang Kai-shek gang said mournfully two years after Lin Piao's death: "Lin Piao . . . had relatively more human nature. This is evidence of the Confucian ethics lying deep in men's hearts." This praise by the Chiang Kai-shek gang best explains what Lin Piao's human nature really was.

Doing their utmost to advocate the theory of human nature, the reactionary classes dress themselves up as "virtuous sovereigns" who care for the people so as to hide their man-eating features. On the other hand, they hoist the banner of "benevolence, righteousness and virtue" to denounce the revolutionary violence of the progressive classes. Did not Confucius curse the newly emerging landlord class as "rebels with courage but

[3] A state under the slave system in the Spring and Autumn Period, Lu was in the southern part of the present Shantung Province.

without righteousness" and the insurgent slaves as "robbers with courage but without righteousness"? Mencius went even farther. He hurled abuses at revolutionary violence, saying "they slaughter men till the fields are filled with bodies," and "they slaughter men till a city is filled with bodies," and they "devour human flesh." He said they should be given capital punishment, crying: "Death is not enough for such a crime." Lin Piao took over the mantle of Confucius and Mencius. With the reactionary theory of human nature as his theoretical basis, he cried: "Those who rely on virtue will thrive and those who rely on force will perish." He accused the dictatorship of the proletariat as "not benevolent." " *'You are not benevolent!' Quite so. We definitely do not apply a policy of benevolence to the reactionaries and towards the reactionary activities of the reactionary classes.*" The proletariat must resolutely and mercilessly suppress all reactionary elements of the reactionary classes who dare to resist. Otherwise, we shall lose our state power, and the landlord and capitalist classes will come back to power. Did not Lin Piao, under the camouflage of sham benevolence and righteousness, attempt to use counter-revolutionary violence to overthrow the dictatorship of the proletariat? In dealing with the counter-revolutionary violence of the reactionaries, we have no alternative but, as the saying goes, to deal with a man as he deals with you, namely, use revolutionary violence to suppress counter-revolutionary violence. We must uphold the Marxist theory of class struggle and dictatorship of the proletariat and persist in the Party's basic line so as to continuously consolidate and strengthen the proletarian dictatorship. This is our conclusion.

Resorting to Expediency of the Confucian School, Forming a Clique for Selfish Purposes, Engaging in Intrigues and Conspiracy

Lin Piao's political line and ideological line were revisionist. This inevitably led him organizationally to carry out splitting activities and form a clique to pursue his selfish interests, and tactically to resort to double dealing and engage in intrigues and conspiracy. In order to entrench himself in the Party and to pull together his counter-revolutionary ranks, waiting for the opportunity to achieve his ambition of "restoring the rites," Lin Piao directed his sworn followers and others to comb through the Four Books and Five Classics,[4] histories of China and other countries, and even novels and proverbs for material to help him find ways and means for carrying out his counter-revolutionary conspiracies. All the tricks the slave-owning class and the

[4] The Four Books—four "classical canons" of the Confucians—include the *Great Learning*, the *Doctrine of the Mean*, the *Analects* of Confucius and *Mencius*.

The Five Classics refer to the following five Confucian "classics"—the *Book of Songs*, the *Book of History*, the *Book of Rites*, the *Book of Change* and the *Spring and Autumn Annals*. Feudal rulers after the Han Dynasty called them the *Five Classics*, using them as an ideological tool to control the people.

The *Book of Songs* is China's earliest collection of songs. It was said that Confucius deleted certain songs in this book.

The *Book of History*, also known as the *Shang Shu*, is a collection of political documents and records of history prior to the Spring and Autumn Period and the Warring States Period.

The *Book of Rites* contains the *Rites of Chou*, the *Book of Ceremony* and the *Records of Rites*. The *Rites of Chou* records the stipulations for government offices and functions of officials of the Chou Dynasty. The *Book of Ceremony* records the ceremonies for marriage, funeral, sacrifices and social intercourse during the Chou Dynasty. The *Records of Rites* contains essays on rites by Confucians before the Chin and Han Dynasties.

The *Book of Change*, also known as the *Chou Yi*, is a book for fortune-telling in ancient China.

The *Spring and Autumn Annals* were the annals recording contemporary history written by the State of Lu in the Spring and Autumn Period. Deletions and alterations were made by Confucius to safeguard the slave system.

feudal landlord class had accumulated for their reactionary rule and their double-dealing tactics became his important ideological weapons for carrying out splitting activities and conspiracies.

In an effort to preserve the dying slave system, Confucius said that "a prince should employ his ministers according to propriety and ministers should serve their prince with loyalty," using this as the criterion in handling relations within the ruling clique of slave-owning nobility. That was precisely what Lin Piao practised in his anti-Party clique.

Lin Piao made use of Confucius' trash that "a prince should employ his ministers according to propriety"; but this was only a hypocritical gesture. An out-and-out fascist dictator, Lin Piao made stupendous efforts to establish his "absolute authority." He drew a line between those he favoured and those he disfavoured according to the attitudes shown towards him, and followed the principle that "those who are obedient shall thrive and those who resist shall perish." Yet he played the tune of "employing ministers according to propriety" and put up the signboard of "seeking wise men." The fact is that the "propriety" he talked about meant handing out official posts and making promises and granting special favours, inviting guests and giving them presents, wining and dining, and trafficking in mutual flattery and commendation. In short, it meant using personal fame, gains and position as lures to buy over and draw together a group of people to serve his undertaking for a counter-revolutionary restoration. When his sworn followers were exposed by the masses, he used his position and power to shield and protect them and help them slip away unpunished. By "seeking wise men," he meant recruiting deserters, renegades and monsters, organizing a bourgeois headquarters and rigging up big and small counter-revolutionary "fleets"

(Lin Piao's secret agencies—translator) to meet the needs of capitalist restoration.

By preaching that "a prince should employ his ministers according to propriety," Lin Piao wanted his sworn followers to act as "ministers serving their prince with loyalty." Like all previous reactionary rulers, Lin Piao used the idea of "loyalty to the prince" as the ideological pillar to maintain his rule in the ranks of counter-revolutionaries. He lauded Confucius and Mencius for their preachings of the concept of "loyalty and filial piety" which meant "respect for superiors" and "obedience," and advocated absolute obedience. He forced members of his secret agencies to swear allegiance and pledge "eternal loyalty" to the Lin family, father and son. Even when the downfall of Lin Piao's anti-Party clique was imminent, he issued the counter-revolutionary order of "success or death," vainly calling on members of his counter-revolutionary "fleets" to die as funerary objects for the "Lin dynasty." These facts show that an important organizational principle of the Lin Piao anti-Party clique was the moral obligations and preachings of Confucius and Mencius.

Lin Piao set great store by Confucius' saying: "Want of patience in small matters confounds big plans." He copied it and hung it on the wall as a counter-revolutionary maxim. Towards the many painstaking criticisms and education given him by Chairman Mao and the Party Central Committee, he nursed his hatred and waited for an opportunity to counter-attack. Plotting to usurp Party leadership and state power, he repeatedly reminded himself "to have patience" so as not to permit the "foolhardiness of common men" to confound his big plan of "restoring the rites" and "spoil one's great plan of a lifetime." Behind the "patience," Lin Piao gritted his teeth, sharpened his knife and watched how the wind blew to achieve his aim. This was actually a repeat performance of the counter-revolutionary trick of "seeking survival in forbearance" of Hu Feng.[5]

Lin Piao highly valued the "stratagem of *tao hui* (concealment)" in order to "seek survival in forbearance" and realize his "big plan." In March 1970 when the Lin Piao anti-Party clique was busy drawing up its scheme to usurp Party leadership and state power, Lin Piao directed his diehard conspirator to write the words *"tao hui"* in one of the notebooks, and personally copied a poem from the *Romance of the Three Kingdoms* that praises Liu Pei for having deceived Tsao Tsao[6] by the "strategem of *tao hui"*: "Constrained to lodge for a time in the tiger's lair, the hero was alarmed when his ambitions were laid bare. Using the thunderclap to cover up his panic, he rose to the occasion, clever and quick." Here Lin Piao maligned the proletarian headquarters as the "tiger's lair" and compared himself to a "hero" who "lodges for a time in the tiger's lair." This shows that he was a bourgeois careerist and conspirator who nestled beside us. This also shows his ferocious features in using double-dealing tactics to disguise himself and cover up his counter-revolutionary aims and

[5] Hu Feng was the ringleader of the Hu Feng counter-revolutionary clique. Under the leadership of the Party Central Committee headed by Comrade Mao Tsetung, the people of the whole country in 1955 exposed and waged struggles against this counter-revolutionary clique hidden in the revolutionary ranks.

[6] The *Romance of Three Kingdoms*, a long Chinese historical novel, takes its material from the history between the latter years of the Eastern Han Dynasty and Three Kingdoms (184-280). The author is Lo Kuan-chung who lived in the 14th century.

Liu Pei (161-223) was the founder of the Kingdom of Han (Shu) in the period of the Three Kingdoms. Tsao Tsao (155-220) was the prime minister in the latter years of the Eastern Han Dynasty and father of Tsao Pi who founded the Kingdom of Wei in the period of Three Kingdoms. Tsao Tsao was post-humously given the title Emperor Wu of Wei.

waiting for an opportune moment to execute his murderous plan against the proletarian headquarters.

In order to disguise his real self, he was quick to change to suit the occasion, and he secretly formulated a series of counter-revolutionary double-dealing tactics in line with the admonition of Confucius and Mencius, which said: "To love those others hate and to hate those others love. . . . Calamities will certainly come down on him who does so." "A great man may not be true to his words or consistent in his action," "one cannot accomplish great things without telling lies" and "keep a smile on the face"—all these, without adding a single word, are sufficient to vividly expose Lin Piao as a counter-revolutionary double-dealer who "never showed up without a copy of *Quotations* in hand and never opened his mouth without shouting 'Long Live' and who spoke nice things to your face but stabbed you in the back."

Why Did the Revisionist Chieftain Lin Piao Seek Help From Confucius and Mencius?

Like chieftains of opportunist lines in the past, Lin Piao was a representative of the bourgeoisie within our Party, a devout worshipper of Confucius. People will naturally ask: Why did a representative of the bourgeoisie seek ideological weapons from the slave-owning and feudal landlord classes? And why do all the revisionist chieftains within the Party invariably seek help from the doctrine of Confucius and Mencius? This is a question worthy of attention.

That the revisionist chieftain Lin Piao and his like worshipped Confucius was not strange at all. It has deep class and historical roots.

In the first place, it should be pointed out that the devotion of Lin Piao and company to Confucius was closely linked to the historical characteristics and class status of the Chinese bourgeoisie and especially the big bourgeoisie, which they represented. The world entered the era of imperialism and proletarian revolution in the late 19th and early 20th centuries. The Chinese bourgeoisie, which then lived in a semi-colonial, semi-feudal society, had its class character formed right from its inception. The Chinese bourgeoisie was very weak economically and politically, and in the ideological and cultural sphere it was incapable of establishing an ideological system powerful enough to replace feudal culture. The big bourgeoisie, which held the dominant position in old China, grew out of a combination of imperialism and feudalism, and its fundamental character was comprador and feudal in nature. The big bourgeoisie all along stubbornly supported and enthusiastically hawked the imperialist philosophy of enslavement and the feudal culture characterized by the worship of Confucius and the study of Confucian classics. In the period of the socialist revolution when the contradiction between the proletariat and the bourgeoisie has become the principal internal contradiction in China, whoever dreams of restoring capitalism in China must politically exercise a feudal, comprador and fascist dictatorship, and in the ideological and cultural sphere, seek weapons from imperialism and feudalism. Chen Tu-hsiu, Wang Ming, Liu Shao-chi, Lin Piao and company, who represented the interests of the bourgeoisie, invariably reflected this class character in practising revisionism and resorting to the doctrine of Confucius and Mencius. This was especially true of Lin Piao who came from a landlord-capitalist family and who all along refused to remould his world outlook.

Secondly, from the point of view of history, the doctrine of Confucius and Mencius was the ideology of the declining slave-owning class, a highly deceptive ideological system of the exploiting classes. Essentially it stands for retrogression and against progress, for conservatism and against reform, for restoration of the old order and against revolution. It is a doctrine of exploitation and oppression, of staging a counter-revolutionary come-back. It was later utilized by the decadent landlord class and the big bourgeoisie as well as by the imperialists who tried to vanquish China, and it became the dominant ideology in China's feudal society and semi-colonial, semi-feudal society of the past 2,000 years and more, the spiritual fetters used by all the past reactionary rulers to enslave the working people, and the ideological weapon of all reactionaries who conspire for a come-back and oppose communism. Because all the past reactionary rulers energetically advocated and forcibly pushed the doctrine of Confucius and Mencius, this doctrine became an age-old, traditional concept that had penetrated into every sphere of social life in old China. All reactionaries who advocated retrogression invariably took up the tattered banner of worshipping Confucius and used the doctrine of Confucius and Mencius in every possible way to deceive the masses with demagogy. Therefore, it is not surprising that all the chieftains of opportunist lines in our Party who opposed the revolution and advocated retrogression should worship Confucius. The revisionist chieftain Lin Piao was a big Party tyrant and big warlord who did not read books, newspapers and documents and who had no learning at all. But he tirelessly collected quotations from Confucius and Mencius and preached their doctrine, because his reactionary thought was the same as that of Confucius and Mencius, his counter-revolutionary nature was to bring about a capitalist restoration, and his vicious desire was to use reactionary traditional ideas in an effort to subvert the dictatorship of the proletariat and restore capitalism.

With the deepening of the movement to criticize Lin Piao and rectify the style of work, it is quite natural that we criticize the doctrine of Confucius and Mencius and the notion of exalting Confucianism and opposing the Legalist school. The current struggle to criticize Lin

Piao and Confucius is a life-and-death struggle between the two classes and the two lines and an event of paramount importance for the entire Party, the entire army and the people of the whole country. Not to criticize Confucius and the idea of exalting Confucianism and opposing the Legalist school is, in effect, not to criticize Lin Piao. A deep criticism of the doctrine of Confucius and Mencius and the idea of exalting Confucianism and opposing the Legalist school is of great significance in thoroughly exposing and criticizing the ultra-Rightist nature of Lin Piao's revisionist line, strengthening education in ideological and political line, consolidating and expanding the achievements of the Great Proletarian Cultural Revolution, and doing a good job in the revolution in the superstructure. Under the leadership of Chairman Mao and the Party Central Committee, we must develop the thoroughgoing revolutionary spirit of the proletariat and win new victories in the struggle to criticize Lin Piao and Confucius! (*Translation of an article in "Hongqi," No. 2, 1974*)

WORKERS, PEASANTS AND SOLDIERS ARE THE MAIN FORCE IN CRITICIZING LIN PIAO AND CONFUCIUS*

High Tide of Criticism in a P.L.A. Company

The Party branch of an anti-chemical warfare company of a P.L.A. unit stationed in Chekiang Province has launched a massive criticism of Lin Piao and Confucius. With firm fighting will, commanders and fighters criticized Lin Piao's crimes in using the doctrine of Confucius and Mencius to carry out counter-revolutionary activities for a capitalist restoration.

The commanders and fighters studied works by Marx, Engels, Lenin and Stalin and Chairman Mao's works during the traditional Spring Festival and wrote

* From *Peking Review,* No. 7, 1974.

articles and outlines of speeches criticizing Lin Piao and Confucius. They held a series of meetings in the squads, platoons and the company, and wrote more than 200 articles. They pledged: "Under the personal leadership of our great leader Chairman Mao, we will carry through to the end the socialist revolution in the superstructure and the struggle against Lin Piao and Confucius."

How did this vigorous struggle of criticism develop in the company?

First, the Party branch enthusiastically helped the fighters understand the nature of the struggle. It gave talks to guide them in making clear the connection between the criticism of Confucius and that of Lin Piao and the relation to today's class struggle and the struggle between the two lines. The commanders and fighters were helped to see what kind of man Confucius was, what his reactionary ideas were, how Lin Piao used the doctrine of Confucius and Mencius—a reactionary ideological weapon—to conspire to usurp Party leadership and state power and restore capitalism, why reactionaries at home and abroad frantically oppose the criticism of Confucius and why they have whipped up an adverse current of exalting Confucianism and opposing the Legalist school. To make these questions clear, cadres and fighters had animated discussions. They pointed out that criticism of Confucianism is an important component of criticism of Lin Piao and an acute class struggle and struggle between the two lines. It is of profound immediate significance and far-reaching historical importance for consolidating and developing the fruits of the Great Proletarian Cultural Revolution, opposing restoration and retrogression, consolidating the dictatorship of the proletariat and dealing blows at imperialism, revisionism and reaction. Commanders and fighters of the company expressed firm class hatred for the doctrine of Confucius and Mencius. The fighters said: "Confucius wanted to re-

store the rites and Lin Piao wanted to restore capitalism; they were one of a kind." "Criticizing Lin Piao
without repudiating Confucius is like cutting weeds
without removing the roots." Members of a platoon
said: "For more than 2,000 years, the reactionary ideas
of Confucius have been used to poison the minds of
the labouring people and impede the progress of revolution. We must completely eliminate Confucius' per-
nicious influence and propel the revolution forward."

Second, the Party branch guided all members of the
company to do away with all fetishes and superstitions,
emancipate their minds and strengthen their determination and confidence to be the main force in criticizing
Lin Piao and Confucius. They discussed such questions
as: "Are the workers and peasants capable of criticizing books by Confucius and Mencius which are very
difficult to read and understand?" and "Does the criticism of Confucius concern only cultural and educational
circles, historians and the leadership?" They raised
their understanding and enhanced their confidence and
determination after doing the following three things:

One. They studied the instructions given by Chairman Mao and the Party Central Committee on criticizing Lin Piao and Confucius and restudied the passages
from the documents of the Tenth Party Congress dealing with grasping class struggle in the superstructure,
thereby arming themselves politically and ideologically.

Two. They familiarized themselves with instances of
how the working people in Chinese history struggled
against Confucius and discussed the great role of the
workers, peasants and soldiers since liberation in criticizing feudalism, capitalism and revisionism. In this
way they came to see their own strength. Fighters in
the tenth squad said: "The working people are the
makers of history. It is they who have overthrown the
reactionary ruling classes one after another. The Liu
Shao-chi and Lin Piao bourgeois headquarters were
both shattered by the workers, peasants and soldiers

under the guidance of Chairman Mao and the Party Central Committee. How can it be said that we the working people lack strength?" Medical orderly Chao Hsueh-chung said: "The working people suffered most from the doctrine of Confucius and Mencius. They hate it the most once they see its reactionary essence, and their criticism is most penetrating."

Three. They further emancipated their minds and drew more encouragement by criticizing Confucius' idealist conception of history represented by his preaching that there are "the highest, who are wise, and the lowest, who are stupid." Fighter Wang Shou-hao said: "In the past I used to consider myself dumb and obtuse. Now I realize those with rich practical experience are the wisest and most talented. That concept of Confucius' was a vicious slander against the working people."

Third, the Party branch guided the commanders and fighters to link the criticism with concrete struggles. They were unanimous that the criticism of Lin Piao and Confucius must be linked with reality. To do this, it is necessary first of all to link this criticism with the conspiracies and crimes of the Lin Piao anti-Party clique, putting particular stress on criticizing the ultra-Rightist nature of Lin Piao's revisionist line. This is the main reality to deal with.

They also agreed that to link the criticism with concrete struggles it is necessary to grasp the cardinal issues in the current struggle between the two lines, criticize the Right deviationist trend of thought which negates the achievements of the Great Proletarian Cultural Revolution, opposes new socialist things and tries to turn back the wheel of history. If these errors are not criticized, it is impossible to carry out Chairman Mao's instructions, put into practice the principles laid down at the Tenth Party Congress and grasp well ideological and political work in the armed forces.

The fighters said that it was also necessary to combat the influence of the reactionary thinking of Confucius and Mencius, break with old, traditional ideas and remould one's world outlook. They said: "If careerists in the future use the doctrine of Confucius and Mencius to conspire to turn back the wheel of history, we will be able to see through their machinations and fight them once we have wiped out the evil influence of Confucius and Mencius and sharpened our vision."

Cadres in the company led the fighters in their conscientious studies and criticisms. Hsu Pan-chung, secretary of the Party branch and political instructor of the company, roundly criticized the bourgeois theory of human nature preached by Lin Piao in connection with the "benevolence, righteousness and virtue" preached by Confucius and Mencius. He said: "In the old society, my father worked as a hired labourer for landlords for more than two decades. He was barely able to keep himself alive. But no landlord showed any benevolence. Thousands upon thousands of poor people died of cold and starvation in the old society. But none of the capitalists showed any benevolence. Lin Piao preached the reactionary absurdities of Confucius and Mencius in his criminal plot to usurp Party leadership and state power and restore capitalism. This shows Lin Piao and Confucius had the same reactionary ideas and both were arch enemies of the working people."

After studying the teachings of Marx and Engels that the reactionaries' purpose in spreading the idealist conception of history was to prove that *"the final answer is that the noble, wise, and learned ones should rule,"* they pointed out that Confucius advocated that some were "born with knowledge" in order to dress himself up as a "sage" representing the will of heaven and to restore the reactionary rule of the slave-owning class. As for Lin Piao, he peddled the theory of "innate genius" to palm himself off as a "genius" so that he could "command everything" and let the overthrown landlord and capitalist classes once again ride on the backs of the people. Comparing the fallacies of Lin Piao with those of Confucius, the fighters discussed and criticized them one by one, and their fighting will grew in the course of such criticism.

The company's commanders and fighters have further raised their consciousness of class struggle and two-line struggle through the criticism of Lin Piao and Confucius. After criticizing the concept that "he who excels in learning can be an official" and other fallacies peddled by Confucius and Lin Piao's venomous slanders against educated young people settling in the countryside, the commanders and fighters wrote revolutionary letters to their families to encourage their relatives to follow the road charted by Chairman Mao unswervingly. All this enabled them to be more conscious of resisting bourgeois ideology and developing the style of plain living and hard struggle. Thanks to the strengthening of their revolutionary unity and sense of organization and discipline, work in various fields in the company is forging ahead vigorously as never before.

Shanghai Workers Active in the Struggle

Workers in China's biggest industrial city Shanghai are full of militancy in the struggle to criticize Lin Piao and Confucius.

Workers at the Cast Steel Section of the No. 2 Electric Furnace Workshop in the No. 5 Iron and Steel Mill, an advanced collective among Shanghai's iron and steel enterprises in studying works by Marx, Engels, Lenin and Stalin and by Chairman Mao, overcame difficulties in reading the *Analects* of Confucius, *Mencius, Great Learning* and *Doctrine of the Mean* in classical Chinese to deepen the criticism of Lin Piao's crime in using the doctrine of Confucius and Mencius to restore capitalism. They collected 250 examples of fallacious viewpoints from these books and criticized them in relation to Lin Piao's reactionary views. The more they criticized, the more clearly they recognized that Lin Piao was a devout disciple of Confucius.

The workers in this section, more than 200 in all, have in the past few years read the four volumes of the *Selected Works of Mao Tsetung,* the *Manifesto of the Communist Party, Imperialism, the Highest Stage of Capitalism* and other Marxist-Leninist works. They used the sharp weapon of Marxism-Leninism-Mao Tsetung Thought to roundly criticize Lin Piao and Confucius.

One of the workers said at a criticism meeting: "Lin Piao and Confucius were sworn enemies of the working people. We workers will stand at the forefront in the struggle to criticize them. We workers are determined not only to overthrow all systems of exploitation of man by man but to criticize thoroughly the ideologies of all exploiting classes."

Workers at the Chiuhsin Shipyard, who have persevered in studying Chairman Mao's works for a long time, in the past few months criticized Lin Piao's concept of "innate genius" and fallacies that viciously slander the workers and peasants by linking them to the sinister stuff spread by Confucius and Mencius such as some are "born with knowledge" and "those who labour with their minds govern others, those who labour with their strength are governed by others." The criticism was focused on the struggle between defending socialism and attempts to restore capitalism.

Workers at the Electric Appliance Workshop read up material by domestic and foreign reactionaries extolling Confucius and compared it to Lin Piao's praise of the doctrine of Confucius and Mencius. This helped them see more clearly that Lin Piao wanted capitalist restoration and retrogression. They said: "The reactionaries want retrogression and restoration, so they worship Confucius. We want to advance and make

revolution, so we must criticize Lin Piao and Confucius."

A veteran worker at the Shanghai Grinding Wheel
Plant recalled that when he was a boy he had studied
San Tzu Ching, an elementary textbook in classical
Chinese, which begins with "When a man is born, his
nature is good." He and his workmates said: "This is
the so-called 'theory of human nature' and idealist
apriorism of the exploiting classes spread by Confucius
and Mencius. They are the same as Lin Piao's reactionary theories."

With this as their starting point, the workers combined criticism of Lin Piao with criticism of Confucius.
In their spare time they looked up material on the words
and deeds of Confucius and Mencius and criticized
them by linking them with the contents of the *Outline
of Project "571,"* the plan for a counter-revolutionary
armed coup d'etat drawn up by Lin Piao and his gang.
The more they criticized, the deeper they went, and
they clearly saw that Lin Piao's reactionary ideas were
exactly the same as those of Confucius.

Veteran worker Huang Chin-tao, who has had only
three years of schooling, read and collected articles
from newspapers and took an active part in criticizing
Lin Piao and Confucius. He also discussed the criticisms with his children at home.

Workers in many enterprises have organized study
classes and held meetings to deepen the criticism of Lin
Piao and Confucius. The workers said: "Lin Piao and
Confucius sang the same tune and took the same road.
Confucius advocated 'restraining oneself and restoring
the rites' and Lin Piao explicitly said that 'of all things,
this is the most important: to restrain oneself and restore the rites.' He wrote this on a scroll and hung it in
his bedroom. This shows that, like Confucius, he
dreamt all the time of a counter-revolutionary restoration. Lin Piao considered capitalist restoration the most
important thing. We the working class and revolutionary

people must wage a tit-for-tat struggle against this. We must bear in mind Chairman Mao's revolutionary line and never forget that the most important thing of all is to combat and prevent revisionism."

Peking Peasants Criticize Lin Piao and Confucius

Poor and lower-middle peasants and other members of the Hsuchiawu Production Brigade in Peking's outlying Pingku County held a meeting on the evening of January 28 to criticize Lin Piao and Confucius. Many of them were eager to take the floor the moment the meeting started.

Yang Ching-chuan, leader of Production Team No. 2, said: "Confucius was the dutiful son of the reactionary slave-owning class, and Lin Piao was the dutiful son of the landlords, rich peasants, counter-revolutionaries, bad elements and Rightists. Both wanted to reinstate the overthrown reactionary classes. Anxious to see the slave-owners back in power, Confucius talked about the 'heaven's will,' 'the highest, who are wise, and the lowest, who are stupid' and uttered such nonsense as whether one belonged to the highest or lowest order was preordained and therefore could not be changed. In other words, a slave-owner should always remain a slave-owner and a slave for ever a slave. Then there was Lin Piao who described himself as a 'genius,' a 'heavenly horse,' saying he had a 'good head' which was 'especially clever.' He dreamt of becoming an emperor and worked for capitalist restoration."

"Heaven's will indeed!" Chen Yung-hsiang, secretary of the brigade's Party branch who presided at the meeting, cut in. "All this is bunk meant to fool us labouring masses. Remember the seven landlord households in our village? Before liberation, didn't they keep singing the tune of Confucius that they were 'born under a lucky star' and therefore were entitled to 'enjoy' while we poor and lower-middle peasants were 'born under an unlucky star' and were destined to 'suffer'? Hooey! 'Lucky star' 'unlucky star' my foot! What they had in mind was to make us work willingly for them like beasts of burden. Led by our great leader Chairman Mao, we carried out land reform and overthrew all seven landlords. Where are their 'lucky stars' now? And where are our 'unlucky stars' now? How did this change come about? It has nothing to do with 'lucky or unlucky stars,' it's the revolution that counts. This Lin Piao and his gang talked about 'heaven's will' to oppose revolution and progress. His intention was to pull us back into the evil old society. But he was only day-dreaming!"

Chia Huai-tung, deputy leader of Production Team No. 3, said: "And this same Lin Piao also viciously attacked the proletarian dictatorship with the rubbish he found in his master's sayings. He talked about 'virtue,' 'benevolence and love,' 'loyalty and forbearance,' hoping we would 'love men' irrespective of the classes they belonged to. Chairman Mao told us long ago: *'There is absolutely no such thing in the world as love or hatred without reason or cause. As for the so-called love of humanity, there has been no such all-inclusive love since humanity was divided into classes.'* This is absolutely true! There is no supra-class love or hatred. Confucius talked glibly about 'benevolence, righteousness and virtue,' but he had a knife in his hand all the time. Only seven days after he became an official he killed a reformer called Shaocheng Mou who opposed slavery. What Confucius loved was the handful of slave-owners and what he hated was the broad masses of slaves and reformers. Now about Lin Piao and his plan for a counter-revolutionary armed coup d'etat entitled *Outline of Project '571'*. In it he planned to kill the revolutionary people and 'liberate' the land-lords, rich peasants, counter-revolutionaries, bad elements and Rightists under our dictatorial rule. Isn't it very clear who this fellow loved and who he hated?"

Yang Feng-hsien, a 59-year-old poor peasant, said: "I worked for a landlord in the old society. That landlord liked to quote Confucius' sayings. He had a tongue as sweet as honey and a heart as venomous as a scorpion. He often told us: 'Compromise and patience are the best. You must be patient in everything and learn to give in. In this way you'll be able to keep yourself out of trouble.' This fellow wanted to bleed us white and at the same time told us not to revolt. This is what Confucius and Lin Piao meant by 'love all men.' It is the great Communist Party of China, it is our great leader Chairman Mao, it is socialism and it is the revolution that really love and take good care of us labouring people. In the old society, not one of my forefathers was literate and after they had a meal they didn't know when they'd have the next. Today, in our new society, all my six children have gone to school, some are now teachers themselves. But this Lin Piao picked up the rubbish of Confucius and tried to make us docile and submissive. He wouldn't let us struggle against the reactionaries so that he and his gang could practise revisionism and drive us back to the old society. . . ."

"That can't be done!" echoed the angry crowd.

It was getting late, but the meeting continued as many people wanted to have their say.

CHANGES IN MY UNDERSTANDING OF CONFUCIUS*

BY FUNG YU-LAN

The May 4th Movement of 1919 was directed against China's centuries-old feudal culture. Opposed to the decadent and reactionary morals, culture and literature, it raised the slogan "Down with Confucius' Shop!", for Confucius was regarded as the chief representative of

* From *China Reconstructs*, August 1974.

all these old things. Since then, to smash or protect the "Confucius Shop"—Confucian doctrine and all those who worshipped it and tried to revive the old order of things—has been a central part of the struggle between the proletarian and bourgeois classes and their two lines in the sphere of ideology. Before the cultural revolution, I had always stood for the protection of "Confucius' Shop". In effect this meant that I served the big landlords, bourgeoisie and Kuomintang reactionaries before liberation and the counter-revolutionary revisionist line of Liu Shao-chi and other political swindlers after liberation.

It was the cultural revolution that enabled me to raise my understanding of Confucius. My present criticism of Confucius is at the same time a criticism of my own thoughts and actions in defending the "Confucius Shop" in the past.

There are many aspects to Confucius' thought. Let us start with the "governing by virtue" he advocated.

Confucius said, "If you govern the people by virtue, you may be compared to the north star, which keeps its place while all the other stars bow to it." (*The Analects*) Again, "If you lead the people by laws and keep them in order by penalties, they may keep away from wrong-doing yet have no sense of shame for it. If you lead them by virtue and keep them in order by the 'rites', or rules of propriety, they will have a sense of shame for wrong-doing and live up to standard." (*The Analects*) These are Confucius' explicit references to "governing by virtue".

My understanding and evaluation of these words have undergone three stages.

In 1957 when I lectured on the "Problems of Inheriting the Legacy of Chinese Philosophy", I put forward the "abstract method", according to which one should pay attention only to the face value and literal interpretation of the textual passage without considering the actual historical conditions, particularly the class content. Now I understand that this is contrary to the Marxist-Leninist method of class analysis. I had always used this method in my lectures on the history of Chinese philosophy. In the old edition of my book *A History of Chinese Philosophy,* for instance, I interpreted the "virtue" Confucius spoke of as the moral qualities of individuals, and the "rites", or rules of propriety, as social standards, including social customs and habits and the political and social system. What Confucius said about "lead the people by virtue" meant to raise the moral qualities of the people to a higher level. "Keep them in order by the 'rites', or rules of propriety" meant using social standards to strengthen the control of individual conduct and creating social customs and habits and public opinion to inculcate into the people a sense of shame for wrong-doing or law-breaking. In this way, the people naturally will not violate the laws. His method, I maintained, was to stress raising the people's moral qualities and strengthening the social influence, and this was much better than forcing the people not to dare to violate the laws by prohibition and punishment. This meant Confucius' respect for "man".

This was a literal interpretation of what Confucius said of "virtue" and "rites", or rules of propriety, taking them as abstract ideas at their face value. This method is used by practically all who revere Confucius. It covers up the class content of different schools of thought, confuses the line of demarcation in the class struggle of the time, and distorts the law of development in the history of philosophy. This is not merely a question of methodology. In the final analysis, it is a question of class stand, that is, on which side one stands in the struggle between two classes and two lines.

Though I made some superficial criticisms of this abstract approach before the cultural revolution, I did not change my exploiting-class stand. In my new edition of *A History of Chinese Philosophy*, I stuck to this approach, especially when referring to Confucius.

During the cultural revolution I gradually came to understand the significance of Lenin's teaching, "Truth is always concrete". The "virtue" and "rites" or rules of propriety Confucius advocated had concrete historical content. The class content was especially important. The moral qualities, for instance, which are promoted by different social classes have different class content. Those encouraged by the proletariat aim at serving the people, overthrowing all exploiting classes and establishing a socialist and communist society. In the eyes of the exploiting classes these qualities "create disorder against the rulers" and are the greatest crime. Different classes also have different social standards. The proletarian revolution aims at replacing the social standards of the exploiting classes with those of its own.

Only after realizing this fact did I see that "lead the people by virtue" and other measures Confucius advocated were intended to benumb and trick the working people so that they would neither dare nor want to oppose the existing order. Confucius' purpose was to eradicate all ideas and acts which "create disorder against the rulers".

Lenin said, *"All oppressing classes need two social functions to safeguard their rule: the function of the hangman and the function of the priest. The hangman is required to quell the protests and the indignation of the oppressed; the priest is required to console the oppressed, to paint for them the prospects of mitigation of their sufferings and sacrifices (this is particularly easy to do without guaranteeing that these prospects will be 'achieved'), while preserving class rule, and thereby to reconcile them to class rule, wean them from revolutionary action, undermine their revolutionary spirit and destroy their revolutionary determination."* (*The Collapse of the Second International*) In other words, the ruling class must have two ways to rule the people: one being persecution and suppression, and the other deception and paralyzing their revolutionary will. What Confucius defined as the two methods of ruling the people—"lead the people by laws" and "lead the people by virtue"—are the two social functions Lenin pointed out. In suggesting ways and means to the rulers of his time Confucius was really maintaining that the function of the priest was more effective than that of the hangman. In a certain sense and under certain conditions, the function of the priest is even more vicious than that of the hangman.

However, Confucius also regarded "punishment" as indispensable. The State of Cheng at that time was suppressing the slave uprisings with armed force. "Excellent!" Confucius applauded. "If the rule is too lenient, the people will be insolent. If the people are insolent, correct them by force." (*Tso Chuan,* a historical work in the period of Confucius) When Confucius himself was in power, he had Shao-cheng Mou, an anti-slavery reformer, put to death.

The Confucian scholars in the Han dynasty (206 B.C.—A.D. 220) maintained that "rites, music, laws and punishment" were all needed to rule the people and consolidate the feudal regime. They also maintained that the ultimate aim of all four was the same, i.e., rule over the people. In other words, it was necessary to have the functions of both the hangman and the priest.

In the present deepening of the criticism of Confucius, my understanding of him has been raised further.

I feel now that the above criticisms of Confucius can be applied to all the later feudal philosophers. To stop with these criticisms, one has not yet laid bare all the characteristics of his thought. Our criticism must go deeper.

When Fan Chih, one of Confucius' disciples, said that he wanted to learn farming and vegetable growing, Confucius spurned him as an "inferior man". Then he expressed his opinion in a passage: "Fan Hsu (Fan Chih) is indeed an inferior man! If the ruler loves the 'rites', or rules of propriety, the common people will not dare to be irreverent. If he loves righteousness, they will not dare to disobey. If he loves sincerity, they will not dare to hide what is in their minds. If he does all this, the common people will flock to him from all quarters, carrying their children on their backs. What need has he to know farming?" (*The Analects*)

In this passage, Confucius endorsed the two opposing social classes of his time. One he called the "superior men" (meaning "lords" at that time), "those above" (meaning the rulers, the oppressors) who did no farming (meaning exploiters who did no physical labor). Opposed to them were the "inferior men", "those below", the "common people" (meaning the ruled, the oppressed) who did the farming (meaning the exploited laboring people).

From the above passage we can see that the rites, righteousness and sincerity which Confucius spoke of concerned only "those above". In his opinion, if "those above" made these gestures, they would influence the people to respect and obey them and work for them faithfully. Confucius said, "The superior men's virtue is like the wind and the inferior men's virtue is like grass. When the wind blows over the grass, it will inevitably bend." (*The Analects*) This is his real meaning of "leading the people by virtue".

In his opinion on Fan Chih, Confucius repeated "dare not" three times. This exposes the repressive nature of his "superior men".

Confucius regarded "benevolence" as the supreme virtue. The many references to "benevolence" in *The Analects* were not identical. Let us cite a few important examples:

1. "Yen Yuan asked about benevolence. Confucius said, 'Benevolence means to restrain oneself and return to the rites. Once self-restraint and return to the rites are achieved, all under heaven will submit to the benevolent ruler.'"

2. "Chung Kung asked about benevolence. Confucius said, 'When you go out, deal with others as if you were receiving great guests. When you order people, do so as if you were attending a great sacrifice. Don't do unto others what you don't want others to do unto you.'"

3. "Fan Chih asked about benevolence. Confucius said, 'Love Man.'"

4. "Tzu Chang asked Confucius about benevolence. Confucius said, 'It consists in being able to practice five virtues under heaven.' He asked what they were. Confucius answered, 'Gravity, generosity, sincerity, industry and charity. If you are grave, you will be treated with respect. If you are generous, you will win all. If you are sincere, you will be trusted by others. If you are industrious, you will succeed in what you do. If you are charitable, you will be able to order people.'"

Quotations 1, 2 and 4 show that the "benevolence" Confucius spoke of referred to "superior men" only. The first quotation says that if you could make your words and actions conform to the rites of the Western Chou dynasty, all under heaven would submit to the "benevolent ruler". This of course referred to only those in high political positions. An "inferior man" could in no way obtain the submission of others under heaven.

The second quotation says that ordering people was a grave matter, like a great sacrifice. This also referred only to those in high political positions. The "inferior man" were the "common people" who could only be ordered around and could never order others.

In the fourth quotation, Confucius said that if you were generous, you would win all, and if you were charitable you would be able to order others. This also referred to those in high political positions. Being the masses themselves, the "inferior men" needed not and could not "win all". They themselves were the ordered who could never order others.

From what Confucius said about "generosity" and "charity", we can see that his "love Man" meant at most giving sops to the laboring people so as to win them over and make it easier to order them around.

It is obvious that Confucius' "benevolence" referred to the morals of the "superior men" while excluding the "inferior men". He clearly stated that "There are superior men who are not benevolent, but there is never an inferior man who is benevolent" (*The Analects*). Again he said, "The common people should be directed to do things but not made to comprehend them." Again, "When a superior man learns a little about the Way (ideology of the superior men), he will love people (meaning giving sops to the laboring people). When an inferior man learns a little about the Way, he will be more easily ordered around." (*The Analects*) All these statements clearly demonstrate the class content of his "benevolence".

Not only Confucius' "benevolence" but his other moral qualities referred only to "superior men". "Don't do unto others what you don't want others to do unto you" in the second quotation meant a gentlemen's agreement among "superior men".

We can see from the above that Confucius' "superior men" referred to the slave-owning aristocrats, for the attitude of the "superior men" toward the "inferior men" was that of the slaveowners toward the slaves. His relation between "superior men" and "inferior men" was that between slaveowners and slaves. The slaves were no more than tools of production. In the eyes of the slaveowners, there was no virtue to speak of when they dealt with slaves. If the slaves had any virtue, it was obedience to the orders of the slaveowners. In the west, Plato (427-347 B.C.), a typical slave-owning philosopher of ancient Greece, had the same ideas.

On this point, the thinking of the feudal philosophers differed sometimes from that of the slave-owning philosophers. For instance, Wang Yang-ming (1472-1528), a philosopher of the land-owning class in the Ming dynasty, said that "sages are everywhere in the street" and "everybody has a conscience". (While admitting on the surface that everybody had a conscience, he actually thought there was a basic distinction between sages and the ordinary people. Sages could only come from the ruling class but never from the laboring people.) His words went further in benumbing and deceiving the laboring people. Likewise, the "liberty, equality and fraternity" advocated by the bourgeois philosophers was also a further attempt to benumb and deceive the laboring people. In the past, some people, including myself, when speaking of Confucius' "benevolence", imagined that Confucius also had conceived of "equality and fraternity", that Confucius had discovered "man". It seemed as if a philosopher could hatch ideas from his brain in isolation from his social position. This is impossible. It is an idealist conception of history instead of a materialist one.

Toward the end of the Spring and Autumn period (770-476 B.C.), slave society in China was in a state of rapid collapse. The slaveowners were then of course declining. The ideas advocated by Confucius served the interests of the slaveowners. He was a philosopher of the declining slaveowners.

In *The Analects* Confucius extolled the achievements of King Wu of the Chou dynasty, saying that he "revived states that have been extinguished, restored families whose line of succession has been broken, and recalled to office those who have fallen into obscurity". This was part of Confucius' political program for the restoration of the old order of the slaveowners. He would restore the extinct slaveowner states, revive the descendants of the slave-owning nobles who had lost their political positions, and lift up the slave-owning nobles who had sunk into the ranks of the common people. This was tantamount to the complete restoration of the old order of slave society.

I used to explain Confucius' "love of Man" as meaning love for all people. We can see from the above that this was impossible. Those Confucius did love were in fact a handful of slave-owning aristocrats. He also said "overflowing in love to all" (*The Analects*). This meant nothing more than giving sops to the laboring people.

Why should the slaveowners give sops? It was because the slave system at that time resembled a dying person who was sinking fast, like the sun setting beyond the western hills. The slaveowners had lost control of the slaves, who either rebelled or fled. To reduce the revolt and flight of the slaves and win over more toilers from the then rising feudal class, Confucius laid great stress on giving some sops to the slaves. Confucius' idea was a reflection of the class struggle at that time.

In *The Collapse of the Second International*, Lenin quoted Feuerbach, ". . . *whoever consoles the slave instead of rousing him to rise up against slavery is aiding the slaveowner.*" This statement aptly applies to Confucius, too.

In feudal society after the Han dynasty, Confucius became the "supreme master" of feudal ideology. In the twentieth century, Yuan Shih-kai, leader of the northern warlords, Chiang Kai-shek, chief of the Kuomintang reactionaries, as well as the renegade Liu Shao-chi and the counter-revolutionary Lin Piao continued to revere Confucius. This is because all of them advocated that exploitation and oppression were justified and rebellion was unjustified.

In the Confucian temple in Chufu county, Shantung province, there are inscriptions on stone tablets recording the honors bestowed posthumously on Confucius by emperors of various dynasties. They all eulogize Confucius' "meritorious deeds" in behalf of the feudal ruling class, which in fact serves to expose Confucius' crimes against the laboring people.

Chiang Kai-shek, Liu Shao-chi and Lin Piao all glorified Confucius with the same political purpose—to deceive and benumb the people in order to restore the old system, the old order, and oppose revolution and social progress.

The 1957 Forum on the History of Chinese Philosophy and the 1962 Tsinan Conference to Commemorate Confucius manifested the revisionist trend of the time to return to the old. At the former, I advocated the "abstract method" of inheriting the past against the Marxist approach of class analysis. In the latter, I spread the viewpoint on Confucius that I had elaborated in my new edition of *A History of Chinese Philosophy*. I argued that Confucius was the ideological representative of the feudal landlord class, that the "benevolence" he preached conformed to a "universal pattern" and had played a progressive role at that time. This only strengthened the deification of Confucius and served the revisionist line.

The great proletarian cultural revolution aimed to remold the people's world outlook by criticizing and repudiating the old ideas and concepts in history. My understanding of Confucius has been raised as a result of the education I received from the cultural revolution.

The cultural revolution is broadening and deepening. In the current movement to criticize Lin Piao and Confucius, Chairman Mao is personally giving leadership and showing us the orientation. A new revolution is taking place in the study of the history of Chinese philosophy. I am now nearly 80. After spending half a century studying and teaching the history of Chinese philosophy, it is a source of great satisfaction for me to be able to witness this great revolution. My happiness is even greater that I am able to take part in it. Studying Marxism-Leninism-Mao Tsetung Thought and remolding my world outlook, I am revising my new edition of *A History of Chinese Philosophy,* and will complete the unfinished parts as my contribution to China's socialist revolution and construction.